COLLEGE STUDY SKILLS

SIXTH EDITION

James F. Shepherd

Queensborough Community College, Emeritus
The City University of New York

HOUGHTON MIFFLIN COMPANY   Boston   New York

This book is dedicated to Earl Kemppainen.

Publisher: Alison Zetterquist
Assistant Editor: Melissa Plumb
Packaging Services Supervisor: Charline Lake
Senior Project Editor: Janet Edmonds
Senior Production/Design Coordinator: Jennifer Waddell
Senior Manufacturing Coordinator: Priscilla J. Bailey

Cover design: Nina Wishnok
Cover images (clockwise): Photo by Neil Robinson, Tony Stone Images; Photo by Frank Saragnese, FPG International; Georgia Deaver Calligraphy and Illustration, San Francisco, Courtesy of Van Dyke Company

Photo Credits
Page 1: Paula Lerner/The Picture Cube
Page 89: Len Rubenstein/The Picture Cube
Page 117: Jean-Claude Lejeune/Stock, Boston
Page 241: Arthur Grace/Stock, Boston

Text Credits
Excerpts from *Core Concepts in Health,* 7th ed., 1996 Update by Paul M. Insel and Walton T. Roth. Copyright © 1996 by Mayfield Publishing Company. Reprinted by permission of the publisher.

Excerpts from *Communicate!,* 8th ed., by Rudolph F. Verderber, copyright © 1996, and excerpts from *Communicate!,* 6th ed., by Rudolph F. Verderber, copyright © 1990. Reprinted by permission of Wadsworth Publishing Company.

Adaptation of material on page 111 and Figure 5.1 and Figure 5.2 on The Cornell Note Sheet from *How to Study in College,* 5th ed., by Walter Pauk, copyright © 1993 by Houghton Mifflin Company. Used with permission.

Excerpt and classification chart from Douglas A. Bernstein et al., *Psychology,* 3rd ed. Copyright © 1994 by Houghton Mifflin Company. Reprinted with permission.

Excerpt from James F. Shepherd, *RSVP: The College Reading, Study, and Vocabulary Program,* 5th ed. Copyright © 1996 by Houghton Mifflin Company. Used with permission.

Credits continue on page 332, which constitutes an extension of the copyright page.

Printed in the U.S.A.

Library of Congress Catalog Card Number: 97-72546

Student Text ISBN: 0-395-84066-X
Instructor's Edition ISBN: 0-395-84996-9

23456789-WC-01 00 99 98

Contents

9 Develop Organizational Skills   73

PART II *Use Time Wisely*   89

10 Work Toward Goals   91

11 Manage Your Time   99

12 Increase Concentration   111

27 Essay Questions 289

Preface

College Study Skills teaches the study and test-taking skills that are needed for success in college and it promotes the improvement of reading comprehension and analytical skills. Written in a supportive tone and in language that is easy for almost all college students to understand, it contains one hundred forty-eight practical exercises that help students to acquire skills through practice. *College Study Skills* in its various editions has been used with great success by thousands of students, both in classes under the supervision of instructors and in other settings, including learning centers and skills laboratories.

Improvements in the Sixth Edition

This new edition of *College Study Skills* includes updated exposition, improved exercises, new textbook passages for skills practice, and many other changes.

Organizational Changes The book is now organized into four parts rather than five.

- Part I, "Organize for Success," orients students to college life, provides an introduction to study skills instruction, and lays the foundation for improving organizational skills.
- Part II, "Use Time Wisely," explains how to make better use of time by setting goals, scheduling time, and increasing ability to concentrate while studying.
- Part III, "Study Effectively," explains how to listen in class, take good class notes, preview before reading, underline or highlight books, make notes of information in books, anticipate test questions, and recite and rehearse in preparation for tests.
- Part IV, "Do Well on Tests," explains methods for answering true-false, multiple-choice, matching, fill-in, and essay questions.

New Chapter This edition includes an entire chapter devoted to developing classroom listening skills—Chapter 14, "Listen in Class." The chapter explains how to be an active listener by preparing for each lecture, eliminating physical and mental distractions, and using effective strategies to focus on teachers' messages. Building the foundation for instruction in taking class notes, the chapter concludes with exercises students can use to evaluate and improve listening skills.

Expanded Instruction   Additions and changes have been made to the instruction in most chapters, including the following:

- Chapter 1, "Adjust to College," now includes information about types and sources of financial aid and advice for older students returning to college.

- Chapter 2, "Do Your Best," contains more ideas about how to select the right courses and an explanation of the advantages in using a word processor.

- Chapter 4, "Find Help if You Need It," explains the benefits of studying with groups and it suggests how to go about forming them.

- Chapter 8, "Use the Library," is revised to help students understand how to access information about a library's holdings that is stored in databases.

- Chapter 13, "Use Effective Study Methods," has been substantially revised and introduces guidelines for mathematics and science courses.

- Chapter 15, "Take Good Class Notes," provides a fuller explanation of the Cornell note-taking system and it includes an explanation of the need to adapt note taking to each subject.

- Chapter 17, "Preview Chapters," now includes explanations, figures, circle graphs, and tables.

- Chapter 18, "Mark Your Books," features ten new excerpts from popular college textbooks for instruction and practice in marking and making notes for books.

Combined Chapters   Another important change in this new edition of *College Study Skills* is that the chapters titled "Learn to Label Outlines" and "Make Well-organized Outlines" are now combined in Chapter 9, "Develop Organizational Skills," located at the end of Part I, "Organize for Success."

Distinctive Features

College Study Skills has several features that distinguish it from other textbooks.

- It provides more detailed instruction and practice for the development of test-taking skills than is available in any similar textbook (see Chapters 21 through 27).

- Words in the textbook selections in Chapter 18 that may be unfamiliar to students are underscored in blue and they are defined in the Vocabulary List on pages 322–326.

- A complete textbook chapter in the appendix is used as the basis for instruction in previewing (Chapter 17), marking books (Chapter 18), making notes for books (Chapter 19), reciting and rehearsing (Chapter 20), and taking tests (Chapter 21).

The textbook chapter in the appendix and the Vocabulary List are followed by a glossary, an index, a form for keeping records of assignments, and a form for planning study schedules.

Teaching Suggestions

The chapters are arranged in a logical teaching sequence, but they are written so that students can study one of them without first having studied any others. Thus, skills may be taught in any sequence that a teacher prefers. I recommend, however, that students read about basic study procedures in Chapter 2, memory in Chapter 5, and effective study methods in Chapter 13 before they study Chapters 14 through 20, which explicate the steps in the study process.

Instructor's Resource Manual

College Study Skills is accompanied by a manual for instructors, which contains teaching suggestions, quizzes, tests, and a complete answer key to exercises. The tests include six based on the words underscored in blue in Chapter 18 and one based on the contents of the textbook chapter located in the appendix. The manual is printed on 8½-by-11-inch paper to facilitate duplicating materials in it for classroom use.

Acknowledgments

In preparing this revision of *College Study Skills*, I am especially grateful to Alison Zetterquist, Melissa Plumb, and Nancy Benjamin for their generous support and expert guidance. I am also indebted to the following reviewers for their comments and suggestions that helped me in revising this book:

Maureen Connolly, Aurora University (IL)
Raymond DeLeon, California State University–Long Beach
Kristine Fuller, Edmonds Community College (WA)
Lois Hassan, Henry Ford Community College (MI)
Kathryn S. Hawes, The University of Memphis (TN)
Carlotta Hill, Oklahoma City Community College
Larry Ludewig, Kilgore College (TX)
Cheryl McLean, Edmonds Community College (WA)
Susan L. Neste, University of North Dakota
Susan L. Smith, Black Hawk College (IL)
Sharon Van Enoo, El Camino College (CA)

In writing this revision, I was once again inspired by the continued interest in this book, which had its beginning in materials I created to teach students at Queensborough Community College in the 1960s.

I want *College Study Skills* to be as useful to you as I can make it. If you write to me to let me know what I should or should not change when I prepare the next edition, I will answer you. Address your letter to James F. Shepherd, c/o Marketing Services, College Division, Houghton Mifflin Company, 222 Berkeley Street, Boston, Massachusetts 02116-3764.

J.F.S.

To the Student

The skills presented in *College Study Skills* are the ones that thousands of college students told me helped them most to do well in their courses.

You may, at first, find it difficult to believe that you should modify your study procedures in the ways that are recommended in this book. If so, read Chapter 5 and Chapter 20 to understand what you must do to remember all the things you will be required to learn in college. Those chapters should help you understand that the study strategies I suggest can help you do your best in college and learn more in less time!

Also, I hope you will carefully work out the exercises that are provided in this book, even the ones that aren't collected by your instructor. Then, when you study or take tests, practice using the skills you have learned in this book. If you do these things, I believe that your chances for earning a degree will be greatly increased.

It is not possible to learn, all at once, everything in *College Study Skills*. When you have a study problem, consult the table of contents at the beginning of the book or the index at the end. For instance, if you know that you must answer multiple-choice questions for a test, consult the index to find where multiple-choice questions are discussed, and study those pages.

As soon as possible, read the chapters about how to do your best in each course (Chapter 2), how to use effective study methods (Chapter 13), how to improve classroom listening (Chapter 14), and how to take good class notes (Chapter 15). These chapters explain information that is essential for you to know in order to succeed in each of your courses.

I would enjoy knowing your reactions to *College Study Skills*. If you take the time to write to me, I will take the time to answer you. Address your letter to James F. Shepherd, c/o Marketing Services, Houghton Mifflin Company, 222 Berkeley Street, Boston, Massachusetts 02116-3764.

I sincerely hope that you use what you learn in this book to do your best in school. I and many others you have never met want you to enjoy the benefits of a college education.

J.F.S.

PART

Organize for Success

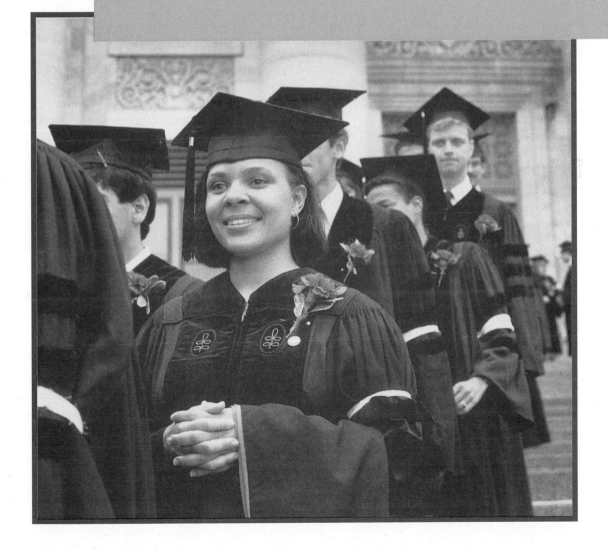

Preview of PART I

This first part of *College Study Skills* explains basic methods you may use to successfully pursue a college education.

- Chapter 1, "Adjust to College," suggests ways to make a smooth transition to college life.
- Chapter 2, "Do Your Best," summarizes procedures used by successful college students.
- Chapter 3, "Know Degree Requirements," helps you learn about the academic standards at your school.
- Chapter 4, "Find Help If You Need It," discusses sources of help that are available to you in case you have academic difficulty.
- Chapter 5, "Understand Your Memory," explains how memory functions and how it can be improved.
- Chapter 6, "Analyze Your Learning Style," gives you an opportunity to analyze your study procedures.
- Chapter 7, "Deal with Stress," includes suggestions for adapting to and coping with stress.
- Chapter 8, "Use the Library," is an introduction to library facilities and services.
- Chapter 9, "Develop Organizational Skills," helps you to develop understanding and abilities that are necessary for taking good class notes, underlining books accurately, and doing many other study tasks efficiently.

If this is your first year in college, you will probably find a great many facts about college that are new to you as you study these nine chapters in Part I.

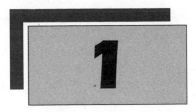

Adjust to College

The first weeks of college may be disturbing to you—they are for most students. You will need to make new friends, and you will have new teachers to get used to. You will need to learn where classrooms are located and to find the easiest way to travel from one place to another. You will want to buy your books, plan where you will study, and schedule when you will study. Also, you may feel uncomfortable because you don't know the difference between a *bursar* and a *registrar* or where to go for help if you have a problem.

This chapter suggests some basic ways to adjust to college life, and it explains the meanings of some important words you may not know.

Free Time

Some of the most noticeable differences between high school and college are that in college your report card is not sent home to your parents and you are not required to go to study hall or to carry a hall pass. In addition, you probably will not have classes scheduled every day, and you may sometimes have long breaks between classes.

You will be responsible for deciding what you will do during the time that you are not in classes. Will you waste your free time, or will you use it studying, exercising, working, or engaging in other constructive activities. Only you can decide!

This is why *College Study Skills* provides many ideas for making effective use of time. Chapter 11 explains basic strategies for managing time, Chapter 12 gives suggestions for making better use of time by increasing concentration, and Chapter 7 describes methods for coping with stress that interferes with your ability to use your study time well. In addition, Chapters 13 through 20 teach study techniques that you may use to learn material more thoroughly and quickly.

The Catalog or Bulletin

Your college publishes a book called a **catalog*** or **bulletin** that contains important information, such as descriptions of courses, graduation requirements, names of instructors, and locations of buildings and offices. If you do not have a copy of your school's catalog, obtain one immediately. It is probably available at the admissions office of your school.

Refer to your catalog when you have questions about the regulations at your school or about your graduation requirements. Do not rely on other students for answers to questions of these kinds; they require an answer that is printed in your catalog or that is stated to you by a qualified faculty member.

Keep a copy of the catalog dated for the year you **matriculated** at your college. If your college changes degree requirements while you are enrolled there, the requirements that apply to you will be the ones that were in effect the year you were accepted to study for a degree.

The School Calendar

Colleges prepare calendars that list holidays and other important days, such as the ones for **orientation,** registration, and final examinations. If you do not find a calendar printed in your catalog, ask a **counselor** or **adviser** for a copy. It is important for you to familiarize yourself with your school's calendar. For one thing, holidays at your school are not necessarily the same as the holidays at local public schools or at other colleges in your community. Record important dates in your calendar (see page 102).

Academic calendars are divided into **terms,** which are periods of study that usually end with final examinations. A term may be a semester, a quarter, or a trimester. When a school uses the **semester system,** the school year is divided into two parts, usually a fall and a spring term of about fifteen weeks each. When either the **quarter system** or the **trimester system** is used, the school year is usually divided into fall, winter, and spring terms of about ten weeks each.

Some colleges offer students opportunities to study during summer sessions or intersessions, which are not regarded as terms for the purposes of school business. A **summer session** is a period in the summer during which students may take courses; an **intersession** is a short session of study offered between two terms, such as a four-week session offered in January between a fall term and a spring term.

New Friends

You will enjoy school more if you have friends to talk with before and after classes. In addition, you need friends in your classes whom you can call to learn about assignments given when you are absent and from whom you can copy notes given on days you are not in class. You may also find it is helpful

---

*Boldface terms are defined in the glossary on pages 327–331.

to discuss assignments or to study for tests with students who are taking the same courses you are taking. Therefore, put a high priority on making friends in each class you take.

Older Students

If you are returning to school after spending several years in the work force or raising a family, you bring with you real-life experiences that will enhance your appreciation and enjoyment of your college education. However, because you have been away from school for some time, you may be concerned about what you can do to smooth your adjustment to college life. If so, the following hints may be helpful to you in making this transition.

Hints for Older Students

- If you are concerned about the demands of full-time college study, begin as a part-time student, taking only one or two courses.
- Prepare for your entry to college by taking a study-skills course.
- Review foreign languages, mathematics, and writing skills by taking courses or by studying the subjects on your own.
- If you are working, tell your employer about your educational plans; some employers offer financial assistance or other support to employees.
- If you have children, elicit their help with chores such as doing the laundry, shopping for groceries, and making beds.
- Determine if your college provides a child-care service or help in finding child care.
- Involve your family or friends in your education by informing them about your schedule, requesting them to give you privacy when you study, giving them a tour of your campus, and taking them to athletic or cultural events at your college.

The following chapters in this first part of *College Study Skills* include many more ideas for dealing with problems that you may encounter in adjusting to college.

Social Activities

Your college experience will be more enjoyable if you make the effort to attend social functions, join clubs, and participate in sports.

Your student government sponsors social events, such as movies, concerts, athletic events, and dances. These and other activities are available to you at little or no cost. Read student newspapers and notices on bulletin boards for announcements of these events.

In addition, the students at your school have organized clubs for interests that may range from bowling to creative writing and from photography to karate. There are probably organizations for students who want to learn more about various religions, countries, or hobbies, and opportunities for students to swim or to play basketball, baseball, volleyball, or other team sports. Information about clubs may be printed in a brochure or pamphlet that was distributed during orientation. Clubs not only provide you with opportunities to participate in activities you enjoy, they are also a way for you to meet people and to make new friends.

If you have difficulty learning about social events and clubs, visit the student government office, student activities office, or the student affairs office. Somebody there can give you the information that you need to involve yourself in campus life.

Counseling Services

Most colleges have counselors who provide students with guidance in achieving their educational and occupational goals and in resolving their personal problems. In addition, counselors are usually experts in helping students with such matters as changing curriculums and dropping courses.

If any of the statements in the following "Checklist for Counseling Services" describe you, a counselor at your school can either help you or tell you where you can find help. You may be advised to visit another office on campus. For instance, if you have difficulty in paying tuition, a counselor may refer you to a financial aid office. Or, if you have a problem for which your school provides no services, you may be advised to visit an agency in the community that can give you the assistance you need.

Checklist for Counseling Services

Check any statement in this list that describes you.

- ❑ I need a part-time job.
- ❑ I need a place to live.
- ❑ I need financial assistance.
- ❑ I need somebody to care for my children.
- ❑ I want to improve my grades.
- ❑ I am very anxious when I take tests.
- ❑ I want an explanation of my placement test scores.
- ❑ I need help in understanding my required curriculum.
- ❑ I want help in deciding what occupation to pursue.
- ❑ I want help in deciding what I should study in college.
- ❑ I want to know about job opportunities after I graduate.
- ❑ I want to transfer to another college.
- ❑ I am extremely displeased with one of my instructors.
- ❑ I have a serious physical disability or chronic illness.
- ❑ I have been out of school for years, and I feel lost.
- ❑ I feel very lonely.
- ❑ I have a serious problem with my parents (or spouse).

❑   I have poor relations with members of the opposite sex.

❑   I want help to overcome my drug (or alcohol) problem.

A counselor at your school can help you with your problems or tell you where you can find help.

Financial Aid

Personnel at the counseling center or financial aid office at your school can help you learn about and obtain grants, scholarships, loans, and other forms of funding for your college expenses.

Types of Financial Aid

- **Grants** are gifts that do not need to be repaid, such as tuition assistance grants funded by state and federal governments to assist students who demonstrate financial need.

- **Scholarships** are grants of financial assistance that are awarded to students who meet specific criteria, such as outstanding academic, athletic, or artistic achievement.

- **Loans** are lent sums of money that must be repaid with interest; they include long-term loans funded by the federal government that are available to qualifying students at reasonable interest rates.

Financial aid counselors can help students learn if funds may be available to them through a work-study program, the Veterans Administration, the Social Security Administration, state vocational rehabilitation offices, state employment offices, or other sources. If you have not already investigated the availability of financial aid, do so immediately—it often takes several months to process an application for financial aid.

Health Services

Most colleges have an office that provides health services for students who become ill or injured while they are on campus. Call this office if you have an illness or injury that prevents you from attending classes for an extended period. Someone in the office may notify your instructors so they can make special arrangements for you to keep up with course work during the time you are unable to attend classes.

Departments, Divisions, and Schools

The courses you are taking are probably offered by several departments. A **department** is an organizational unit that offers courses in a specific subject or a specific group of subjects. For example, a history department may offer courses only in history, but a social science department may offer courses in psychology, sociology, anthropology, and other subjects.

At some colleges, departments are organized in groups called **divisions.** For example, the social science division of a college may include a psychology department, a sociology department, an anthropology department, and other departments. Some universities refer to divisions as **schools.** For instance, schools of business, schools of law, and schools of medicine are usually divisions of universities.

The President and Deans

The senior administrative officer at most colleges and universities is the **president,** who has ultimate responsibility for all aspects of the functioning of a school. **Deans** are members of the administration who are in charge of specified areas of the school's activities, such as a dean of students or a dean of instruction. Sometimes, there are also deans of divisions or schools within a college or university. At most schools, students come in contact with deans only when they are given awards or are in serious trouble.

At some schools, the senior administrative officer is called a **chancellor,** and deans are sometimes called **vice chancellors** or **vice presidents.** At a few colleges and universities, a chancellor or **ombudsperson** serves as a special assistant to the president.

The Registrar and the Bursar

The administration includes a **registrar,** who oversees registering students for courses and keeps records of the courses students take and the grades they receive. Shortly after you complete each term, the registrar will send you a **transcript,** which is a report of your grades for the courses you took. The registrar may be located in the registrar's office, the admissions office, or the student records office. Visit the registrar when you have questions about your transcript or your registration in courses, and when you want a transcript mailed to an employer or another school.

The **bursar,** or **cashier,** is the person who is responsible for money transactions; he or she may be located in the bursar's office, the cashier's office, the business office, or the office of the treasurer. Visit the bursar when you have questions about tuition or fees and when you need to pay a bill.

Teachers, Professors, and Doctors

College teachers may be called "professor" or "doctor." "Professor" is sometimes an honorary or courtesy title, but more often it is a title for faculty members who hold the rank of **professor, associate professor,** or **assistant professor. Doctor** designates a person who has earned the highest degree awarded by a college or university, such as the Doctor of Philosophy (Ph.D.). In *College Study Skills,* I use "teacher," "instructor," and "professor" interchangeably when I refer to a person who teaches in a college or a university.

EXERCISE 1.1   Your Instructors and Required Textbooks

List the following on a sheet of notebook paper:

1. your instructors' names, telephone numbers, and office locations
2. the titles of the textbooks and any other materials that you are required to purchase for the courses you are taking this term

EXERCISE 1.2   Your School's Calendar

The following questions are about your school's calendar, which may be printed in the front of your catalog.

1. What is the last day this term you can add a course to your program? _____

2. What is the last day this term you can drop a course from your program and get a full tuition refund? _____

3. What is the next day when there will be no classes because your school is observing a holiday? _____

4. What is the next week when there will be no classes because your school is observing a recess of one week or longer? _____

5. What is the last day of classes for the current term? _____

6. On what days will final examinations be given for the current term at your school? _____

EXERCISE 1.3   Office Locations

The answers to these questions are probably in your catalog and in materials that you got during orientation.

1. Where are the counselors' offices located? _____

2. Where is the registrar's office located? (It may be called the admissions office or the student records office.) _____

3. Where is the bursar's office located? (It may be called the cashier's office, the business office, or the office of the treasurer.) _____

4. Where is the financial aid office located? _____

5. Where is the office of testing located? (It may be
   called the office of assessment.) _____

6. Where is the student activities office located? _____

7. Where is the health services office located (and
   what is its telephone number in case you must
   report that you are unable to attend classes for
   an extended period because of illness)? _____

EXERCISE 1.4   Other Services

1. Where can you obtain a student identification
   card? How much does one cost? _____

2. Where on campus can you go to use a computer? _____

3. Where is the bookstore located? _____

4. Where is the lost-and-found office located? _____

5. If lockers are available on campus, where do you
   go to rent one? _____

6. If your school makes medical insurance available
   to you at special rates, where do you purchase it? _____

7. If students need parking stickers for their cars,
   where are the stickers purchased and how much
   do they cost? _____

8. If your school has a child-care center, where is it
   located and whose children does it serve? _____

9. What exercise, swimming, or sports facilities
   are available for your use and what hours are
   they open? _____

Do Your Best

Many of today's famous entertainers had to work at everyday jobs in restaurants, construction, offices, and factories before they became successful in show business. At one time, Tom Hanks was a hotel bellboy, Whoopi Goldberg was a cosmetologist, and Harrison Ford was a carpenter. However, we don't think of these celebrities as a bellboy, cosmetologist, and carpenter; we think of them as the famous performers they have become by doing the things that are necessary to succeed in the entertainment industry.

The same is true of you in your pursuit of a college degree. Today others may think of you as a recent high school graduate, working person, or homemaker, but you can become known as a successful college student by doing what successful college students do. These things are explained in this chapter.

Know Why You Are Attending College

It may seem obvious that the reason people go to college is to acquire an education, but the reasons for attending a college or university are actually extremely varied. Young people who have recently completed high school may go to college because they cannot find work; older people may go to college because the opportunity has been made available to them by their employers. The following checklist lists the reasons students most often give for being in college.

Checklist of Reasons for Attending College

Check the boxes in front of the three reasons that best describe why you are in school.

❑   I want to earn a college degree.
❑   I need a better education to get a good job.
❑   I want to prepare myself for a specific occupation.

11

- ❑ I want to be a well-educated person.
- ❑ I want to learn to think more clearly.
- ❑ I want to be the first in my family to graduate from college.
- ❑ I want to be more responsible for my own life.
- ❑ I want a job better than the one I have now.
- ❑ I want to be promoted at the place where I work.
- ❑ I want to decide what I will do with my life.
- ❑ I want to use the money that is available for my tuition.
- ❑ I cannot find a job right now.
- ❑ I do not want to go to work right now.
- ❑ My parents want me to go to college.
- ❑ I like the social life at college.
- ❑ I like the feeling it gives me to be on campus.
- ❑ I want to find a boyfriend or girlfriend.
- ❑ I want to find a husband or wife.

Most students check three boxes in front of the first ten reasons, which are all ways of saying "I want to improve myself."

Did you check boxes in front of the reasons that are ways of saying "I want to improve myself"? If so, you believe in the possibility of a better life for yourself, and you believe that if you attend college, your life will be better for it. However, if you are attending school *only* to please your parents, *only* because you cannot find work, *only* for some reason other than self-improvement, you may not have sufficient motivation to do well in school.

Enroll in the Right Curriculum

You will be awarded a **degree** when you satisfactorily complete all the course work and other requirements in your **curriculum,** or program of study.

Following is an example of a program for first-semester students enrolled in an accounting curriculum:

		Credits
BU-101	Principles of Accounting I	4
BU-210	Business Organization	3
BU-205	Business Management	3
EN-101	English Composition I	3
HE-202	Health Education	1
PE-	Physical Education	1
		15

If you do not have a copy of your curriculum, ask your counselor or adviser where you can get a copy of it. It is extremely important for you to know exactly what courses you must take to earn a degree. When you obtain a copy of your curriculum, refer to your college catalog to read the descriptions of your required courses to decide if they are the types of things that you want to study. You will benefit from college more if your required courses are ones that you want to take.

If you are not pleased with your curriculum, examine the courses that are required for *other* curriculums at your school; you may find a program of study that is more appealing to you and change to that curriculum. For most people, college is a time to explore possibilities and to learn about themselves; as a result, more than half of all college students change their curriculum at least once during their college careers.

Professions such as nursing and electrical engineering require studying specific curriculums; however, most career paths do not. My first three jobs after graduating from college with a bachelor's degree in English Literature were for a publisher, a telephone company, and a law firm. After ten years of working in business, I returned to college to earn the degrees I needed to become a college teacher. College teaching led me to writing—a career for which I received no training in college beyond required freshman writing courses. I developed my writing skills while working for the publisher, telephone company, and law firm in jobs that required a great deal of writing!

Take the Right Courses

In addition to enrolling in the right curriculum, it is important that you take the right courses. Use the following suggestions to guide you during course **registration** each term:

Suggestions for Selecting Courses

- **Enroll early.** Enroll in courses as early during the registration period as you can; if you wait until the last minute, the courses you want to take may be closed because they are filled with other students.

- **Enroll in prerequisite courses.** A **prerequisite** is a course for which you must receive a satisfactory grade before you can enroll in some other course. For instance, the prerequisite for Accounting II may be a grade of C or better in Accounting I. It is essential for you to enroll in prerequisites so that you will take courses in the correct sequence and not be delayed in graduating from college.

- **Take learning-skills courses.** Colleges usually test students' reading, writing, and mathematics skills when they apply for admission. After testing, many students are required or advised to improve learning skills. Take full advantage of any learning-skills instruction that you are offered. The faculty of your school believes that this instruction will help you do your best and earn a degree.

- **Satisfy your degree requirements.** Your college offers many courses that cannot be applied for credit in your degree program. If your goal is to earn a college degree, first take prerequisite courses and learning-skills courses, and then take only courses that apply toward your degree.

- **Prepare for possible change.** If you believe you might eventually change your curriculum, study your catalog to find courses that apply to any curriculum to which you may someday transfer, and take those courses as electives.

- **Consider your strengths.** During the first term or two, try to take only courses in which you are confident you will do well. Ease yourself into college by taking courses in your areas of strength; don't put yourself under the unnecessary pressure of taking courses in subjects that you know are especially difficult for you.

- **Accommodate your learning style.** Enroll in difficult classes at the times you are most alert and concentrate best. If you like to get up early, schedule difficult classes as early in the day as you can. However, if you are not fully awake until noon, schedule your most challenging courses after lunch, late in the afternoon, or even in the evening.

Also, resist the temptation to schedule classes with no free periods between them. It is tiring to sit in one class after the other without sufficient breaks, and you need free time after each class to prepare for the one that follows. If you don't have breaks between classes, you may often go to a class under-prepared or you may sometimes find yourself cutting one class to prepare for another.

Choose Your Instructors Carefully

Some students who take great care in selecting who will cut their hair or repair their automobile give no thought to choosing who will teach their courses. However, a good teacher can make any subject more enjoyable and satisfying to study. When two or more instructors teach a course, you have a chance to pick the one you prefer.

You probably already have a good idea about the characteristics you like in a teacher. Most students prefer instructors who are well organized and easy to understand, enthusiastic about their subject matter, available to answer questions, fair in testing, and reasonable in grading. However, students often report that they try to avoid teachers who come to class unprepared, conduct aimless class discussions, read aloud from the textbook, talk in an expression-less voice, ramble from topic to topic, show a preference for certain students, have unnecessarily difficult course requirements, or are disrespectful or condescending to students.

Other students are your best source of information about the teachers at your school; therefore, if at all possible, enroll in courses taught by instructors who have been recommended to you by students whose judgment you trust. If you are unable to get recommendations from other students, investigate whether students' evaluations of the instructors at your school are published by your student government.

Purchase Textbooks Immediately

One important way that college differs from high school is that college students must buy their own **textbooks.** Some students encounter unnecessary difficulties because they wait too long to purchase required books or because they try to get by without buying the books they need.

Textbooks are expensive, but they are a small cost of attending college in comparison to tuition, housing, and other expenses. Do what experienced students do—purchase your required books immediately and get a head start in your classes by beginning to read them even before your teachers give reading assignments.

Know Your Teachers' Requirements

Students who don't know what their instructors require usually don't do all the things that are expected of them. As a result, they usually do not earn very good course grades.

During the first class meeting, instructors usually give an overview of the course, explain course requirements, and distribute a **syllabus** or other handout. A syllabus is a printed outline of the main topics of a course. When course requirements are listed in a syllabus or on other printed pages, keep them in a safe place; when they are presented orally, maintain accurate and complete notes about them. In either case, understand them completely and follow them exactly.

Use the following checklist to make certain that you know exactly what your teachers expect of you. Some teachers require only that students take **midterm** and final examinations, but other instructors require most of the items that are mentioned in the checklist.

Checklist for Course Requirements

Write checks in pencil so you can erase them and use this checklist for each course.

- ❑ I know what books or other materials I must purchase.
- ❑ I know what books or materials I must take to class.
- ❑ I must take notes during class.
- ❑ I must participate in class discussions.
- ❑ I must do homework assignments.
- ❑ I must read materials that are on reserve in the library.
- ❑ I must attend a laboratory (and I know where it is located and when I must attend it).
- ❑ I must have conferences with the teacher (and I know when and where I must go for the conferences).
- ❑ I must write a paper (and I know the format for the paper and when it is due).
- ❑ I must go on field trips or to concerts or museums.
- ❑ I know the class policy on missed and late assignments.
- ❑ I know the class policy on lateness and absence.
- ❑ I know how many tests I must take and when they will be given.
- ❑ I know how my final grade will be determined.

If you are uncertain about requirements for a course, ask the instructor to explain them.

Attend Classes Faithfully

At some colleges there are teachers who do not take attendance, thus giving students the impression that it is not important for them to go to class. However, even teachers who don't take attendance are not likely to be sympathetic toward students who cut class. Students who are frequently absent should not expect their teachers to do favors for them if they have a problem, and chances are that they will have a problem.

Faithful class attendance is essential because you are responsible for everything that happens in each of your classes, even if you are absent. For instance, you are expected to know about all assignments and tests even if they are announced on a day you are not in class! In addition, it is only by attending class that you can know what material your instructors emphasized by writing it on the board, by repeating it, or by other means; you cannot get this information from another student's notes. If you don't know what material your teachers consider to be most important, you will not know what to emphasize when you study for tests.

What to Do If You Miss a Class

- Contact a classmate to learn about assignments or tests announced in your absence.

- Hand-copy or photocopy notes taken by a classmate while you were absent.

- Deliver due assignments to the instructor as soon as possible.

- When you return to a class, check with your teacher to make certain that your classmate gave you correct information about assignments and tests, and ask the instructor for suggestions about how you can catch up with work you missed.

Following an absence, do not ask an instructor, "Did I miss anything?" The answer is yes. Also, do not tell a teacher that an absence is "excused" because of illness or some similar reason. Excused absences are noted in high schools but not in most colleges and universities. When a serious student is absent from a college class, the teacher assumes that the absence is unavoidable.

If an injury or illness makes it impossible for you to attend class for an extended period, contact the health services office of your school—someone in that office may notify your instructors why you are not attending classes. If your school has no health services office, call each of your instructors to inform them why you are not attending classes. When you must be absent for an extended period, your teachers may make special arrangements for you to catch up with course work; however, if your teachers do not make special arrangements, you may need to withdraw from your courses (see pages 36–37).

In addition to attending all classes, arrive on time. Students who are frequently late to class communicate the message to their teachers and classmates that they are disorganized, inconsiderate, or immature. Do not create an unfavorable impression of yourself; arrive at class on time.

Use the Right Study Equipment

Professional chefs don't try to cook gourmet meals without the right cooking utensils and qualified carpenters don't try to build houses without the tools of their trade, but many students try to pursue a college career with not much more than a ballpoint pen and a spiral notebook.

You will find that it is easier to be a student if you have the equipment that you need to do the work of a student efficiently. The following checklist may include some items that you need to purchase.

Study Equipment Checklist

Check the boxes in front of the items you own.

❑ Desk or table	❑ Staple remover
❑ Desk chair	❑ Ruler
❑ Reading lamp	❑ Hole punch
❑ Word processor or typewriter	❑ Notebook
❑ Bulletin board	❑ Notebook paper
❑ Bookshelves	❑ Typing paper
❑ File	❑ Index cards
❑ Required textbooks	❑ File folders
❑ Dictionary	❑ Pencils and pens
❑ Thesaurus	❑ Pencil bag
❑ Calculator	❑ Highlight pens
❑ Pencil sharpener	❑ Eraser
❑ Paper clips	❑ Rubber bands
❑ Transparent tape	❑ Scissors
❑ Household glue	❑ Clock or watch
❑ Stapler and staples	❑ Backpack, bag, or briefcase

Figure out how you can acquire any of this equipment that you need but don't have.

Select a Notebook

When you purchase study equipment, take special care in selecting a notebook; the notebook you choose can help or hinder you in maintaining the well-organized records of class notes you need to do well in your college courses. Though most students choose spiral notebooks, a ring binder is probably a better choice.

Reasons for Using a Ring Binder

- A ring binder can hold all the notes for all of your classes.
- Because you will have only one ring binder, you will always take the right notebook to class.
- Using a hole punch, you can insert papers that teachers distribute exactly where they belong in your notebook.
- You can add paper to a ring binder. As a result, you can always have enough paper in your notebook for courses in which teachers give long lectures.
- If you are absent, you can insert notes you copy from a classmate exactly where they belong.

- You can have an assignment section in a ring binder, so you don't have to have a separate assignment book.
- It is less expensive to buy paper for a ring binder than to buy spiral notebooks.

When a desk is too small to accommodate a ring binder comfortably, remove some paper from the binder for note taking. Or leave your ring binder at home, take notes on loose-leaf paper that you carry in a folder with double pockets, and insert the notes where they belong in your ring binder when you return home.

If you decide to use spiral notebooks, it is a good idea to purchase a separate notebook for each class. Buy notebooks with pockets on the inside covers so you will have a place to keep papers your teachers distribute, or use transparent tape to attach these papers to inside covers. Purchase a notebook of a different color for each course, and write the names of your courses in large print on the outside front covers of your notebooks to further ensure that you take the right notebooks to your classes.

Organize Your Notebook

Organize your notebook so that notes for each class are completely separate from the notes for your other classes. For example, notes for a biology, a math, and an English course should be kept in three separate sections of a notebook. If you mix your notes for one class with your notes for another class, your notes will not be properly organized when you study them to prepare for tests. In addition, be sure you set aside in your notebook a place to keep records about assignments, tests, instructors, and classmates.

Important Records for Your Notebook

- Information about assignments should explain exactly what they are, how they are to be done, and when they are due.
- Information about tests should include exactly what materials and topics will be covered on each test and the dates, times, and places that the tests will be given.
- Information about instructors should include their names, office locations, office telephone numbers, and office hours.
- Information about classmates should include the names, addresses, and telephone numbers of at least two people in each class whom you can contact for assignments and notes you miss when you are absent.

An explanation of a method you may want to use to keep accurate records of your assignments is on pages 103–105, and a form for keeping assignments is found in the back of this book.

Start a Reference Library

In addition to textbooks, you need reference books to help you in doing your college assignments. Your basic reference library should include a standard desk dictionary, a thesaurus, and an English handbook.

A Basic Reference Library

- In addition to a paperback dictionary to take to classes, you need a standard desk dictionary to use where you study. When you shop for a desk dictionary, pay special attention to the clear definitions, usage notes, word histories, and illustrations in *The American Heritage Dictionary of the English Language,* Third Edition (Boston: Houghton Mifflin, 1992).

- Your library should include a **thesaurus,** which is a book that lists synonyms; it will provide you help in finding the best words to express your ideas. I recommend *The Random House Thesaurus* because it is complete and easy to use.

- A good English handbook is an essential reference book because it contains a great deal of information, including answers to your questions about grammar, usage, and the correct format for term papers. *The Riverside Handbook,* published by Houghton Mifflin Company, is an excellent English handbook.

Eventually, you should add an almanac, atlas, and other books to your reference library. An **almanac,** such as *The World Almanac,* is an annual publication that contains a wealth of information on many topics, including facts and statistics about famous people, history, the countries of the world, and various sports. An **atlas,** such as *The Rand McNally World Atlas,* is a collection of maps of all the countries of the world followed by a detailed index that assists in locating the thousands of places indicated on the maps.

Keep Up-to-Date with Course Work

College terms start out slowly. They gradually get busier and busier, reaching a peak of activity at final examination time. If you fall behind in the work for a course, you may find yourself trying to catch up just when you are very busy with all of your other courses. Don't fall behind—keep up-to-date with work in all your courses.

This is doubly important when you must master information or **skills** taught early in a course in order to learn information or skills that are taught later in the course. Mathematics, science, technology, and foreign language courses are some of the courses that fall into this category. When you study, ask yourself this question: "Do I need to learn this information or skill in order to learn other information or skills later in the course?" If the answer to that question is yes, learn the information or skill immediately and review it often.

Do Assignments on Time

Instructors give assignments to provide practice for skills and for other purposes. They expect students to have assignments ready on time; many teachers do not accept late work, and other instructors give lower grades for assignments that are turned in late.

Some teachers give assignments that they review in class but do not collect and grade. Do these assignments faithfully; their purpose is to help you acquire a skill or to learn other things that you need to know.

Teachers sometimes require students to write papers that are five, ten, or more pages long. The grades for papers such as these usually account for substantial proportions of course grades. Therefore, before you start work on any paper for which you will receive college credit, make certain that you know the answers to the following questions.

Questions to Ask Before Starting a Paper

- How many pages long must the paper be?
- What topics are acceptable for the paper?
- In what format must the paper be presented?
- When is the paper due?

When you are uncertain about the requirements for a paper, schedule a conference with the teacher to receive the clarification you need.

English handbooks, such as *The Riverside Handbook*, mentioned on page 19, explain the steps in writing papers and reports of various kinds. It is wise to begin work on long papers as soon as they are announced. If you put off writing a paper, you may need to devote many hours to it just when you want to prepare for midterm tests or final examinations. If you are unable to complete a paper on time, you may need to ask your instructor to give you an incomplete grade (see page 37).

Keep a photocopy of each paper you write or store the final version of each paper in your computer so you will not need to rewrite it if a teacher misplaces or loses it. You will then have a record of references and other information in the paper to which you may want to refer in the future.

Submit Neat Assignments

Before you submit any written work, keep in mind that college instructors usually give higher grades to papers that are neat in appearance and free of errors than to ones that are sloppy looking and full of mistakes. Therefore, ask a friend or relative to proofread your written work before you give it to an instructor, and submit only papers that are as neat as you can make them.

When you do assignments for mathematics, science, or engineering courses, show all the steps you used in arriving at the solutions to problems. Also, leave plenty of space before and after each problem for your instructors to make comments and suggestions when they grade your work.

Use a Word Processor

If you do not know how to use a word-processing program, it would be a good idea for you to learn. Purchase a personal computer, if you can. If you cannot, one may be available for your use in an instructional resource center or in some other facility on your campus.

When you use a word processor to write papers, you don't need to waste your time recopying or retyping them. It is very time consuming to rewrite or retype an entire page when you want to make a change; however, changes can be made very easily and quickly on a word processor, and a corrected page can be printed by simply pushing a button. When you use a word processor, you can also easily move phrases, sentences, or paragraphs from one place to another if you decide to rearrange material.

In addition, the spelling checkers that accompany word-processing programs are invaluable for detecting misspellings and typographical errors. The limitation of spelling checkers is that they cannot differentiate words that are correctly spelled but inappropriately used. For instance, a spelling checker will locate only one of the two errors that are italicized in the following sentence:

> My best friend possesses two qualities *than* I *especially* admire: he is honest and kind.

A spelling checker will not identify *than* as a misspelling because, though it is used incorrectly, it is spelled correctly.

If you have never used a word processor, you are in for a delightful surprise. They make writing easier, and papers written using a word processor tend to receive higher grades because they usually have fewer errors than typed or handwritten papers.

Do Extra-Credit Work

When instructors offer special assignments or projects for extra credit, be certain that you do them. By giving extra credit for special work, teachers have a convenient way to find out which students are most eager to earn high course grades. Thus, the good work you do for extra credit might raise your final course grade from C to B or from B to A. However, doing only extra-credit assignments is not enough; students who do failing work all term are not likely to raise their grades much by doing extra-credit assignments at the last minute.

Be Prepared for Tests

Some first-year students make the mistake of not preparing properly for the first test their teachers give. Being poorly prepared, they do not go to class on test days, or they take tests and receive low grades. Either way, they start the term at a great disadvantage.

If you are absent the day a test is given, you may be required to take a make-up test that is more difficult than the test the other students took. Or if a teacher does not offer make-up tests, you may be given a failing grade for the test you missed.

If you receive a low grade for the first test in a course, you might become discouraged because you realize that it may be extremely difficult for you to earn a good grade in the course. Do not create an unnecessary source of discouragement for yourself. Be prepared to do your best on all tests.

Chapters 13 through 20 explain how to prepare for examinations, and Chapters 21 through 27 describe methods for answering test questions.

Participate in Discussions

Some instructors evaluate students on the contributions they make to class discussions. If an instructor announces there will be a class discussion, prepare for it by reading assigned material about the discussion topic before you go to class.

You do not need to do a great deal of talking during a discussion. It is usually better to say too little than to say too much. Make statements and ask questions that are directly related to the points under discussion and that keep the discussion moving toward the goal that has been established. Try using some of the following strategies.

How to Participate in Discussions

- If somebody says something that you do not fully understand, ask for a more complete explanation.
- If somebody gives information on a topic and you have additional information about the same topic, offer the information.
- If somebody asks a question that you can answer, give the answer.
- When it is appropriate, ask any question you have about the discussion topic.

You may grow weary of some students who try to dominate discussions by talking too much and by always trying to put in the last word on every point. This is inappropriate behavior during a discussion. Teachers may ask students who talk too much to give others a chance to speak, and they may also correct students who engage in other inappropriate behaviors, such as the following: being unprepared by failing to read required material about the topic, not paying attention while other students speak, stating opinions and experiences without referring to information in required reading material about the topic, interrupting others while they are speaking, doing anything that is distracting while others are speaking, engaging in arguments with others, and making unkind statements to others.

Polite disagreement is appropriate during a discussion, but unkindness is not. When people discussing a topic disagree, they are more likely to make a statement such as "I understand your point, but I don't fully agree because . . ." rather than "That's the dumbest idea I've ever heard."

Build Good Relationships

It is to your benefit to have good relations with your instructors. Should a problem arise, teachers will be more interested in helping you find a solution if you have made a favorable impression on them. Also, when they can't decide which of two grades to give you, they are more likely to give you the higher grade if they have positive feelings about you.

One way to make favorable impressions on your teachers is to pronounce and spell their names correctly and to address them using the titles they prefer. Notice the titles they place before their names on materials they distribute to you. If your instructors show their names as "Prof. Joseph Hosey," "Dr. Elaine Morton," "Mr. John Snyder," or "Ms. Kitty Bateman," they probably would like you to use these titles when you say their names.

Students also create a good impression on instructors when they show that they are willing and ready to learn by attending class faithfully, arriving on time, sitting in an attentive position, and contributing to the class by asking and answering questions. Most of your teachers will also appreciate it if you smile and say hello when you see them on campus. Following is a list of student behaviors that are a source of annoyance to many college teachers.

Behaviors That May Annoy a Teacher

- Cutting class
- Arriving late or leaving early
- Being unprepared for class
- Holding a conversation
- Not paying attention
- Making comments about the teacher's private life

- Acting bored or going to sleep
- Studying something for another class
- Criticizing the course or subject matter
- Eating, drinking, or chewing gum noisily
- Passing notes or making wisecracks
- Not having a notebook or pen

Work at creating a good impression of yourself; there are few assets more valuable than the good opinion others have of you.

EXERCISE 2.1 ### Checklist for Course Requirements

Use the "Checklist for Course Requirements" on page 15 to analyze what your teachers require. Use your analyses to write a summary of the requirements for each of your courses.

EXERCISE 2.2 ### Attendance Requirements

Write the answers to the following questions on notebook paper.

1. What are the official attendance requirements at your college? (Refer to your catalog.)
2. If any of your teachers have attendance requirements that are more or less strict than those stated in your college catalog, list those requirements.

EXERCISE 2.3 ### Your Study Equipment

Which items that you didn't check on the "Study Equipment Checklist" (page 17) do you intend to purchase? List them on a piece of notebook paper.

EXERCISE 2.4 **Your Teachers' Names**

List the names of all your teachers and the titles by which they prefer to be addressed.

1. _____

2. _____

3. _____

4. _____

5. _____

EXERCISE 2.5 **Course Information Chart**

List information about your courses, instructors, classmates, and tests on the "Course Information Chart" on the inside back cover of this book.

Know Degree Requirements

To graduate from your college or university, you must satisfy requirements that are stated in your school's catalog or bulletin (see page 4). The information and exercises in this chapter will help you learn what you must do to earn a degree at the school you are attending.

Degrees

When students graduate from colleges and universities, they are awarded **degrees,** which are ranks for those who successfully complete specified courses and other requirements.

If this is your first year in college, you are probably studying for an associate degree or a bachelor's degree. **Associate degrees** are usually offered by two-year and community colleges. They are most commonly the A.A. (Associate of Arts), the A.S. (Associate of Science), and the A.A.S. (Associate of Applied Science). **Bachelor's degrees** are offered by four-year colleges and universities. They are usually the B.A. (Bachelor of Arts) and the B.S. (Bachelor of Science). Some colleges and universities offer **master's degrees** and **doctoral degrees.**

You will be awarded a degree when you satisfactorily complete all the course work and other requirements that are listed in your **curriculum,** or program of study.

Credits and Hours

Credits and hours are assigned to most college courses. **Credits** are units given for the satisfactory completion of study that applies toward a degree. **Hours** are units that designate time spent in classrooms, laboratories, or conferences—they may be shorter or longer than sixty minutes. For example, at many colleges, students earn three credits when they satisfactorily complete a three-credit English composition course. However, the students devote four *hours* each week to the course—*three* hours in class and *one* hour in conference with their composition teachers.

25

FIGURE 3.1

The Usual Correspondences Between Letter Grades, Number Grades, and GPA Values

Letter grades	Meaning	Number grades	GPA values	
			System 1	System 2
A	Excellent	96–100	4.00	4.00
A−		90–95	4.00	3.70
B+		87–89	3.00	3.30
B	Good	84–86	3.00	3.00
B−		80–83	3.00	2.70
C+		77–79	2.00	2.30
C	Satisfactory	74–76	2.00	2.00
C−		70–73	2.00	1.70
D+		67–69	1.00	1.30
D	Passing	64–66	1.00	1.00
D−		60–63	1.00	0.70
F	Failing	0–59	0.00	0.00

Letter and Number Grades

Instructors evaluate papers, tests, and other student work using letter or number grades. Figure 3.1 shows the correspondences between letter grades and number grades used at most schools. Notice, for example, in Figure 3.1 that the **letter grade** of B+ corresponds to the **number grades** 87, 88, and 89. Study your catalog to learn the correspondences between letter grades and number grades that are used at your school. Sometimes there are important differences between colleges. For instance, some schools offer the letter grade of A+ and do not offer the grade of D−.

The Grade Point Average (GPA)

Most colleges compute students' average grades using the **grade point average** or **GPA,** which is a number that ranges from 0.00 to 4.00. Following final examinations, instructors submit letter grades to the registrar, who enters the grades on students' transcripts and assigns numerical values to them for the purpose of computing GPAs.

At the end of each term, your transcript will show two GPAs: one for the current term and a cumulative GPA for all the terms you have been in college. For instance, at the end of your third term in college, your transcript will report your GPA for the third term and a cumulative GPA computed on all the courses you took during your first three terms of college study. If you change curriculums, your transcript may show yet another GPA for the courses you have taken that apply toward the degree in which you are currently enrolled.

Figure 3.1 shows two widely used methods for assigning **GPA values** to letter grades. Notice in Figure 3.1 that when system 1 is used, letter grades have

How to Compute the GPA

Letter grades	Credits		GPA values		Grade points
A	3	×	4.00	=	12.00
B−	6	×	2.70	=	16.20
C−	6	×	1.70	=	10.20
	15				38.40

$$\frac{38.40}{15} = 2.56 \text{ GPA}$$

The grade point average is computed using the following procedures:

- Assign GPA values to letter grades.
- Multiply GPA values by credits.
- Add credits and add grade points to find totals.
- Divide total grade points by total credits.

In this example, the GPA of 2.56 was found by dividing total grade points (38.40) by total credits (15).

the same value whether they are accompanied by a plus or a minus (for example, B+, B, and B− all have a value of 3.00). But when system 2 is used, letter grades have more value when they are accompanied by a plus and less value when they are accompanied by a minus (for example, B has a value of 3.00, but B+ has a value of 3.30 and B− has a value of 2.70). "How to Compute the GPA" above explains methods you may use to compute your grade point average.

Final Course Grades

It may surprise you to learn that most instructors find grading to be their most painful responsibility. A few teachers avoid the discomfort of grading by giving all students high grades. But most accept the obligation to compare students and to award the highest grades to students who do the best work and the lowest grades to students who do the poorest work.

Instructors use a variety of methods for computing final grades; it is impossible to list them all. Following are descriptions of three commonly used methods:

1. *An instructor may determine final course grades by finding the averages for students' test grades.* For example, if a student has test grades of 77, 82, 86, and 75, an instructor will add the scores (320) and divide by the total number of scores (4) to find the average, which is 80. Figure 3.1 shows that a number grade of 80 is equivalent to a letter grade of B−; this is the final course grade the instructor will submit for the student.

2. *An instructor may determine final course grades by finding the average for letter grades students have received.* For example, if a student has the three letter grades of C+, B−, and B+, the instructor may convert these letter grades to the GPA values shown in Figure 3.1 (2.70, 3.00, and 3.30), add the values (9.00), and divide by the total number of grades (3) to find the average, which is 3.00. Figure 3.1 shows that 3.00 is equivalent to a letter grade of B. The instructor will enter a final course grade of B.

3. *An instructor may give extra value to one score in a set of scores.* For example, one psychology professor computes final grades from scores on a term paper, a midterm examination, and a final examination, giving double value to the final-examination score. Following is an example of how the teacher computed a student's final grade:

Term paper	B+	= 3.30 × 1	=	3.30
Midterm exam	B	= 3.00 × 1	=	3.00
Final exam	A	= 4.00 × 2	=	8.00
		4		14.30

The professor divided 14.30 by 4 to find the average, which is 3.575. Figure 3.1 shows that 3.575 is equivalent to B+ (3.70 is needed for an A−). The student's final course grade is B+.

These are only three examples of the many different methods instructors may use to determine final course grades. If an instructor does not tell you how he or she will determine your final grade, ask, so you will know what you must do to earn the grade you want for the course.

The Importance of Your GPA

In high school, students pass from one grade to the next if they pass all of their courses. However, college students can fail out of school even if they pass all of their courses because most colleges require students to maintain a minimum GPA of 2.00. Students who have passing grades of D, D+, or C− often have GPAs lower than 2.00.

Strive to maintain a good grade point average. An unsatisfactory GPA will have a devastating effect on your college career, and it may cause you to have a poor opinion of yourself. Following are some reasons you must have a satisfactory GPA.

Reasons for Having a Satisfactory GPA

- to graduate
- to avoid probation and dismissal
- to transfer credits to another school
- to participate in athletics
- to join certain clubs
- to be eligible for scholarships and grants
- to run for class or student government offices
- to qualify for interviews with employers who use GPAs to screen job applicants

When a student's GPA drops below 2.00, it is usually difficult or impossible to raise it to a satisfactory level. For example, students who complete fifteen credits in their first term with a GPA of 1.65 must have a GPA of at least 2.35 for fifteen credits in their second term to bring their GPA up to 2.00. Unfortunately, students who have a D+ average in their first term seldom have a C+ average in their second term. However, the GPA works to the advantage of students who earn good grades. If you have a GPA in the 2.50 to 3.50 range for many courses, you can receive a D, D+, or C− in one or two courses and still have a good average.

EXERCISE 3.1   **Credits and Hours**

The answers to questions 3, 4, and 5 are probably printed in your catalog.

1. For how many credits are you registered this term? _____

2. For how many hours are you registered this term? _____

3. How many credits are required in your curriculum? _____

4. What is the minimum number of credits for which you must register to be classified as a full-time student? _____

5. What is the maximum number of credits for which you can register without receiving special permission? _____

EXERCISE 3.2   **Letter Grades and Number Grades**

Study your catalog to learn the correspondences between letter grades and number grades at your school. Then write the letter grades that correspond to the following number grades.

1. 85 ____	7. 84 ____	13. 89 ____
2. 70 ____	8. 90 ____	14. 76 ____
3. 77 ____	9. 79 ____	15. 73 ____
4. 63 ____	10. 83 ____	16. 69 ____
5. 74 ____	11. 64 ____	17. 60 ____
6. 59 ____	12. 67 ____	18. 87 ____

<u>EXERCISE 3.3</u> ## Letter Grades and GPA Values

Study your catalog to learn the correspondences between letter grades and GPA values at your school. Then write the GPA values that correspond to the following letter grades.

1. C _____   5. D _____   9. C− _____

2. B+ _____   6. B _____   10. F _____

3. A− _____   7. D+ _____   11. A _____

4. C+ _____   8. D− _____   12. B− _____

<u>EXERCISE 3.4</u> ## Minimum Grade Requirements

1. What is the minimum GPA required for graduation? _____

2. Most schools have lower minimum GPA requirements for the first term or two of study and higher requirements for subsequent terms. If your school has such a policy, describe it below.

    _____

    _____

3. A college may require students to have minimum grades in specified courses (such as for courses in the subject areas in which students specialize). If your school has minimum grade requirements for specified courses, state them below.

    _____

    _____

4. List the grades that have a value of 0.00 for computing the GPA at your school.

    _____

5. When students are put on probation because of low grades, how much time are they given to raise their grades?

    _____

6. What action is taken against students who fail to raise their grades sufficiently during the time they are on probation?

    _____

EXERCISE 3.5   Your Teachers' Grading Practices

Find the answers to the following questions and write the answers on note-book paper.

1. What grading policies do your teachers have for assignments that are turned in late?

2. What grading policies do your teachers have for students who are frequently late to class?

3. What arrangements do your teachers make for students who are absent on the days when tests are given?

4. How will your final grades be determined for the courses you are taking this term?

EXERCISE 3.6   Computation of the GPA

Compute GPAs for the following problems, using the method that is used at your school. If you own a calculator, use it to help you make the computations.

1.

Letter grades	Credits		GPA values		Grade points
A	12	×		=	
B	8	×		=	
C	<u>15</u>	×		=	_____

   GPA = _____

2.

Letter grades	Credits		GPA values		Grade points
B	10	×		=	
C	6	×		=	
D	<u>2</u>	×		=	_____

   GPA = _____

3. | Letter grades | Credits | | GPA values | | Grade points |
   |---|---|---|---|---|---|
   | B | 6 | × | | = | |
   | C | 6 | × | | = | |
   | D | 6 | × | | = | |
   | F | 3 | × | | = | _____ |

   GPA = _____

4. | Letter grades | Credits | | GPA values | | Grade points |
   |---|---|---|---|---|---|
   | B | 6 | × | | = | |
   | C | 7 | × | | = | |
   | D | 4 | × | | = | _____ |

   GPA = _____

5. | Letter grades | Credits | | GPA values | | Grade points |
   |---|---|---|---|---|---|
   | B+ | 5 | × | | = | |
   | C | 4 | × | | = | |
   | C− | 6 | × | | = | _____ |

   GPA = _____

Find Help If You Need It

Most students have difficulty with a course at some time during their college careers. Academic difficulty often begins when a student falls behind in doing assignments, misses a quiz or test, or is absent from classes.

Get Help at the First Sign of a Problem

The first step in solving a problem is to acknowledge that it exists. Don't make the mistake of thinking that the problem will go away—it probably won't. If you have trouble in a course during the third week of a term, you are likely to be in worse trouble later on. Therefore, begin immediately to explore possible solutions to your problem. Don't be hasty; take time to investigate all possible remedies to your situation and weigh the advantages and disadvantages of each alternative before you set a course of action. Following is a summary of the strategies for solving academic problems that are explained in this chapter.

Strategies for Solving Academic Problems

There are six basic strategies you may use to help yourself resolve an academic problem.

1. **Study a book**. Investigate whether the answer to the problem is printed in a book you own, borrow from a library, or purchase in a bookstore.
2. **Talk with helpful people**. Confer with a teacher, counselor, adviser, experienced student, or other person who may suggest a solution to your problem.
3. **Study with a group.** You may be able to give and receive help from classmates by studying with some of them in a group.

4. **Improve your learning skills.** If your learning skills are deficient, take advantage of instruction your school provides in writing, mathematics, reading, or studying.
5. **Drop a course**. You may find it necessary to drop a course and take it again later; the withdrawal grade is provided for this purpose.
6. **Request more time.** If you request, a teacher may give you additional time to complete a term project or to study for a final examination; special grades are provided for this purpose.

Study a Book

Your first source of answers to study problems is books you may own, purchase, or borrow from a library.

College Study Skills provides help for taking class notes, studying for tests, answering test questions, and many other study problems. You may also own other books that contain answers to problems you encounter in college courses. For example, your English handbook should explain the format to use for a research paper you must write for a psychology course, and a math book you own may provide the review of mathematics you need for a chemistry course.

When you have extreme difficulty understanding the textbook for a course, visit the library and bookstore to locate other books on the same subject, and use the methods explained on page 127 to find a book you can more easily understand. If you are unable to find a more suitable book, use one of the other strategies explained in this chapter.

Talk with Helpful People

Counselors, advisers, teachers, and other students are sources of help when academic difficulties arise. The services counselors provide are explained on pages 6 and 7.

Most schools provide students with academic advisers who help them to understand their program requirements and to register in courses each term. You should also always consult with your adviser when you have any problem that pertains to your education and before you add a course, drop a course, change your major, withdraw from school, or transfer to another college.

It is important that you have an adviser whom you trust, with whom you feel comfortable, and who helps you in finding satisfactory solutions to your problems. If you are assigned to an adviser with whom you are unable to develop a comfortable, trusting relationship, find out what you must do to change advisers and make the change. It is essential that you have an adviser with whom you can communicate openly and who gives advice you trust.

Teachers can sometimes offer solutions that do not occur to students. A young man told his chemistry teacher that he was having trouble because his laboratory sessions were taught by an inexperienced laboratory assistant. His teacher arranged for him to sit in on laboratory sessions taught by another assistant. Instead of attending one laboratory each week, he attended two, but he did well in his chemistry course.

If you have established a good relationship with a teacher, you may be able to make a special arrangement with him or her. For instance, if you didn't do well on an important test, you might schedule a conference with your instructor to explain why you didn't do your best and to ask whether there is anything you can do to offset the low test grade. Some teachers take an interest in students who show that they are concerned about doing good work.

Teachers, counselors, and advisers also usually know if there are study groups, laboratories, **tutors,** or other sources of help available. If they do not know, they may advise visiting the office of the department that offers the problem course. Or they may suggest visiting an office of academic skills, a learning center, a tutorial service, or some other department or service on your campus.

Also, students who have already taken a course that gives you trouble may sometimes be your best source of help—they have already solved problems you are having. Make friends with second-, third-, and fourth-year students who are enrolled in your curriculum and who will give you suggestions on how to study for courses they have already taken.

Study with a Group

Some people learn better when they study with another student or with a group. A study group can help you become more involved in a course. It can also be a source of ideas about what to study, and it can provide you with a stimulating setting for learning. However, study groups can also become places for complaining, gossiping, and joking around, and they can be a waste of time unless all members are properly prepared. Study groups are most effective when they are limited to no more than five members and when all members have the same academic goals, are prepared and serious about studying and learning, and are available to participate in the group at the same time.

Sometimes groups are formed to study for a specific test. In this case, the group gets together a week or two before the test for members to discuss class notes and to make up a list of questions that might appear on the test. Group members then study alone to work out and learn their answers to the questions devised by the group. Then, the group gets together a day or two before the test to discuss each member's answers and to test one another.

If you organize a study group, discuss and agree on the group's purpose the first time it meets. Then, at the beginning of each meeting, decide what you will study, how long you will study, and when and for how long you will take a break. At the end of each session, summarize what was accomplished, discuss ways the next meeting might be more productive, and plan what you will study the next time the group meets.

If forming a study group for each of your classes is not practical, consider finding one student in each of your classes with whom you can study. Most experiences are more enjoyable when they are shared—studying can be, too.

Improve Your Learning Skills

Colleges usually test students' reading, writing, and mathematics skills when they apply for admission. After testing, many students are required or advised to improve learning skills. Take full advantage of any learning-skills instruction that you are offered. The faculty of your school believes that this instruction will help you do your best and earn a degree.

Some students who do poorly in college are the ones who do not take reading, writing, and mathematics instruction when they are supposed to because they aren't aware of how important these skills are to their success in college. Other students believe that their skills are better than they actually are. For instance, it is fairly common for students to complain about being required to take a special writing course even though they did well in high school English classes. The misunderstanding arises because sometimes high school and college teachers use different criteria for evaluating student writing. For instance, a high school teacher might read students' work looking especially for original thinking, whereas a college teacher might give as much attention to whether written work is free of grammatical errors and misspellings as to the ideas presented in it.

When learning-skills instruction is offered for no credit or for partial credit, students sometimes believe that they will learn nothing or that the courses are extremely easy. However, learning-skills courses usually are not easy because they require students to master skills that they did not master earlier in their schooling. You may need to work as hard in these courses as you do in courses that you take for full academic credit.

Drop a Course

When an academic problem cannot be solved in any other way, you may find that it is necessary to drop a course and take it again later. It is always advisable to drop a course when a final course grade is likely to be an F, and it is usually better to drop a course than to end up with a low grade, such as a D. The grade of D is acceptable only for an extremely difficult course that is not in your area of specialization. For example, students who specialize in computer technology may be satisfied with a grade of D in a very difficult history course but not in a computer course.

Before you drop a course, discuss the matter with your instructor—he or she may have suggestions about how you can deal effectively with whatever problem you are having in the course. However, keep in mind that effective teachers are often people who have an indestructible belief in students' ability to succeed. As a result, students sometimes complain that they have failed a course they wanted to drop but were convinced by a teacher not to drop. Therefore, take responsibility for your own decisions. After you discuss your intention to drop a course with an instructor, trust your own judgment about whether to drop it.

It is essential to drop courses officially, by making the proper arrangements with the admissions office or the registrar's office. If you just stop going to a class without officially dropping it, you will receive a grade of F or some other grade that has the same value as F in computing your GPA.

For the first few days of a term, dropped courses are usually not recorded on students' transcripts. After this period, it is necessary to request a **withdrawal grade,** or **W.** The W grade is not usually used to compute grade point averages; thus, it usually does not lower (or raise) GPAs. However, there are strict limitations on the time period during which this grade may be requested.

Before you request a W grade, keep in mind that when you drop a course, the total number of credits in your program may be reduced to fewer than you need for full-time student status. If you lose full-time status, you may lose important benefits, such as financial aid or the privilege of playing varsity athletics. Therefore, before you withdraw from a course, you may want to discuss your intentions with a financial aid counselor or other adviser.

Also, it is not a good idea to develop the habit of withdrawing from courses frequently. A transcript with several W grades creates the impression that it belongs to a person who had difficulty following through on commitments—an impression you do not want to convey to prospective schools or employers who examine your transcript.

Request More Time

If your problem in a course is that you need more time to finish a term paper or other project or to study for a final examination, your professor may give you additional time if you request it.

The **incomplete grade,** or **INC,** is provided for students who did satisfactory work in a course but who did not complete a term paper or other important project (and at some schools it is given to students who miss work because of an extended illness or family problems). For instance, when students do satisfactorily on all tests for a course but do not submit a required written report, a teacher may give them INC grades rather than grades such as B or C. When the report is completed, the INC grade is changed to A, B, C, or some other letter grade.

However, there are deadlines after which past-due work is not accepted. At most schools, INC grades are automatically changed to Fs when work is not turned in by deadlines. It is much better to keep up-to-date with course work than to request an INC grade and to run the risk of having it changed to an F.

Some schools also give students a chance to take make-up final examinations if they are absent from the final for a course in which all of their other work is satisfactory. They are given a course grade that is similar to the INC grade; when a make-up test is not taken by a specified deadline, the grade is automatically changed to an F. Investigate whether your school makes provisions for students who are absent from final examinations.

EXERCISE 4.1   **Using This Book**

Consult the table of contents of this book to answer the following questions.

1. What chapter explains how to take good lecture notes?   _____

2. What chapter explains how to remember and recall information?   _____

3. What chapter explains methods for selecting correct answers to multiple-choice questions?   _____

4. What chapter explains how to write good answers to essay questions?   _____

EXERCISE 4.2   **Finding Helpful People**

Seek the help of others if you have academic problems. List the following on a sheet of notebook paper:

1. the names of all your current teachers with whom you would feel comfortable in discussing any difficulty you might have in fulfilling the requirements for their courses

2. the names of two counselors, advisers, or former teachers with whom you would talk if you were having difficulty with a course

3. the names of at least three second-, third-, or fourth-year students enrolled in your curriculum from whom you would seek help if you were having difficulty with a course

4. the name of at least one person in each of your courses with whom you might study or who might help you in starting a study group for the course

---
EXERCISE 4.3   **Learning Skills**

If you have taken a writing, mathematics, reading, or study-skills course in college, write an explanation of whether you believe the course helped you improve learning skills.

EXERCISE 4.4   **Dropping a Course**

The answers to the following questions are probably printed in your catalog.

1. What is the last day this term you can drop a course and not have the course recorded on your transcript?   _____

2. What is the last day this term to request a W grade (or drop a course without academic penalty)?   _____

EXERCISE 4.5   **Requesting More Time**

The answers to the following questions are probably printed in your catalog.

1. What is the deadline for completing past-due work for INC grades students receive at the end of this term?   _____

2. To what grade is the INC grade changed when past-due work is not completed by the deadline?   _____

3. If your school has a grade for students doing satisfactory work who are absent from the final examination, write the grade on the line.   _____

5

Understand Your Memory

Have you ever wondered why you sometimes forget people's names a few seconds after you are introduced to them or why you are unable to recall the answers to test questions that you have studied thoroughly? This chapter gives the answers to questions such as these, and it also provides general background for your study of Chapters 13 through 20 of *College Study Skills*, which are devoted to helping you improve your ability to analyze, organize, remember, and recall information. Chapter 20, "Remember and Recall Information," provides practical suggestions for applying the information you will read about memory in this chapter.

The Three Stages of Memory

The most generally accepted theory about human memory is that it consists of three stages: sensory memory, short-term memory, and long-term memory. The characteristics of these three stages are summarized in Figure 5.1 on page 40.

Sensory memory registers all information that enters through the five senses: sight, hearing, taste, touch, and smell. Each bit of incoming information stays in sensory memory for a fraction of a second so that we experience consecutive bits of information in a smooth, uninterrupted flow. For example, when you listen to a speaker, your sensory memory holds each speech sound for a fraction of a second so that you experience a smooth flow of words and sentences rather than a series of unconnected sounds. Sensory memory is essential for interpreting experiences, but it is not useful for remembering information or events. For something to be remembered, it must first be transferred from sensory memory to short-term memory.

Short-term memory holds between five and nine pieces of information for about twenty seconds. The information stored in short-term memory is usually meaningful groupings of letters or numbers, such as "The Boer War was fought from 1899 to 1902." After information has been in your short-term memory about twenty seconds, you will forget it unless it is transferred to long-term memory.

39

FIGURE 5.1

The Three Stages
of Memory

Sensory Memory	Short-Term Memory	Long-Term Memory
Registers incoming information for a fraction of a second.	Holds up to nine pieces of information for about twenty seconds.	Stores a vast amount of information for as long as a lifetime.

$\rightarrow$ between Sensory Memory and Short-Term Memory, $\rightarrow$ between Short-Term Memory and Long-Term Memory.

When people use the word *memory*, they usually mean **long-term memory,** which is the stage of memory that holds an enormous amount of information for long periods, even a lifetime. The following discussions in this chapter are about long-term memory, because it is in long-term memory that you keep information to recall for answering test questions. *In the following discussions, the word* memory *refers to long-term memory.*

The Information-processing Model

The **information-processing model** applies to human memory the processes that pertain to computer memory: encoding, storage, and retrieval. The characteristics of these basic memory processes are summarized in Figure 5.2 on page 41.

Encoding

Encoding is the process by which information enters memory. Many kinds of information are encoded, including memories about how to ride a bicycle and memories of events that took place on birthdays and vacations. However, the focus of this discussion is on college subject matter, which is usually encoded into memory through the use of semantic codes or visual codes.

Semantic Codes   The word *semantic* means "pertaining to meaning in language," and a **semantic code** is a representation of information by its general meaning. For instance, a student wanted to learn the following definition for a business course:

A Definition

Selective advertising promotes the sale of brand-name products, such as Bayer aspirin.

She encoded this definition in the following way, using the general meaning of the statement rather than the exact words:

Semantic Coding of a Definition

Selective advertising is used to sell specific brand-name products, such as Macintosh computers and Skippy peanut butter.

FIGURE 5.2

The Three Basic
Memory Processes

Encoding
Information is put
into memory.

→

Storage
Information is held
in memory over
time.

→

Retrieval
Information is
recalled from
memory.

Compare the definition of *selective advertising* and the semantic coding of the term to notice that they are identical in meaning though they are worded differently. The comparison illustrates the basic characteristic of a semantic code—it is a general representation of a meaning rather than a rote, word-for-word memorization of it.

Visual Codes   A **visual code** is a mental image of information or an event. My memory of meeting my newborn sister was encoded as an image. When I want, I can visualize the moment I first met my sister many years ago. Visual coding can be used to remember many kinds of information. For example, an effective way to learn the locations of the countries of South America is to visualize a map of the continent with the names and boundaries of countries clearly marked on it. Or, the function of *selective advertising* could be remembered by visualizing the images of brand-name products, such as Bayer aspirin, Macintosh computers, Skippy peanut butter, and Nike shoes.

Storage

In the information-processing model, the act of holding information in memory over time is called **storage.** Any facts you can recall, any events of the past that you can recollect, and any information you can use to answer test questions are stored in your memory.

Automatic Processing   Information is stored in memory in a variety of ways. Some is stored by **automatic processing,** which is an effortless transfer of information. My memory of my baby sister was no doubt stored in my memory through automatic processing. Your recollection of the places you were yesterday was also stored in your memory by this means unless you made a conscious effort to remember those places.

Recitation and Rehearsal   Most information is stored in memory through recitation and rehearsal. **Recitation** is the act of repeating information over and over. For instance, when you are introduced to somebody and repeat that person's name several times to remember it, you use recitation.

Recitation is most effective when it is used together with **elaborative rehearsal,** or **rehearsal,** which is the act of analyzing information and relating it to information that is already stored in memory.

To **analyze** is to separate something into its parts for the purpose of studying the parts or understanding how they are related. A great deal of the instruction in *College Study Skills* is designed to help you improve your analytical skills. For example, you analyze information when you make outlines of written material and when you make notes for class lectures or textbooks. Rehearsal also includes relating new information to information previously stored in memory as, for instance, in rehearsing the following definition:

Morphemes are the smallest meaningful units of language, such as *un-*, *truth*, and *-ful* in *untruthful*.

In rehearsing this statement, you might observe that *un-* is a prefix, *truth* is a word, and *-ful* is a suffix. Then, you might recall other words that consist of these three kinds of morphemes, such as *indirectness* and *retelling*, which contain the prefixes *in-* and *re-*, the words *direct* and *tell*, and the suffixes *-ness* and *-ing*. An analysis such as this used together with recitation is very effective for storing information in memory.

One barrier to using rehearsal is that you may sometimes not have in your memory information to which you can productively relate new information. For instance, you can rehearse the dates of the Boer War (1899–1902) by relating them to the dates of the Spanish-American War (1898) and World War I (1914–1918) *only if* the dates of these other wars are in your memory. When college courses are difficult for you, it may be partly because you have insufficient information in your memory to which you can relate the new information you must learn.

Retrieval

In the information-processing model, **retrieval** is the act of recalling or recollecting information stored in memory. You retrieve information when you search your memory for it and recall it. Retrieval is aided by good organization and retrieval cues. Look at the following list of sixteen words.

An Unorganized List of Words

long, wine, chemistry, pear, algebra, narrow, grape, beer, milk, orange, wide, history, apple, psychology, soda, short

Compare this unorganized list with the following logically organized lists of the same words.

Organized Lists of Words

psychology	orange	wine	long
algebra	apple	milk	short
history	grape	soda	wide
chemistry	pear	beer	narrow

The words in these well-organized lists are the same as the words in the unorganized list, but, because they are organized, they are easier to store in memory and they are easier to retrieve.

Retrieval is further facilitated by using **retrieval cues,** which are words or images that help in recalling information. Each of the following lists of words is headed with a retrieval cue.

Subjects	Fruits	Beverages	Dimensions
psychology	orange	wine	long
algebra	apple	milk	short
history	grape	soda	wide
chemistry	pear	beer	narrow

When all these words are stored in memory, each retrieval cue can be used to recall four words. For instance, *fruits* can be used as a cue to retrieve *orange, apple, grape,* and *pear.*

Forgetting

Forgetting occurs very rapidly. Psychologists have documented that we forget about 70 percent of what we learn within two days of learning it! Three main theories have been offered to explain why we forget: decay, interference, and retrieval failure.

Decay theory proposes that if we don't use information stored in memory, we will not be able to retrieve it because it fades away from disuse. It's as though old memories crumble and disappear to make way for new ones. On the surface, this explanation seems reasonable. For instance, I was good at solving algebra problems when I was in high school, but it seems reasonable to me that I've forgotten virtually everything I knew about algebra because I haven't used it since I was a teenager. However, the other two theories about forgetting propose that once information is stored in memory, it remains there even though we may not be able to recall it.

Interference theory advances the idea that information stored in memory sometimes cannot be retrieved because other memories stored there interfere with retrieval. If you imagine your memory as books on a shelf, interference theory suggests that when new books are added, old books fall off the shelf into a place where they cannot be located. This theory is now more highly regarded than decay theory; psychological research seems to support the conclusion that we forget, not so much because memories decay, but because new memories interfere with recalling old memories (and old memories interfere with recalling new ones). According to interference theory, I still remember what I knew about algebra, but other memories interfere with my ability to find my memories about the subject.

Retrieval failure theory holds that when stored memories cannot be recalled, it is because proper retrieval cues are not available. This is a hopeful theory because it suggests what you can do to remember more and forget less. When you store information,

- organize it in a logical manner.
- include an effective retrieval cue.
- use elaborative rehearsal—analyze the information and relate it to other information that is already in your memory.

These are all skills you will improve when you study Chapters 13 through 20.

LEARNING CENTRE

<u>**EXERCISE 5.1**</u>   **Long-term Memory**

According to information-processing theory, the information in this chapter is not stored in your long-term memory unless you expended some effort to store it there. Test this theory by attempting to write the answers to the following questions without referring to the chapter for the answers. After you have attempted this exercise, do Exercise 5.2 before you study the chapter for correct answers.

1. How much information can be stored in (a) sensory memory, (b) short-term memory, and (c) long-term memory?

   a. _____

   b. _____

   c. _____

2. How long is information stored in (a) sensory memory, (b) short-term memory, and (c) long-term memory?

   a. _____

   b. _____

   c. _____

3. What is the main function of sensory memory?

   _____

   _____

   _____

4. What is encoding?

   _____

   _____

5. What is a visual code?

   _____

   _____

6. What is automatic processing?

   _____

   _____

7. What is elaborative rehearsal?

   _____

   _____

   _____

8. What are the two aids to retrieval?

   a. _____

   b. _____

9. What percentage of the information we learn do we forget within two days after we learn it?

   _____

10. What are the names of the two theories of forgetting that propose that once information is stored in long-term memory, it remains there even though we may not be able to recall it?

    a. _____

    b. _____

EXERCISE 5.2   Retrieval Cues

According to information-processing theory, retrieval cues help in retrieving information that is stored in memory. The questions in Exercise 5.1 were written to include no retrieval cues. In contrast, all the following questions contain retrieval cues that may help you retrieve information you remember as a result of reading this chapter. Check the box in front of the correct answer.

1. How many pieces of information can be stored in short-term memory?
   - ☐ a. one to five
   - ☐ b. three to six
   - ☐ c. five to nine
   - ☐ d. eight to twelve

2. Information is stored in sensory memory for
   - ☐ a. a fraction of a second.
   - ☐ b. one second.
   - ☐ c. twenty seconds.
   - ☐ d. up to a lifetime.

3. Which stage of memory provides a means for connecting bits of incoming information so that we experience them in a smooth, uninterrupted flow?
   - ☐ a. sensory memory
   - ☐ b. short-term memory
   - ☐ c. long-term memory
   - ☐ d. both a and b

4. The process by which information enters memory is called
   - ☐ a. storage.
   - ☐ b. encoding.
   - ☐ c. retrieval.
   - ☐ d. automatic processing.

5. A mental image of information or an event is called
   - ☐ a. a daydream.
   - ☐ b. an elaboration.
   - ☐ c. a hallucination.
   - ☐ d. a visual code.

6. The effortless transfer of information into memory is called
   - ☐ a. semantic coding.
   - ☐ b. visual coding.
   - ☐ c. automatic processing.
   - ☐ d. simplified processing.

7. The storing of information in memory by analyzing it and relating it to information already stored there is called
   - ☐ a. semantic coding.
   - ☐ b. visual coding.
   - ☐ c. maintenance rehearsal.
   - ☐ d. elaborative rehearsal.

8. The retrieval of information in memory is aided by
   - ☐ a. good organization.
   - ☐ b. retrieval cues.
   - ☐ c. semiautomatic processing.
   - ☐ d. both a and b

9. What percentage of information do we forget within two days after learning it?
   - ☐ a. 80 percent
   - ☐ b. 70 percent
   - ☐ c. 30 percent
   - ☐ d. 20 percent

10. Which theory of forgetting proposes that once information is stored in memory it remains there even though we may not be able to recall it?
    - ☐ a. decay theory
    - ☐ b. interference theory
    - ☐ c. retrieval failure theory
    - ☐ d. both b and c

EXERCISE 5.3   **Rehearsal**

Rehearsal, or elaborative rehearsal, involves analyzing information and relating it to information that is already stored in memory. When you answer the following questions using the information in this chapter, you will engage in rehearsal of that information.

1. What information is registering in your sensory memory at this moment?

_____

_____

2. You promised a friend that you would meet her in the cafeteria at noon, but you completely forgot that you had made this promise. Why did you forget?

_____

_____

3. What is your earliest memory from childhood?

_____

_____

_____

4. Name three fairly complicated procedures, such as the ability to ride a bicycle, that are stored in your memory.

   a. _____

   b. _____

   c. _____

5. Describe the room in which you sleep. As you do so, notice whether your memory is mostly in visual images or in some other form.

_____

_____

_____

6. Recollect some of the places you were yesterday. Were those places stored in your memory using automatic processing, recitation, or rehearsal?

_____

_____

7. How would recitation help you avoid the embarrassment of forgetting people's names when you are introduced to them?

_____

_____

8. Is there any course you will be required to take that will be difficult because you have little information stored in your memory to which you can relate the new information you must learn? If so, what is the course?

_____

9. If you forgot to take your shopping list with you to the grocery store, what are some retrieval cues you would use to remember the things that were written on your list?

_____

_____

_____

10. Think of a telephone number that you once knew and called often but that you can no longer recall. Why do you believe you are unable to recollect the number now?

_____

_____

Analyze Your Learning Style

A student came to me one day upset because she had not done well on a test in her psychology course. I was surprised. She was an outstanding study-skills student; she knew how to make notes and how to mark her textbooks and had learned all the other study procedures she needed for doing well in her psychology course. I set up an appointment for her to come to my office so we might find the source of her problem.

It was not long into our conference that the reason for her difficulty became obvious. When I opened her psychology textbook, I found no highlighting, underlining, or other marks in it. And, when I asked to see the notes she had made to learn the information in the book, she told me that she hadn't made any notes. Rather, she had tried to learn the information in the book by reading and rereading it, as she had done in high school. Her problem was that her learning style did not include using all the learning strategies she knew!

In case you have never thought about your learning style, this chapter is designed to give you insight into three aspects of it. You will find out about

- the learning strategies you prefer to use.
- your preferences for learning by visual, auditory, or kinesthetic means.
- the environmental conditions under which you prefer to study.

The following discussions and exercises will help you understand your learning style and give you an opportunity to think about whether you want to make any changes in it.

Learning Strategies and Styles

A **learning strategy** is a set of procedures for accomplishing a learning task, such as the procedures that are used to learn information for tests. A **learning style** is the set of procedures that a particular person actually uses to accomplish a learning task.

Students cannot use study strategies that they do not know, but, like my student who failed a psychology test, they sometimes do not use study strategies that they do know. Use Exercises 6.1 and 6.2 to think about and analyze the learning strategies you use.

Three Kinds of Learning

Most of what we learn, we learn through reading, watching, hearing, touching, or moving. When you read or watch, you use your sense of seeing; when you hear, you use your sense of hearing; and when you touch and move, you use your senses of touch and kinesthesia. **Kinesthesia** is the sensory experience that comes from moving muscles, tendons, and joints.

Some teachers provide students with visual, auditory, and kinesthetic learning experiences. For instance, a swimming instructor would probably teach you a new stroke by demonstrating it, explaining it, and having you practice it. You would receive the instruction *visually* by watching the demonstration, *auditorily* by hearing the explanation, and *kinesthetically* by making the movements of the swim stroke.

Though we all learn by these three means, some students have a definite preference for one of them:

- **Visual learners** prefer to learn by reading and watching demonstrations. Because they would rather read a textbook than listen to a lecture, they enjoy lecture courses more when they take many notes to study after class.
- **Auditory learners** prefer to learn by listening and discussing. Because they would rather listen to a lecture than read a textbook, they enjoy reading more after they listen to a background lecture on the subject matter.
- **Kinesthetic learners** prefer to learn by being physically involved, such as by doing something or by handling and manipulating things. Because they prefer to learn by experimenting on their own, they benefit most from listening to lectures and reading textbooks when they understand how these activities benefit them in their experimentation.

The primary advantage of knowing your instructional preference is that it will help you in adjusting to the demands of college study. For instance, in a discussion with a student I uncovered that his dissatisfaction with his history professor's lectures was not due to any fault in the lectures but to the student's preference to learn by reading rather than by listening. He adjusted to the history course by taking more notes and comparing what his teacher said to what was written in course reading material.

Use Exercises 6.3 and 6.4 to analyze whether you prefer to learn visually, auditorily, kinesthetically, or by using a combination of these means.

Environmental Conditions

Over the past twenty-five years, educational psychologists have studied learning style in a variety of ways. For instance, one area of research investigates how students' performance is affected by studying at times they prefer rather than at other times. This branch of research, called chronobiology, has produced clear evidence that students perform much better when they study or take courses at the times of day when they are most alert than when they study or take courses at other times.

It used to be commonly believed that everybody learns best when they study in a quiet place, seated at a desk. Today, these assumptions are questioned. Researchers have found that some students study better with the distraction of background music and that others learn just as well when they study sitting in an easy chair as they do when they study sitting at a desk.

Some of the other environmental conditions that affect studying include room temperature and the presence or absence of noise, food, or other people. Exercise 6.5 provides an opportunity for you to think about the environmental conditions under which you prefer to study.

EXERCISE 6.1   ## Learning Strategy Checklist

Following is a list of fifty-four learning strategies that are explained in *College Study Skills*. They are organized into the topics taught in nine chapters of this book. Check the boxes next to the strategies that you *actually use* and total the boxes you check in each category. You will use the totals when you do Exercise 6.2.

I use this strategy

A. Basic Strategies (Chapter 2)

1. At the beginning of each term, I find out exactly what teachers require. ☐
2. I attend all classes unless I am sick. ☐
3. I purchase all required books and other materials at the beginning of the term. ☐
4. I keep up-to-date with course work. ☐
5. I have all assignments ready on time. ☐
6. I am always prepared for tests. ☐

Total checks _____

B. Time Management (Chapter 11)

7. I schedule time for doing assignments and preparing for examinations. ☐
8. I keep a daily list of things that I need to do. ☐
9. I keep a record of the assignments for all of my courses in one convenient place. ☐
10. I set priorities for the order in which I do assignments. ☐
11. I schedule the study of difficult subjects at the time of day when I am most alert. ☐
12. I schedule major projects to complete them a step at a time over as long a period as possible. ☐

Total checks _____

C. Preparing for Tests (Chapter 13)

13. I use class notes as a guide about what to study for tests. ☐
14. When studying for tests, I emphasize information teachers said was important or difficult to learn. ☐
15. I use learning goals and review questions in textbook chapters as a guide in deciding what to learn in them. ☐
16. I always learn the meanings of important terminology in textbooks. ☐
17. I master skills by doing exercises and problems in textbooks. ☐
18. I always attend test reviews when they are offered. ☐

Total checks _____

D. Class Notes (Chapter 15)

19. I read about topics in textbooks before class lectures on them. ☐
20. I begin each day's notes with a heading that includes the date and lecture topic. ☐
21. I make major thoughts stand out clearly in my notes. ☐
22. I use simplified handwriting and abbreviations to write notes quickly. ☐
23. I review class notes immediately after class. ☐
24. I study class notes thoroughly before tests. ☐

Total checks _____

E. Previewing Textbooks (Chapter 16)

25. I know how to determine if a book is sufficiently up-to-date for a specific purpose. ☐
26. I read the table of contents in books to get an overview of the topics in them. ☐
27. I read prefaces and introductions in preparation for studying books. ☐
28. I locate and use appendixes. ☐
29. I locate and use glossaries. ☐
30. I locate and use subject indexes and name indexes. ☐

Total checks _____

F. Previewing Chapters (Chapter 17)

31. I use the title, introduction, and headings in a chapter to learn the topics in it. ☐
32. I use learning goals or chapter previews as guides for studying chapters. ☐
33. I study tables, graphs, diagrams, and other visual materials in a chapter before reading it. ☐
34. I read a chapter summary before reading the chapter. ☐
35. I identify the important terminology introduced in a chapter. ☐
36. I use review questions, exercises, and problems to check my learning. ☐

Total checks _____

G. Marking Textbooks (Chapter 18)

37. I underline, highlight, or otherwise mark information I want to learn in a book. ☐
38. I read a section of a book before I mark it. ☐
39. I use a variety of techniques to avoid underlining or highlighting too much. ☐
40. I try to mark information in a book that will help me make good notes later. ☐
41. I mark definitions of terminology in books. ☐
42. I mark examples in books. ☐

Total checks _____

H. Making Notes for Books (Chapter 19)

43. I make notes for information I want to learn in my textbooks. ☐
44. I use a variety of formats for notes. ☐
45. I begin notes with a title that accurately describes the information in them. ☐
46. I make major thoughts stand out in notes. ☐
47. I include examples in notes. ☐
48. I make notes in the classification chart or time-line format when appropriate. ☐

Total checks _____

I. Remembering and Recalling (Chapter 20)

49. I learn information by reciting it over and over. ☐
50. I learn information by analyzing it into its parts to study the parts and understand how they are related. ☐
51. I learn information by relating it to information I already know. ☐
52. I review information to guard against forgetting it. ☐
53. I use effective methods to learn virtually all kinds of information. ☐
54. I use a variety of effective techniques to recall information when I take tests. ☐

Total checks _____

EXERCISE 6.2   Analyzing Your Learning Strategies

Put a check in each box under the number of items you checked in each category in Exercise 6.1. For example, if you checked four of the basic strategies in Exercise 6.1, put a check in the box under "4" for "A. Basic Strategies."

	Number of Checks in Exercise 6.1					
	1	**2**	**3**	**4**	**5**	**6**
A. Basic Strategies	☐	☐	☐	☐	☐	☐
B. Time Management	☐	☐	☐	☐	☐	☐

C. Preparing for Tests	☐	☐	☐	☐	☐	☐
D. Class Notes	☐	☐	☐	☐	☐	☐
E. Previewing Textbooks	☐	☐	☐	☐	☐	☐
F. Previewing Chapters	☐	☐	☐	☐	☐	☐
G. Marking Textbooks	☐	☐	☐	☐	☐	☐
H. Making Notes for Books	☐	☐	☐	☐	☐	☐
I. Remembering and Recalling	☐	☐	☐	☐	☐	☐

The checks you placed on the lines create a profile of the strategies you use for studying. The checks farthest to the right indicate areas of relative strength, and the checks farthest to the left signify areas of relative weakness. There is room for improvement in any category for which you checked fewer than six items.

EXERCISE 6.3   ## Auditory and Visual Learning

Check one answer for each question.

1. I prefer to learn by
   ☐ a. reading a textbook.
   ☐ b. listening to a lecture.

2. I prefer to learn by
   ☐ a. watching a demonstration.
   ☐ b. listening to an explanation.

3. I like to read maps.
   ☐ a. true
   ☐ b. false

4. When listening to a lecture
   ☐ a. I take many notes.
   ☐ b. I take few notes.

5. I tend to remember people's
   ☐ a. faces but forget their names.
   ☐ b. names but forget their faces.

6. I don't mind studying with noise in the background.
   ☐ a. false
   ☐ b. true

7. I like a classroom seat from which I can
   ☐ a. see what is going on.
   ☐ b. hear what is said.

8. Graphs, charts, and diagrams
   ☐ a. are interesting to me.
   ☐ b. confuse me.

The *a* responses are usually checked by visual learners and the *b* responses are usually checked by auditory learners. If you checked about the same number of visual and auditory responses, you are probably one of the majority who prefer visual and auditory methods of learning about equally.

EXERCISE 6.4 ## Kinesthetic Learning

Check the boxes in front of statements that describe you or that you believe are true.

- ☐ If I bought a new VCR, I would probably try to figure out how it works by playing with it rather than by reading the owner's manual.
- ☐ I prefer a job that keeps me on my feet, moving from place to place, rather than one that gives me a chance to sit most of the time.
- ☐ The best part of studying sciences is doing experiments in a lab.
- ☐ Engineering and construction work interest me.
- ☐ I usually don't enjoy sitting in a classroom listening to a lecture.
- ☐ I like to cook meals.
- ☐ I get great enjoyment from typing or using a computer.
- ☐ When I was in grade school, I could usually find an excuse to get up and move around the room.
- ☐ When I'm in an airplane, I prefer to sit on the aisle so I can get up when I want rather than to sit by a window so I can see out.
- ☐ When I study, I need to take frequent breaks.

Most students check four or five of these statements; if you checked seven or more of them, you are strongly oriented toward learning kinesthetically.

EXERCISE 6.5 ## Your Environmental Preferences

Check the answers to the following questions that best describe you. If no answer to a question describes you, write an answer that does describe you.

1. I am most alert for learning difficult subjects ☐ in the morning, ☐ in the afternoon, ☐ in the evening.
2. I study best in a ☐ dormitory room, ☐ bedroom, ☐ living room, ☐ library, ☐ kitchen, ☐ lounge or ☐ cafeteria.
3. I prefer to study ☐ at a desk, sitting in a chair, ☐ in an armchair or on a sofa, ☐ on a bed or on the floor.
4. I like to study in a place with ☐ bright overhead light, ☐ medium light, ☐ dim light.
5. I prefer to study in a room that is ☐ hot, ☐ warm, ☐ cool, ☐ cold.
6. I learn best when I study with ☐ loud background music playing, ☐ soft background music playing, ☐ no background music playing.
7. When I study, the sound of voices or noise ☐ doesn't bother me, ☐ bothers me a little, ☐ makes it impossible for me to study.

8. When studying, I like to ☐ drink a beverage, ☐ smoke, ☐ chew gum, ☐ eat candy, ☐ eat snack food, ☐ eat a meal, ☐ avoid eating or drinking.
9. I prefer to study ☐ by myself, ☐ with one other person, ☐ with a group of people.
10. I study most efficiently ☐ when I am under the pressure of a deadline, ☐ when there is a little pressure, ☐ when there is no rush to meet a deadline.

From time to time, reevaluate the conditions under which you study best. Some students believe they study best late at night in a hot room under a dim light, only to later find that, in fact, they study more efficiently early in the day in a moderately cool room with bright sunlight flooding through a window. Experiment with a variety of environmental conditions to find the optimal study conditions for yourself.

EXERCISE 6.6　**Your Learning Style**

On notebook paper, write a description of the procedures that you prefer to use when you study. Include the following:

- a summary of the learning strategies you prefer to use when you study
- an explanation of your preference for visual, auditory, or kinesthetic learning
- a description of your environmental preferences when you study

Use your answers to Exercises 6.1 through 6.5 as the primary source of information in writing your description. Include a discussion of ways you might improve your learning style.

Deal with Stress

Stress is the mental or physical strain you experience in response to events that make psychological or physical demands on you. The events or situations that induce stress are called **stressors**; they range from major life changes, such as entering college, to everyday hassles, such as having to deal with an annoying neighbor.

Understanding Stress

- Stress is mental or physical strain that is experienced in response to psychologically or physically demanding events.

- Stress can arise from things that happen at school, at home, at work, or in any other area of life. For example, having a serious argument can be stressful whether it is with a teacher at school, a friend or relative at home, or an employer at work.

- Reactions to stress can be emotional, behavioral, or physical. Emotional reactions include depression and anxiety; behavioral reactions include eating, drinking, or sleeping too much; physical reactions include headaches, indigestion, or skin problems.

- Some ways of coping with and adapting to stress are to eliminate stressors, to manage time effectively, to exercise, to eat a nutritious diet, to value one's ability, to not insist on perfection, to turn threats into challenges, to change goals, and to use relaxation techniques.

We usually think of stress as being undesirable, but that is not necessarily so. The stress of being in armed combat may be harmful to all who experience it. However, some stress is beneficial for people who adapt to it. For example, in adapting to the stress of entering college, some students are challenged to do better in school than they ever thought they could. However, those who cannot adapt to the stress created by entering college may be overwhelmed and defeated by it.

As a college student, you will have many opportunities to experience stress. This chapter explains events that may be sources of stress for you, ways you may react to stress, and methods for adapting to and coping with stress. Following is a summary of the basic facts about stress.

Sources of Stress

Stress can come from problems at school, at home, at work, or in any other aspect of life.

Situations in Which Stress Is Likely to Arise

- You are going through a major change in your life, such as entering college, losing a job, or moving from one place to another
- You are required to do too much in too little time, such as having only one day to study for a test that requires three days of studying
- You are involved in a conflict, such as a serious disagreement with a friend, relative, teacher, employer, or coworker
- You are prevented from getting something you want, such as being unable to attend college because you don't have enough money for tuition

The "Sources of Stress Checklist" on page 59 lists common experiences students have that cause them stress. Read the stressors on the list and check the ones you are experiencing or have experienced in the past twelve months.

People often react very differently to the same situation; an event that is a stressor for one person may not be a stressor for somebody else. For instance, your roommate may study best under the pressure of having to learn a great deal in a short time, whereas you may "freeze up" and be incapable of learning anything when you are rushed. You may enjoy bungee jumping but become nervous on the dance floor, whereas your best friend loves to go dancing but gets sick to her stomach at the thought of making a bungee jump.

Reactions to Stress

When you are under stress, you will always react to it. Emotional, behavioral, or physical reactions may alert you that you are experiencing stress or that you are not coping with it effectively.

Emotional Reactions to Stress   Depression and anxiety are the most common emotional reactions to stress. Events such as a layoff at work, the death of a loved one, or the breakup of a relationship often bring about depression. Depressed people lose interest in life and feel "down," worthless, tired, and hopeless. Anxious people, however, tend to be worried, fearful, and uneasy about the future. They also often experience weakness or dizziness and feel irritable, tense, or nervous. Waiting to take a test, visiting a dentist's office, and asking an employer for a pay raise are examples of stressors that cause anxiety for many people.

Sources of Stress Checklist

The following situations commonly cause mental or physical strain. Check the items that state something you have experienced in the past year.

School

☐ Entered college for first time
☐ Transferred to new school
☐ Too many courses
☐ Too much schoolwork
☐ Serious problem with teacher
☐ Failed a course
☐ Lower grades than expected
☐ Missed too many classes
☐ Worried about grades
☐ Dropped more than one course
☐ On academic probation

Family

☐ Close relative died
☐ Close relative seriously ill or injured
☐ Serious problem with close relative
☐ Moved and left close relatives
☐ Parents divorced
☐ Parent lost job

Friends

☐ Close friend died
☐ Close friend seriously ill or injured
☐ Serious problem with close friend
☐ Moved and left close friends
☐ Not enough friends

Love and Marriage

☐ New love interest
☐ Became engaged or married
☐ Became pregnant
☐ Fathered a pregnancy
☐ Became a parent
☐ Sexual problems

☐ Serious problem with partner
☐ Trouble with in-laws
☐ Divorced or separated
☐ Couldn't find desired partner
☐ Felt physically unattractive

Work

☐ Unemployed
☐ Disliked job
☐ Serious problem with boss or coworker
☐ Fired or laid off
☐ Worried about losing job
☐ Started new job

Money

☐ Not enough money for school
☐ Not enough money for food, clothing, or housing
☐ Not enough money for car or entertainment
☐ Worried about debts
☐ Denied credit card or loan
☐ Took large loan

Living Place

☐ Too many responsibilities
☐ Not enough space or privacy
☐ Annoying neighbor
☐ Bad neighborhood
☐ Moved to new place
☐ Denied living in desired place
☐ Problems with roommate

Health

☐ Seriously ill or injured
☐ Unable to get needed medical or dental care
☐ Abused alcohol or drugs

Behavioral Reactions to Stress When people are under a great deal of stress, they often have difficulty concentrating on their work or studies. They may also have sexual problems or eat too much, drink too much, sleep too much, watch too much television, or spend too much money. Any excessive or self-destructive behavior such as these may be a response to stress.

Physical Reactions to Stress Stress has been identified as a contributing factor in many illnesses, including heart disease, diabetes, hypertension, and cancer.

Common Physical Reactions to Stress

- Aches in the neck or lower back
- Tension or migraine headaches
- Frequent colds or other illnesses
- Allergy or asthma attacks
- Excessive perspiration
- Constant feeling of tiredness
- Indigestion, constipation, or diarrhea
- Acne, psoriasis, or other skin problems

If you suffer any of these physical conditions and are under a great deal of stress, the ailment could be a symptom of the stress.

Coping with Stress

You may be one of the fortunate people who has a natural talent for managing stress by listening to music, gardening, or engaging in a hobby. However, if you want to improve your stress-coping skills, begin by using the "Sources of Stress Checklist" on page 59 to help in making a list of your stressors. The checklist does not include every source of stress, but the examples in it should help you in listing your stressors. Then, identify how you react to these stressors. Do you become depressed or anxious? Do you eat, drink, or sleep too much? Do you have frequent headaches, colds, or allergy attacks? Or, do you have reactions that are not mentioned on pages 58 and 60? Finally, use some of the following suggestions to cope with the stress. There is no one best way to manage stress; select from the following stress-management methods the ones that you feel are best suited to your personality and the kinds of stress you experience.

Eliminate Stressors Sometimes it is possible to eliminate a source of stress. For instance, if you are under extreme stress because of difficulty in a college course, you may be able to drop the course and take it later with a different teacher. Or, if you are upset because a neighbor's noise prevents you from getting a good night's sleep, you may be able to figure out a way to get the neighbor to be less noisy or arrange to move to a quieter place.

Manage Your Time Students who do poorly in college because of their tendency to procrastinate suffer the stress that comes from being underprepared and the embarrassment that comes from doing inferior work. The failure to manage time well is such a widespread problem that Chapter 11 of *College Study Skills* is devoted entirely to this topic. When you study that chapter, you will learn a systematic approach to planning how to make the best use of your time for study, work, and the enjoyment of life.

The natural reluctance to change is a major cause of procrastination; we are naturally attached to the ways that we habitually do things. As a result, many students encounter difficulty when they try to do well in their college courses by using study methods and procedures that helped them succeed in high school. They are reluctant to give up their accustomed study methods and replace them with procedures that are tailored to the demands of college study.

Seek Help from Others   When you are in distress, your greatest source of comfort may be another person who is understanding and can help you deal with your problem. Turn to a friend, relative, teacher, counselor, or other person who might be able to help you in dealing with your problem. See the suggestions on pages 34–35.

Exercise   In addition to its obvious physical benefits, exercise promotes mental and emotional health. Walking and climbing stairs are two forms of exercise that are readily available to students on most college campuses. You should expect to feel an increase in energy and a decrease in fatigue for up to two hours after a brisk walk. Wear comfortable walking shoes and step out smartly; don't stroll. Try to walk one or two miles every day at the rate of at least four miles per hour.

Some people don't exercise because they believe it saps them of their energy and leaves them too tired to meet their other responsibilities. This is a completely false belief. Exercise strengthens you, making you better able to withstand stress and to accomplish the mental and physical tasks that are required of you.

Make exercise an integral part of your life by varying your activity from day to day. For instance, you might stretch your muscles by bicycling on Sunday, walking three miles on Monday, mowing the lawn on Tuesday, shooting hoops on Wednesday, swimming on Thursday, jogging on Friday, and cleaning house on Saturday.

Eat a Nutritious Diet   A nutritious diet promotes well-being and strengthens the body so it can deal more effectively with stress. The key to good nutrition is to eat a variety of foods, emphasizing large quantities of fruit, vegetables, bread, and cereal and small servings of meat, milk, and cheese. Experts also advise not eating too much fat, sodium (salt), and sugar—major ingredients in popular foods such as hamburgers, hot dogs, potato chips, French fries, soft drinks, salad dressings, cookies, muffins, ice cream, and candy.

If you take a health-education course, you will learn the fundamentals of good nutrition. Or, you can learn about a healthful diet by reading books that are available in your college library or bookstore. Also, see pages 198–202 of *College Study Skills.*

Sleep Sufficiently   Lack of sleep weakens you and makes you less able to deal effectively with stress. Some medical doctors recommend nine hours of sleep a night; if you sleep less than you need, you may be creating an unnecessary source of stress for yourself.

By keeping track of how long I slept and how well I functioned the next day, I found that I need eight hours of sleep and that I can function for one day with seven hours of sleep and "get by" on six hours of sleep if it is followed by an undemanding day. If you keep similar records, in a week or two you will know whether insufficient sleep is a source of stress for you and how much sleep you need to function at your best.

Value Your Ability   Some people feel that there are certain things they cannot do or subjects that they are incapable of learning. If you feel there is a subject that you cannot learn, ask yourself this question: "Why do I feel that I cannot learn this subject when I know that people just like me learn it, and do well in it?" If you answer this question, you may discover that the only thing that is preventing you from learning a subject is your erroneous belief that you cannot learn it.

Don't Insist on Perfection   You do not need to be outstanding in every subject you study in college. If you are majoring in business and receive low grades in your business courses, then you have a serious problem. But if you are majoring in business, you don't need to be outstanding in all courses outside your specialization. Also, keep in mind that you do not need to be outstanding at something to enjoy it. For instance, you may have a singing voice that nobody would pay to hear, yet derive great pleasure from singing. The same is true of subjects you study in college. Give yourself permission to enjoy all the subjects you study, even the ones in which you do not excel.

Turn Threats into Challenges   Some stressful situations can be controlled by treating them as challenges. For instance, if you have difficulty with a college subject, develop more effective study strategies rather than dwell on the possibility of failing or doing poorly. A subject that you find difficult to learn may merely require more time than you are devoting to it. Ask yourself this question: "Could I learn this subject if I spent more time studying it?" If so, give the subject the additional time that it requires. You will then have the satisfaction of learning something that you thought you could not learn; you will discover that you can do things that you thought you could not do. This will improve your opinion of yourself and reduce your stress.

Change Your Goals   You may experience stress because you lack the necessary support or ability to achieve a goal. In such instances, you can take pressure off yourself by changing your goal. For example, if you lack the financial support to achieve your goal of graduating from college in four years, you might take a job to earn money and revise your goal to graduate in six years. If you lack the math skills to achieve your goal of becoming a certified public accountant, you might alter your goal to acquire the necessary math skills or to prepare for some other profession. (Chapter 10 of *College Study Skills* explains how to establish and work toward realistic goals.)

Use Relaxation Techniques   Deep muscle relaxation, imagery, and meditation are three relaxation techniques that help the body cope with stress by triggering a calming relaxation response. Instruction in one or more of these methods may be offered by your school's counseling, psychology, or physical education department.

- *Deep muscle relaxation* involves tensing and relaxing each part of your body at least twice, breathing in while tensing and breathing out while relaxing. Begin with your hands and work up to your biceps, shoulders, neck, face, and down to your chest, stomach, buttocks, legs, and feet.
- *Imagery* requires closing your eyes to visualize yourself in a totally relaxed state or performing a difficult task perfectly. For instance, you might relax by imagining yourself sitting on a mountaintop or build confidence by visualizing yourself walking down an aisle in cap and gown to receive your college diploma.
- *Meditation* is a method for telling your mind to be quiet. It requires being in a quiet place, assuming a comfortable position, organizing attention by focusing on something calming (such as your breathing), and allowing your mind to relax without making an effort for it to do so.

Muscle relaxation, imagery, and meditation are all effective in reducing stress. It would be worthwhile to take advantage of relaxation instruction, if it is available at your school. Even if you find that it is inconvenient for you to take time each day to practice a relaxation method, once you master one of the techniques, you will have it as a resource to draw on when you are under stress.

EXERCISE 7.1 Sources of Stress

Check the stressors in the "Sources of Stress Checklist" on page 59 that you are experiencing or have experienced in the past twelve months. What are the greatest sources of stress for you at this time? Write your answer on notebook paper.

EXERCISE 7.2 Reactions to Stress

Read "Reactions to Stress" on pages 58 and 60, and then write the answers to the following questions on notebook paper:

1. Are you experiencing any emotional reactions to stress? Are you depressed or anxious, or are you experiencing other emotions, such as anger, shame, or guilt?

2. Is your behavior affected by stress? Are you having difficulty concentrating? Or, are you eating, drinking, or sleeping too much?

3. Do you have physical problems as a result of stress, such as backaches, headaches, indigestion, constipation, or skin disorders?

EXERCISE 7.3 Coping with Stress

Considering your personality and the kinds of stress you experience, which of the stress-management strategies described on pages 60–63 do you believe may be helpful to you in reducing stress you are under now or may experience in the future? Write your answer on notebook paper.

Use the Library

The library is the center for study and research on most campuses. You will use the library frequently to collect information for papers you write and other projects you do for your courses.

Library Instruction

It is likely that your library offers a service to teach you about its facilities and their proper use. The instruction may be printed in a booklet or in a series of leaflets, it may be recorded on videocassettes or on computer software, or it may be presented by a librarian to small groups of students at various times during the school year. Because the procedures for doing research at your college library may be quite different from the procedures you have used at other libraries, it is important that you take advantage of whatever instruction is available. You will enjoy your visits to the library more when you know what is available there and how to access it.

When you need help in a library, go to a librarian for assistance. Librarians are highly trained professionals who can teach you how to use library facilities, show you how to search for material on a specific topic, and inform you about sources of information and library services that you might overlook. If you find that some librarians are more helpful to you than others, remember who the more helpful ones are and seek them out when you need help in the future.

Computer Technology

In recent years, the computer has become the basic tool for accessing information about the books, magazine articles, and other material available in a library. Information about library holdings that was once available only in printed indexes is now more likely to be stored in **databases** that are accessed using a computer terminal.

Databases have several advantages. Information can be found more quickly by using a database than by any other means and databases eliminate the need for taking notes because the information contained in them can be printed out. In addition, databases can usually be accessed at computer terminals located in departmental offices, learning centers, and other convenient places on a campus.

Advances in technology have provided libraries with index choices that were not previously available to them. For instance, in the past a publication called the *Readers' Guide to Periodical Literature* was the only widely used index to the articles in popular magazines. Today, the information contained in the *Readers' Guide* is also available in various computer databases. A college library may now pick and choose from among many databases to select the particular ones that will best serve the students who use the library. My college library, for instance, uses a service called Infotrac, which provides an index to hundreds of magazines, scholarly journals, and newspapers. However, the databases available at your college library may be quite different from the ones at other libraries.

Popular Magazines

Begin your research by investigating what has been written about your topic in popular magazines. Because the papers you write in college will be closer to the length of articles than to the length of books, magazine articles are likely to give you some good ideas about the ways you can discuss a topic in a paper for a college course. In addition, magazines often contain information that is more up-to-date than the information in books.

Databases   The following reference to an article in *Newsweek* was found by searching a database using the subject "Drugs and Youth."

```
Source:    Newsweek, Feb 12, 1996 v127 n7 p68(2).

Title:     Parents' dilemma; if you did drugs as a kid, how
           do you talk to your children about the dangers?

Author:    John Leland


Abstract: Many baby-boomers who used recreational drugs in the
1960s and 70s are now parents who dread the thought of their
school-age children trying drugs.  They find it difficult to
justify forbidding their children to experiment and to decide
what to tell their children about their own experiences.

Subjects: Drugs and youth - Psychological aspects
```

This printout from a database states that there is an article related to the subject "Drugs and Youth" on page 68 of the February 12, 1996, issue of

Newsweek. In addition, it includes an **abstract**, or summary, of the information contained in the article.

Because your library probably does not subscribe to all magazines that are listed in a database or bound-volume index, it maintains a list, file, or database of all the magazines, newspapers, **journals**, and other **periodicals** that are included in its collection. This list or file will tell you whether your library has the periodical you want and, if so, for which years it owns the publication. If a periodical you want is not available, a librarian may be able to inform you whether it is in the collection of some other library in your community.

Bound-Volume Indexes   In doing research, you will find that it is sometimes necessary to refer to bound-volume indexes. First, your library may have only bound-volume indexes for some of the publications to which you wish to refer. Second, most databases do not include information about articles in all the issues of a publication. For instance, the databases at the library I use do not include information about articles in any magazine published before 1980. If I want to research articles published before 1980, I must use a bound-volume index.

The *Readers' Guide to Periodical Literature* is a bound-volume index to the articles that appear in about two hundred popular magazines, such as *Newsweek*, *Time*, and *Consumer Reports*. Articles are listed by subject and author. Following is an excerpt from the *Readers' Guide*. It shows the entry for the same *Newsweek* article that was used to illustrate the information in databases. Compare the following entry with the printout of the database entry shown on page 65.

DRUGS AND YOUTH
  Parents' dilemma [parents who were hippies talk to their
    children about drugs] J. Leland. il *Newsweek* v127
    p68–9 F 12 '96

Notice that this entry uses different abbreviations than the database entry and it does not include an abstract.

The abbreviations used in the *Readers' Guide* are clearly explained on the first pages of each volume. By consulting those pages, you will learn, for instance, that months are abbreviated using one or two letters. For example, *F* is the abbreviation for February, but *Je* is used for June and *Jl* is used for July.

When you locate an article in a bound-volume index that you want to read, make notes that include (1) the title of the article, (2) the name of the magazine, (3) the volume number of the magazine, (4) the pages on which the article is printed, and (5) the month and year the magazine was published. Following is an example of notes for the *Readers' Guide* entry above.

> "Parents' dilemma"
> Newsweek
> Volume 127, pages 68-69
> February 12, 1996

The *Readers' Guide* and other indexes to periodical literature are published in volumes for various time periods. You may need to consult several volumes of an index.

Specialized Periodicals

Your library also has databases or bound-volume indexes to periodicals that publish articles about specialized subjects. The *Art Index*, for instance, is a bound-volume index that lists articles about fine arts, architecture, photography, film, and many other related subjects. Other such indexes to specialized and professional periodicals include the *Applied Science and Technology Index*, the *Business Periodicals Index*, the *General Science Index*, the *Humanities Index*, and the *Social Science Index*.

When you do research for college courses, it is important to consult indexes such as these. For example, if you write a paper for a business course, you should consult the *Business Periodicals Index* or a database of business periodicals.

Newspapers

When you want to find articles in newspapers, consult the *New York Times Index*. This index, which may be in a database or bound volumes, lists all the articles that have ever appeared in the *New York Times*. Your library may also have CD-ROMs that contain abstracts and even entire articles from the *New York Times* that you can print out or download to your own disk.

All issues of the *New York Times*, beginning in 1851, are available on microfilm at most college and university libraries. Also, because news events are printed in most newspapers at about the same time, the *New York Times Index* may be used to locate articles published in other newspapers. For example, if you learn in the index that the *New York Times* published an important news story on May 15, 1998, you may be confident that your local newspaper also published a story about the event on or about May 15, 1998.

Books

The books owned by a library are located by referring to an index in which they are organized by author, title, and subject. In the past, the index was invariably a **card catalog**, in which information is printed on cards that are stored in filing cabinets. However, today the index is much more likely to be in a database that is accessed by using a computer terminal. Use the following procedure to locate books:

- When you know the author, use the author's name to locate the book.
- When you know a title, use the title to locate the book.
- When you do not know the author or a title, use the subject to locate books.

Figure 8.1 shows the information that was located by searching a database using the title of the book: *Modern Man in Search of a Soul*. The printout in Figure 8.1 includes the information that the library owns two copies of the

FIGURE 8.1

Printout of a
Database Entry
for a Book

```
      AUTHOR      Jung, C. G. (Carl Gustav), 1875—1961.

      TITLE       Modern man in search of a soul, by C.G. Jung.
                  [Translated by W.S. Dell and Cary F. Baynes]

  PUBLISHER       New York, Harcourt, 1933.

  DESCRIPTN       ix, 282 p. 23 cm.

   SUBJECTS       1) Psychoanalysis
                  2) Therapeutics, Suggestive.


              CALL NUMBER        STATUS          LIBRARY
   1.         2nd Floor          Due date        Central Library
              130 J954M          01 Aug 96

   2.         REF -- 2nd Floor   Checked In      Central Library
              SCS Desk (SK)
              R130 J954M
```

book. One copy is located in the **stacks** and the other at the reference desk on the second floor of the central library. One copy of the book is checked out and it is due to be returned on August 1, 1996. The other copy is for reference; it may be read in the library, but it cannot be checked out.

Figure 8.2 shows the author, title, and subject card for Carl Jung's book, *Modern Man in Search of a Soul,* from a card catalog.

Call numbers give specific information about the location of a book. The letters and numbers typed in the upper left corner of the cards in Figure 8.2 on page 69 are call numbers and so are the numbers and letters under the heading "CALL NUMBER" in the database printout in Figure 8.1 above.

Notice that Figures 8.1 and 8.2 show different call numbers for the same book. The reason is that there are two systems used for call numbers: the Dewey Decimal system and the Library of Congress system. The call number in Figure 8.1, which begins with the numbers *130,* is an example of the Dewey Decimal system; the call number in Figure 8.2, which begins with the letters *BF,* is an example of the Library of Congress system. Some libraries use both systems because they switched to the Library of Congress system after first using the Dewey Decimal system.

When you locate a book you want to examine, print out the information from the database or copy the following information from cards in a card catalog:

- The call number
- The name of the author
- The title of the book

Libraries print leaflets or post signs to guide library users to the locations of books. If you have difficulty locating a book, ask a librarian for assistance.

FIGURE 8.2

An Author, Title, and Subject Card

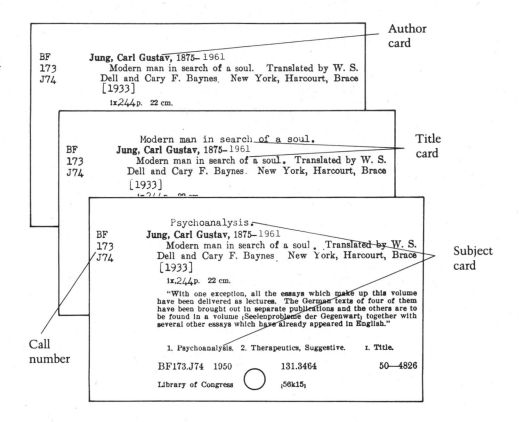

Reference Books

The collection of a library may include specialized encyclopedias, dictionaries, indexes, and other reference books for art, anthropology, economics, education, and other subjects. Some reference books are helpful for researching the life and accomplishments of a person, and some indexes and digests are useful when writing book reports or book reviews. When you do research in a library, ask a reference librarian to suggest specialized reference books that may be helpful to you.

You will usually want to consult at least a general encyclopedia. Articles in encyclopedias may give you good ideas about how you can narrow the topic of a paper, and they sometimes include titles of books or articles that are worthwhile to examine.

The two best-known general encyclopedias are the *Encyclopedia Americana* and the *Encyclopaedia Britannica*. However, some articles in these encyclopedias are written using highly technical language. Therefore, do not overlook *Collier's Encyclopedia*, *Merit Students Encyclopedia*, and *World Book Encyclopedia*. All three of these are easy-to-read and authoritative encyclopedias.

Borrowing and Photocopying

Library materials may be studied in the library, or they may be borrowed or photocopied. When you find information in a book, borrow the book if it is one that circulates. If it is a reference book, you may want to photocopy the pages that you need to use. For instance, if you find a useful article in an encyclopedia, it may be convenient to have a copy of the article to refer to when you are at your usual study place. It is also a good idea to photocopy useful magazine and newspaper articles. For a small investment in photocopying, you can analyze the articles in the comfort of your home rather than in the library.

Whenever you photocopy material, write complete bibliographical information directly on your copy. For instance, if you photocopy pages from a book, write the name of the book, author, publisher, and copyright date directly on the copy.

EXERCISE 8.1   ## Selecting a Topic

Do the following activities to select a topic that you will research in the library.

1. Suppose that you must write a five-page paper about any topic you choose for one of your courses. Which course will you use for this exercise?

    _____

2. Study the table of contents and the index in the textbook for the course you listed above. Select three topics in the book that are especially interesting to you. Write the topics on the following lines together with the page numbers on which the topics are discussed in the book.

    a. _____

    b. _____

    c. _____

3. Read about the three topics in the textbook. Which of the three topics is most interesting to you?

    _____

Do the following exercises using the topic that interests you most.

EXERCISE 8.2   ## Popular Magazines

Search a database or refer to the most recent annual volume of the *Readers' Guide* for magazine articles about the topic you are researching. If you don't find any articles listed for your topic, ask a librarian for help. If the librarian cannot help you find articles for your topic, select one of the other topics you listed in Exercise 8.1.

1. How many articles are listed for the topic? _____

2. If you used a database, print out information about three articles that appear in publications that your library owns.

3. If you used the *Readers' Guide,* make notes of the type illustrated on page 66 for three of the articles. Select articles in magazines that your library owns.

   a. _____

   b. _____

   c. _____

4. Locate the three articles in the library and read them quickly. Which one of the three articles has the most interesting and useful information for writing a five-page paper about your topic?

   _____

EXERCISE 8.3   **Newspapers**

Search a database or refer to the most recent annual volume of the *New York Times Index* for articles about the topic you are researching. If you do not find any articles listed for your topic, ask a librarian for help.

1. How many articles are listed for your topic? _____

2. If you are using a database, print out the information about one article that you want to read.

3. If you are using the *New York Times Index,* write the title of one of the articles, the date it was published, and the page numbers on which it is printed.

   _____

   _____

   _____

4. What procedure must you use to read articles published in the *New York Times* five years ago?

   _____

   _____

EXERCISE 8.4   **Books**

Search a database or refer to the card catalog to locate books for the topic you are researching. Ask a librarian for help if you cannot find them.

1. How many books are there for your topic?   _____

2. If you used a database, print out information for three books that include information about your topic.

3. If you used a card catalog, list the call numbers, names of authors, and titles for three books that include information about your topic.

   a. _____

   b. _____

   c. _____

4. Attempt to locate these three books in the library. How many of them did you find?

   _____

5. Ask a librarian how you can secure a copy of a book when it is not where it is supposed to be in the library. Write the answer on the following lines.

   _____

   _____

   _____

EXERCISE 8.5   **An Encyclopedia**

Find where your topic is discussed in an encyclopedia.

1. To which encyclopedia did you refer?

   _____

2. In which volume and on which pages is your topic discussed?

   _____

Develop Organizational Skills

In this chapter, you will learn how to use Roman numerals, capital letters, and Arabic numerals to make notes in the traditional **outline** format, which is illustrated in the outline titled "Fast Food Restaurants," below.

To make outlines, you must analyze written material—you must study it to understand how statements in it are related. Analysis, you may recall, is an essential step for effectively storing information in memory (see pages 41–42). Thus, the abilities you will develop by learning to make outlines are the ones you will use to take good class notes, to select what to underline in your textbooks, to make well-organized notes for learning information in books, and to store information in your memory.

Major Thoughts and Details

In an outline, major thoughts are labeled with Roman numerals and listed under titles, and details are labeled with capital letters and listed under major thoughts.

Fast Food Restaurants
 I. McDonald's
    A. Big Mac
    B. French fries
    C. Apple pie
    D. Chocolate shake
 II. Burger King
    A. Whopper
    B. Onion rings
    C. Vanilla shake
 III. Dairy Queen
    A. Big Brazier
    B. Fiesta sundae

This outline is organized to show that McDonald's, Burger King, and Dairy Queen are three fast food restaurants and to identify some of the foods each restaurant serves.

Figure 9.1 below illustrates how to check whether the information in an outline is logically organized. Notice in Figure 9.1 that "McDonald's," "Burger King," and "Dairy Queen" logically belong under "Fast Food Restaurants" because they are three fast food restaurants. Also, observe that the various types of food are logically organized under the names of the restaurants that serve them. For instance, "Big Mac" is under "McDonald's," and "Whopper" is under "Burger King." When information is logically organized in this way, it is said to be logically subordinated.

The exercises for outlines in *College Study Skills* are prepared so you will learn to make outlines in which all statements are logically subordinated and logically coordinated.

FIGURE 9.1

Logical Subordination of Details

Coordination in Outlines

Statements in outlines must be logically subordinated and logically coordinated. To coordinate is to put together things that belong together. For instance, when you wear two brown socks, your socks are coordinated. However, if you wear a brown sock and a white one, your socks are not coordinated. Cross out any items that you believe are not logically coordinated in the following outline.

My Summer Vacation
I. California
   A. Los Angeles
   B. Uncle Joe
   C. San Francisco
II. Washington
   A. Swimming
   B. Sailing

C. Mt. Rainier
D. Hiking
III. Yellowstone National Park
IV. Oregon
   A. Crater Lake

You should have made the outline coordinate by crossing out the italicized items in the following list:

- *III. Yellowstone National Park* is not coordinate with the other items following Roman numerals; they are states.
- *B. Uncle Joe* is not coordinate with the other items in the list; they are cities.
- *C. Mt. Rainier* is not coordinate with the other items in the list; they are sporting activities.
- *A. Crater Lake* is not coordinate because there must be at least two items under any category to coordinate.

There must be coordination within the lists of an outline, but there need not be coordination between the lists of an outline. In the corrected outline titled "My Summer Vacation," the items under "California" are coordinate; they are both cities. Also, the items under "Washington" are coordinate; they are sporting activities.

Minor Details

When minor details are added to outlines, they are labeled with Arabic numerals. Minor details in the following outline are the names of college courses.

Social Science and Science Courses
I. Social Science
  A. Sociology
    1. Sociology of the Family
    2. Women in Society
  B. Psychology
    1. Abnormal Psychology
    2. Human Development
    3. The Psychology of Aging
II. Science
  A. Biology
    1. Evolution of Humankind
    2. Anatomy and Physiology
  B. Chemistry
    1. Fundamentals of Chemistry
    2. Inorganic and Analytic Chemistry
  C. Physics
    1. Principles of the Physical Environment
    2. Physics of Life Processes
    3. Basic Atomic and Nuclear Physics

Use the following procedures when you label the outlines in Exercises 9.3 through 9.10 at the end of this chapter.

How to Label Outlines

- Always use at least two Roman numerals in an outline (**I** and **II**). Enter Roman numerals before you enter any capital letters.

- If you use capital letters under a Roman numeral, always use at least two (**A** and **B**). Indent capital letters under Roman numerals, and enter capital letters before you enter any Arabic numerals.

- If you use Arabic numerals under a capital letter, always use at least two (**1** and **2**). Enter Arabic numerals last, and indent them under capital letters.

Also, always place periods after Roman numerals, capital letters, and Arabic numerals in your outlines.

If you follow these suggestions, you will make coordinate outlines. All the exercises at the end of this chapter are prepared to help you learn to make coordinate outlines.

Exercises 9.1 through 9.10 on pages 78–83 are arranged to help you acquire skill in writing titles for outlines and in labeling statements in outlines with Roman numerals, capital letters, and Arabic numerals. You should find the first exercises easy to do; they are included to prepare you for other exercises that are more challenging. Do Exercises 9.1 through 9.10 before you read the following explanations about how to make outlines.

Well-organized Outlines

If you have done Exercises 9.1 through 9.10, you know the traditional method for labeling major thoughts, details, and minor details in outlines. The rest of this chapter provides additional information and practice that will help you learn how to make outlines of textbook selections. As you do exercises 9.11 through 9.19 on pages 84–88, keep in mind that you are doing them to develop skills you will use when you take class notes, mark textbooks, make notes about information you want to learn in textbooks, and store information in your memory.

Topic and Sentence Outlines

Outlines are of two basic types: topic outlines and sentence outlines. The outline in Figure 9.2 on page 78 is a **topic outline**; the statements in it are all phrases. The following outline is a **sentence outline**; the statements in it are all sentences.

Outlines

I. Outlines have two basic characteristics.
   A. They are accurate summaries of information.
   B. They are organized to show how ideas are related.
II. Outlines are written in a specific format.
   A. They begin with titles.
   B. Statements are labeled with numbers and letters.
      1. Roman numerals label major thoughts.
      2. Capital letters label details.
      3. Arabic numerals label minor details.

When you submit an outline to a teacher for a paper you will write or a speech you will give, the statements in it should be all phrases or all sentences. However, when you prepare outlines for your own purposes, you may use a combination of phrases and sentences.

How to Make Outlines

Use the following procedures to make outlines for Exercises 9.11 through 9.19 at the end of this chapter.

How to Make Outlines

1. Use the procedures summarized in "How to Label Outlines" on page 76.
2. Always subordinate items if they can be subordinated.
3. Outline information in the order in which it is written in a passage (rather than rearrange the sequence).
4. Write titles for your outlines that summarize the information in the passage.

All the exercises at the end of this chapter are designed to help you learn how to make coordinate outlines. If you prepare an outline with a **I** but no **II**, an **A** but no **B**, or a **1** but no **2**, you know that you have made a mistake. Also, one of the purposes of the exercises in this chapter is to give you practice subordinating items in outlines. Therefore, practice subordinating at every opportunity. If you can choose between writing an outline that includes Arabic numerals or an outline that includes no Arabic numerals, write the one that includes Arabic numerals.

When you are dissatisfied with an outline you make, refer to these directions; they will help you to make better outlines in the future.

FIGURE 9.2

A Topic Outline

An Outline

I.   Basic characteristics
     A. Accurately summarizes information
     B. Shows relations among ideas

II. Correct format
     A. Begins with a title
     B. Numbered and lettered statements
        1. Major thoughts – Roman numerals
        2. Details – capital letters
        3. Minor details – Arabic numerals

Evaluation of Your Outlines

Figure 9.3 shows an example of a model outline like ones your instructor may give you to score and evaluate the outlines you make. If your instructor makes model outlines available to you, use the following procedures to score your outlines.

1. Score 10 points if you write a title that summarizes the information in a passage.

2. Score 30 points if you have the same number of Roman numerals as a model and if the information next to your Roman numerals is essentially the same as the information in a model.

3. Score the points shown for each set of capital letters or Arabic numerals when you have the same number of capital letters or Arabic numerals as shown in a model and the information next to your capital letters or Arabic numerals is essentially the same as the information in a model.

In the models, the points for sets of details and minor details are distributed so that the maximum score for an outline is always 100.

EXERCISE 9.1   ## Major Thoughts in Lists

Check the word in each list that is the major thought. For instance, check *Coins* in the first list because pennies, nickels, dimes, and quarters are all coins.

1. ☐ Pennies ☐ Nickels ☐ Dimes ☐ Coins ☐ Quarters

2. ☐ May ☐ June ☐ Women ☐ April ☐ Mary

3. ☐ Hat ☐ Shoes ☐ Shirt ☐ Pants ☐ Clothes

4. ☐ Hate ☐ Emotion ☐ Envy ☐ Fear ☐ Love

FIGURE 9.3

A Model Outline for the Outline in Figure 9.2

```
                    10 [  Outlines

              I.  Have two basic characteristics
        ┌     A.  Accurate summaries of information
   30 ┌ 20 [
        │     B.  Organized to show how ideas are related
        └
             II.  Are prepared in a specific format
           ┌  A.  Begin with a title
      20 [
           └  B.  Have statements correctly labeled
                 ┌ 1.  Roman numerals for major thoughts
            20 [   2.  Capital letters for details
                 └ 3.  Arabic numerals for minor details
```

5. □ Second □ Minute □ Day □ Time □ Hour

6. □ Ballet □ Sculpture □ Arts □ Painting □ Opera

7. □ Store □ Grocery □ Bakery □ Pharmacy □ Florist

8. □ Beef □ Meat □ Lamb □ Pork □ Veal

9. □ Eyes □ Lips □ Nose □ Face □ Chin

10. □ Entertainment □ Television □ Movies □ Circuses □ Theater

11. □ Milk □ Coffee □ Beverage □ Soda □ Tea

12. □ Novel □ Poem □ Essay □ Drama □ Literature

13. □ Letter □ Writing □ Newspaper □ Magazine □ Book

14. □ Fowl □ Chicken □ Turkey □ Duck □ Quail

15. □ Seattle □ Boston □ Chicago □ Cities □ Indianapolis

16. □ Steam □ Energy □ Atomic □ Electric □ Gasoline

17. □ Car □ Airplane □ Train □ Bus □ Transportation

18. □ Spain □ Europe □ Germany □ France □ Italy

EXERCISE 9.2

Major Thoughts and Titles

Check the major thoughts and write titles for the lists. For instance, check *Short* and *Long* in the first list and write "Measures of Time" as a title for it.

1. _____

□ Short □ Second □ Minute □ Long □ Week □ Month □ Year

2. _____

□ California □ Los Angeles □ San Francisco □ Sacramento □ Illinois □ Chicago □ Decatur

3. _____

☐ Feet ☐ Socks ☐ Shoes ☐ Torso ☐ Shirt ☐ Sweater ☐ Vest ☐ Jacket

4. _____

☐ Theater ☐ Opera ☐ Ballet ☐ Drama ☐ Musical ☐ Museums ☐ Paintings ☐ Sculpture

5. _____

☐ Africa ☐ Nile ☐ Congo ☐ United States ☐ Mississippi ☐ Columbia ☐ Hudson ☐ Missouri ☐ Delaware

6. _____

☐ Mammal ☐ Beef ☐ Pork ☐ Lamb ☐ Veal ☐ Bird ☐ Chicken ☐ Turkey ☐ Duck

7. _____

☐ Vegetables ☐ Potatoes ☐ Onions ☐ Tomatoes ☐ Lettuce ☐ Beans ☐ Fruit ☐ Apples ☐ Oranges ☐ Bananas ☐ Lemons

8. _____

☐ Arm ☐ Wrist ☐ Elbow ☐ Shoulder ☐ Leg ☐ Ankle ☐ Knee ☐ Thigh ☐ Hand ☐ Fingers ☐ Palm

FIGURE 9.4

Example of How to Do Exercises 9.3 Through 9.5

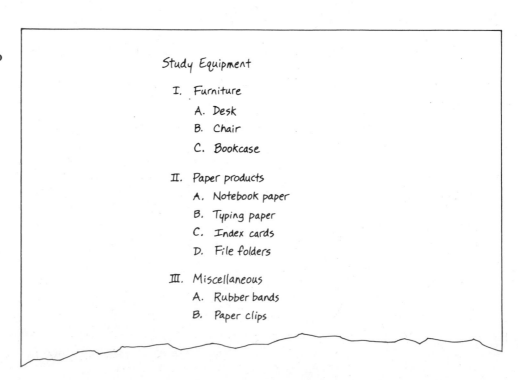

EXERCISE 9.3   ## Labeling Outlines

Write titles for the following lists and label the items in them with Roman numerals and capital letters. See the example in Figure 9.4 on page 80 and read "How to Label Outlines" on page 76.

1. Arm, Wrist, Elbow, Leg, Thigh, Knee, Shin

2. Bird, Cuckoo, Gull, Dog, Greyhound, Terrier, Spaniel, Snake, Asp, Python, Boa constrictor

3. Length, Inch, Foot, Yard, Mile; Volume, Ounce, Cup, Pint, Quart, Gallon

EXERCISE 9.4   ## Labeling Outlines

Write titles for the following lists and label the items in them with Roman numerals and capital letters. See the example in Figure 9.4 on page 80 and read "How to Label Outlines" on page 76.

1. Individual, Hiking, Swimming, Bicycling, Jogging, Javelin, Two-person, Tennis, Badminton, Ping-Pong, Handball, Boxing, Wrestling, Team, Baseball, Football, Basketball, Volleyball, Soccer, Hockey

2. String, Violin, Cello, Viola, Woodwind, Piccolo, Oboe, Flute, Clarinet, Saxophone, Brass, Trumpet, Trombone, Tuba, Percussion, Xylophone, Bass drum, Kettledrum, Snare drum, Tambourine, Castanets

EXERCISE 9.5   ## Labeling Outlines

Write titles for the following lists and label the items in them with Roman numerals and capital letters. See the example in Figure 9.4 on page 80 and read "How to Label Outlines" on page 76.

1. Sex, Male, Female, Marital status, Single, Married, Divorced, Age, Weight, Height, Address, Street, City, State, ZIP code, Education, High school, College, Previous jobs

2. Office, Secretary, Typist, Clerk, Manager, Hospital, Nurse, Doctor, Dietitian, Library, School, Principal, Teacher, Custodian, Factory, Store, Buyer, Salesperson, Stock person

EXERCISE 9.6   ## Labeling Outlines

Write titles for the following lists and label the items in them with Roman numerals, capital letters, and Arabic numerals. See the example in Figure 9.5 on page 82 and read "How to Label Outlines" on page 76.

1. Restaurant, Dining room, Host, Waiters, Dish carrier, Kitchen, Chef, Baker, Dishwasher, Store, Sales floor, Salespeople, Cashiers, Back room, Wrappers, Stock people, Cleaning staff, Hospital, Doctors, Nurses, Lab technicians

FIGURE 9.5

Example of How to Do Exercises 9.6 Through 9.10

Celebrities' Birth Years

I. Born in the 1950s
   A. Men
      1. Kevin Costner, 1955
      2. Denzel Washington, 1954
   B. Women
      1. Debbie Allen, 1951
      2. Kim Basinger, 1953
      3. Madonna, 1958

II. Born in the 1960s
   A. Men
      1. Sean Penn, 1960
      2. Eddie Murphy, 1961
      3. Tom Cruise, 1962
      4. Michael Jordan, 1963
   B. Women
      1. Demi Moore, 1962
      2. Paula Abdul, 1962

2. Individual, Water, Swimming, Diving, Surfing, Land, Hiking, Jogging, Bicycling, Two-person, Table, Ping-Pong, Pool/billiards, Court, Tennis, Handball, Team, Baseball, Football, Basketball, Soccer

---

EXERCISE 9.7 **Labeling Outlines**

Write titles for the following lists and label the items in them with Roman numerals, capital letters, and Arabic numerals. See the example in Figure 9.5 above and read "How to Label Outlines" on page 76.

1. Produce, Fruit, Apples, Bananas, Grapefruit, Vegetables, Potatoes, Lettuce, Onions, Dairy, Eggs, Cheese, Swiss, American, Cheddar, Milk, Meat, Beef, Hamburger, Chuck steak, Pork

2. Nonalcoholic, Milk, Skim, Whole, Buttermilk, Fruit juice, Orange, Grape, Apple, Soda, Cola, Ginger ale, Alcoholic, Beer, Wine, Californian, French, Liquor, Gin, Vodka, Scotch

EXERCISE 9.8   ## Labeling Outlines

Write titles for the following lists and label the items in them with Roman numerals, capital letters, and Arabic numerals. See the example in Figure 9.5 on page 82 and read "How to Label Outlines" on page 76.

1. Hot, Cereal, Oatmeal, Cream of Wheat, Eggs, Fried, Scrambled, Meat, Bacon, Ham, Beverages, Coffee, Cocoa, Cold, Cereal, Cornflakes, Shredded Wheat, Raisin Bran, Juice, Orange, Apple

2. Grooming aids, Mouth, Toothpaste, Mouthwash, Hair, Shampoo, Conditioner, Body, Soap, Deodorant, Drugs, Aspirin, Laxative, Iodine, Beauty aids, Face, Lipstick, Cheek blush, Hands, Nail polish, Hand cream

EXERCISE 9.9   ## Labeling Outlines

Write titles for the following lists and label the items in them with Roman numerals, capital letters, and Arabic numerals. See the example in Figure 9.5 on page 82 and read "How to Label Outlines" on page 76.

1. Field, Baseball, Football, Soccer, Table, Card, Poker, Gin, Rummy, Boxed, Scrabble, Monopoly, Court, Racket, Tennis, Badminton, Nonracket, Volleyball, Handball

2. Fall-winter, November, Veterans Day, Thanksgiving Day, December January, Christmas, New Year's Day, Martin Luther King Day, February, Presidents' Day, Valentine's Day, Spring, Easter, Mother's Day, Memorial Day, Summer, Father's Day, Independence Day, Labor Day

EXERCISE 9.10   ## Labeling Outlines

Write titles for the following lists and label the items in them with Roman numerals, capital letters, and Arabic numerals. See the example in Figure 9.5 on page 82 and read "How to Label Outlines" on page 76.

1. Pie, Fruit, Apple, Cherry, Cream, Banana, Chocolate, Cake, Pound, Angel food, Fruit, Jell-O, Fruit, Ice cream, Sundae, Chocolate, Butterscotch, Strawberry, Soda, Shake

2. Furniture, Seats, Sofas, Chairs, Benches, Tables, Dining, Coffee, End, Bookcases, Beds, Dressers, Accessories, Walls, Pictures, Mirrors, Tabletops, Lamps, Plants, Figurines

EXERCISE 9.11   Advertising

Outline the following passage using the procedures explained in "How to Make Outlines" on page 77. Do not outline the first sentence, which is an introduction. Use the following numbers and letters: I, A, B, C, II, A, B.

> There are three basic types of advertising: selective, primary demand, and institutional.
>
> *Selective advertising* promotes the sale of specific brand-name products, such as Bayer aspirin, Ford automobiles, and Maxwell House coffee.
>
> *Primary demand advertising* encourages the total demand for a product without promoting any single brand. For example, advertisements of the Wool Bureau attempt to convince consumers to purchase clothing made of wool rather than synthetic fibers. Similarly, the American Dairy Association advises us to "Drink More Milk."
>
> The third type, *institutional advertising*, has as its purpose to create good will toward the advertiser. When a utility company runs an ad that explains how to save money on electric bills or when an insurance company sponsors a television commercial that explains how to maintain good health, it uses institutional advertising. Any advertisement designed to make you think well of a company or organization, and that does not request you to make a purchase, is an example of institutional advertising.

EXERCISE 9.12   News Stories

Outline the following passage using the procedures explained in "How to Make Outlines" on page 77. Do not outline the first sentence, which is the introduction. Use only Roman numerals in your outline.

> Doris A. Graber has argued that five criteria are used most often for choosing news stories, and all are related to popular appeal rather than political significance.[1] First, the content of stories must have a *high impact* on the audience. The kidnapping of a local child will usually be more interesting than the deaths of many unknown persons far away. Second, interest will be heightened if a story deals with "natural or man-made *violence, conflict, disaster,* or *scandal.*"[2] People find events of this sort endlessly fascinating in real life as well as in the world of fiction.
>
> *Familiarity* is the third element of newsworthiness. The more the public knows about famous people and institutions, the more they want to know. Thus, established politicians and celebrities receive more coverage than persons who have not yet found a way to public prominence. Fourth, the public likes *novel* and *up-to-date* stories. Interest can wane quickly. Finally, *local events* are generally more newsworthy than stories from far away. As Graber points out, this kind of interest is what keeps small-town newspapers and local television alive. *Local* can be an elastic term, however. Washington and Hollywood have become so familiar that they may seem local to the regular TV viewer.

References

[1]These factors are discussed in Doris Graber, *Mass Media and American Politics,* 2nd ed. (Washington, D.C.: Congressional Quarterly Press, 1984), pp. 78–79.
[2]Graber, *Mass Media,* p. 78.

EXERCISE 9.13　　Property

Outline the following passage using the procedure explained in "How to Make Outlines" on page 77. Do not outline the first sentence of the first paragraph or the first sentence of the second paragraph, which are introductions. Begin your outline as follows: I, A, 1, 2, 3, 4, 5, 6, B.

> Property is of two basic types: real property and personal property. **Real property** includes land, buildings on the land, mineral deposits beneath the land, bodies of water on the land, anything attached to the land (such as fences and oil wells), and the air above the land. By contrast, furniture, clothing, money, automobiles, books, and other property not attached to land is **personal property**.
>
> Property may be acquired by inheritance, legacy, or accession. **Inheritance** refers to ancestry and the acquisition of property under laws of inheritance, which specify who will receive the property of a person who dies leaving no will and who may not be excluded from receiving such property. Property is acquired by **legacy** when it is so specified in a properly executed will. You acquire property by **accession** when there is an increase in something you already own. If your rosebush blooms or your cat has a litter, the roses and kittens are yours by right of accession.

EXERCISE 9.14　　Misspellings

Outline the following passage using the procedures explained in "How to Make Outlines" on page 77. Do not underline the first paragraph, which is the introduction. Use the following numbers and letters: I, A, B, 1, 2, C, II, A, B, 1, 2, C, III.

> Among the most frequently misspelled English words are *two, too, to, they're, there,* and *their*. If you confuse the spellings of these words, you should benefit from the observations made here.
>
> The confusion among *two, too,* and *to* may be overcome by remembering three things. First, use *two* only when counting (as in "*two* heads are better than one"). Second, use *too* when you intend to say "also" or "overly." For example:
>
> "I hope you will come too (also)."
> "She is *too* (overly) kind."
>
> Third, use *to* when you cannot use *too* or *two*!
>
> Problems with *they're, there,* and *their* may also be solved rather easily. Use *they're* only when you wish to say "they are," as in "they're going to the party." Use *there* when you wish to say "at or in that place"—for example, "over *there*" or "it's *there*." Then use *their* when you cannot use *they're* or *there*.
>
> If you have difficulty with the spellings of any of these words, you will probably be interested to know that *a lot* is two words, not one word.

EXERCISE 9.15   **Families**

Outline the following passage using the procedures explained in "How to Make Outlines" on page 77. Do not outline the first sentence, which is the introduction. Use Roman numerals, capital letters, and Arabic numerals in your outline.

There are several basic ways in which sociologists may view families. A **nuclear family** consists of parents and their children. Most people are born into a nuclear family—their family of orientation—and then go on to establish a nuclear family of their own—their family of procreation. The only possible members of a *family of orientation* are a mother, father, brothers, and sisters. Your *family of procreation* may include your spouse, sons, and daughters.

The **extended family** is another term sociologists use to describe family relationships. Exactly who is considered a member of an extended family differs from country to country, but in the United States the extended family is usually considered to include children, parents, and other relatives who live with them in the same house or very near by.

Families may also be viewed in terms of the number of partners in a marriage. In our country we have **monogamous families**—there is only one husband and one wife in a marriage partnership. In some societies, though, there are **polygamous families** with more than two marriage partners. *Polygyny* is the form of polygamy in which there is one husband and two or more wives; *polyandry* is the form in which one wife has two or more husbands.

EXERCISE 9.16   **Tests**

Outline the following passage using the procedures explained in "How to Make Outlines" on page 77. Do not outline the first sentence, which is the introduction. Begin your outline as follows: I, A, 1, 2, B, 1, 2.

Some educators believe that multiple-choice and true-false tests are fairer to students than essay tests.

Critics claim that essay tests have three disadvantages. First, they say, the reader of an essay test may be unduly influenced by the writing talent of the test takers. As a result, students with good writing ability may get high grades although they may not have mastered course content, and students with poor writing ability may get low grades even though they have an excellent grasp of what they were supposed to learn. The second major problem, critics argue, is that the "halo effect" sometimes operates when essay tests are graded. For example, a teacher who has the notion that a student is below average might let this idea influence the grading of the student's essay and give the student's good essay a low mark. However, an instructor who has the impression that a student is capable of superior work might give the student's poor essay a higher grade than it deserves. Finally, teachers are known to vary in their opinions, and, as a result, the same answer to an essay question might be graded high by one instructor and low by another.

Those who favor the use of multiple-choice and true-false tests say that their primary advantage is that they do not require students to be graded on writing ability. Also, the halo effect has no chance to operate because an instructor's opinion of a student does not enter into the grading of the student's test in any way. Finally, because multiple-choice and true-false tests are graded using an answer key, teachers' judgments of students' scores on a test cannot vary if the answer key is used correctly.

EXERCISE 9.17   Products

Outline the following passage using the procedures explained in "How to Make Outlines" on page 77. Do not outline the first sentence, which is the introduction. Use Roman numerals and capital letters in your outline.

The names for products come from a great variety of sources. Many famous brand names such as *Arrow*, *Carnation*, and *Bumble Bee* were chosen by studying the pages of a dictionary. Coined, or invented, words are another major source of brand names. *Vaseline*, *Kodak*, and *Kleenex* are a few of the well-known words in our vocabulary that did not exist until they were coined to name products. *Elizabeth Arden* and *John Hancock* are examples of brand names that come from the names of people; *Pittsburgh* paint and *Olympia* beer are two of the many products that took their names from geographical locations. Even initials and numbers have been used: *IBM*, *Heinz 57*, and *A-1*, for example.

EXERCISE 9.18   Spelling

Outline the following passage using the procedures explained in "How to Make Outlines" on page 77. Do not outline the first sentence, which is the introduction. Use Roman numerals, capital letters, and Arabic numerals in your outline.

There are two important spelling rules that many writers of English never master. Many people are not certain when to drop a final silent *e* before adding a suffix to an English root word and when not to drop it. The final *e* is almost always dropped before a suffix that begins with a vowel. For example, the final *e* in *care* is dropped before *-ing* is added to spell *caring*, and the final *e* in *cure* is dropped before *-able* is added to spell *curable*. The final *e* is not dropped before endings that begin with consonants. Thus, the final *e* in *care* is not dropped before *-ful* is added to spell *careful*, and the final *e* in *white* is not dropped before *-ness* is added to spell *whiteness*.
Confusion also exists about when to change a final *y* to *i* before adding a suffix to an English root word and when not to change it. There are, however, only two simple rules to remember. First, *y* is usually changed to *i* before any suffix if there is a consonant in front of the *y*. Examples are *beauty* and *beautiful*, *happy* and *happier*, and *silly* and *silliness*. Second, *y* is not changed to *i* when there is a vowel in front of the *y*. Examples are *destroy* and *destroyer*, *pay* and *payable*, and *annoy* and *annoyance*.

<u>**EXERCISE 9.19**</u>   ## Behavior Disorders

Outline the following passage using the procedures explained in "How to Make Outlines" on page 77. Do not outline the first paragraph, which is the introduction. Use Roman numerals, capital letters, and Arabic numerals in your outline.

Neuroses are relatively mild behavior disorders. However, they are sometimes sufficiently disturbing that it is necessary for individuals showing the symptoms of neuroses to seek professional help.

Anxiety reactions, constituting the most common neurosis, are found in people who have much more tension than average people have. Sometimes people who suffer from this neurosis are overtaken by the strong feeling that something unfortunate is about to happen. This feeling may be accompanied by physical responses, such as weakness, fast breathing, or the desire to vomit.

There are two basic types of **obsessive-compulsive reactions**: obsessive thoughts and compulsive acts. Obsessive thoughts are unwelcome thoughts that crowd the neurotic's mind to the extent that they interfere with normal activity. The person may, for example, have recurring thoughts of killing a spouse, jumping out a window, or committing a crime. Compulsive acts often serve the purpose of making a person feel better about obsessive thoughts. A man who has continual thoughts about killing his wife may call her several times a day to check on her well-being; people who have the obsessive thought that they will say something "dirty" may brush their teeth many times a day.

Phobic reactions are uncontrollable fears about dangers that do not exist, or fears that are too great in relation to the danger that actually exists. Acrophobia and claustrophobia are two of the many phobic reactions. Acrophobia is the excessive fear of height. A person who cannot look out the window of a skyscraper or cannot cross a bridge without extreme discomfort may be suffering from acrophobia. Claustrophobia is the fear of being in small, closed places. A person who cannot enter an elevator or walk into a large closet without experiencing great distress may be a victim of claustrophobia.

PART

II

Use Time Wisely

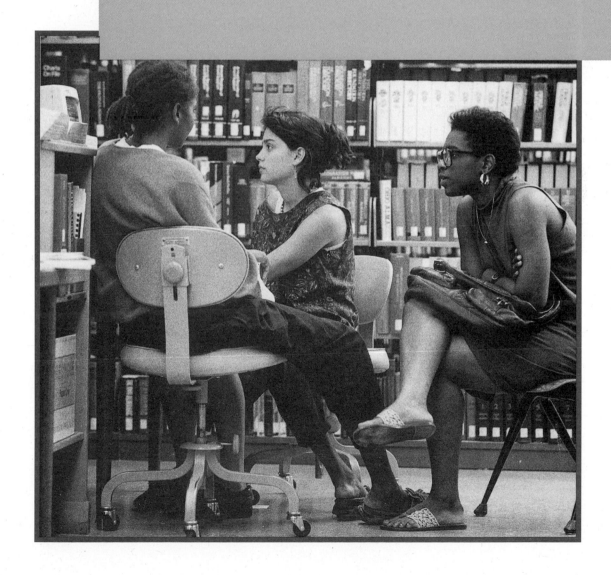

Preview of PART II

Most college students have difficulty in attempting to accomplish all the things they must do during a typical college term. Some students are pressed for time because they have a job, care for a family, or have other responsibilities; others have enough time to do all the things they need to do, but they do not know how to make good use of it. This part of *College Study Skills* examines three ways to make better use of time:

- Chapter 10, "Work Toward Goals," explains how to identify your goals so you can use them to make basic decisions about how you will use your time.

- Chapter 11, "Manage Your Time," describes how to plan and organize your time for studying and achieving your other goals.

- Chapter 12, "Increase Concentration," teaches methods you can use to make better use of study time by keeping your mind focused on studying rather than letting it wander.

When you use time wisely, you will do the things you need to do and have more time to spend with your friends and family and to engage in activities you enjoy.

Work Toward Goals

A fundamental way to make good use of your time in college is to prepare an efficient plan for achieving your goals. Your goals are the accomplishments you work toward or strive for; they are the things you want enough to spend your time, effort, and money to achieve them. Check the boxes in front of any of the following statements that are goals of yours.

Goals I Value

☐ To have a better job

☐ To travel in foreign countries

☐ To earn a college degree

☐ To be healthy and live a long life

☐ To always do my best

☐ To improve in a sport or athletic event

☐ To live in a more desirable house or apartment

☐ To be married and to be a good parent

☐ To make an important contribution to society

Your goals give your life direction by helping you decide how you will use your resources. For instance, if one of your aims is to earn a college degree, this goal will guide you in making decisions about spending time going to classes, spending effort studying, and spending money on tuition and textbooks.

Following is a summary of the suggestions in this chapter for achieving goals of the type that are illustrated in Figure 10.1 on page 93.

Achieving Goals

1. Write primary goals.
2. Make an effective plan for achieving primary goals that is expressed in intermediate and current goals.
3. Use suggestions in Chapter 11 to schedule the exact times you will accomplish your current goals.
4. Write goals that state things you want to achieve.
5. Word goals in ways that make it easy for you to evaluate your success in achieving them.
6. Write goals that
   - you have the ability to achieve.
   - you have enough time to achieve.
   - you will pay the price to achieve.
   - you are in control of the circumstances necessary to achieve.
7. Do not be discouraged by obstacles.
8. Monitor and assess your progress in achieving your goals.
9. Revise your intermediate and current goals when necessary.

The emphasis in this chapter is on the goals that lead to success in college. However, the information pertains to all kinds of goals. Use the suggestions given here to also achieve your objectives for general self-improvement, friendship, health, travel, or any other area of interest to you.

Types of Goals

Figure 10.1 on page 93 gives examples of the three basic types of goals: primary, intermediate, and current.

Primary Goals   A **primary goal** is something that you hope to achieve in the future. Following are examples of primary goals some students have for their education:

> to earn a college degree
> to graduate with at least a 3.00 grade point average
> to prepare for a specific profession

Primary goals are of special importance because they are used as a guide in establishing intermediate and current goals.

Intermediate Goals   An **intermediate goal** is a goal that helps in accomplishing a primary goal. For example, to successfully complete a college course is an intermediate goal that helps in attaining the primary goal of earning a college degree.

FIGURE 10.1
Examples of Goals

Current Goals

Start smoking later in the day.
Smoke only ten cigarettes daily.
Smoke only half of each cigarette.
Drink water rather than smoke.
Chew gum rather than smoke

↓

Intermediate Goal

Become a nonsmoker.

↓

Primary Goal

Live a healthy lifestyle.

Current Goals   A **current goal** is a goal that leads to accomplishing an intermediate goal. To earn a good grade on a test you will take next week is a current goal that helps in attaining the intermediate goal of successfully completing a course you are taking.

As you come close to achieving primary goals, they usually become intermediate goals. For instance, as you draw near to your primary goal of graduating from college, you may set a new primary goal, such as to have a well-paying job or to be admitted to a graduate school. In so doing, your primary goal of graduating from college becomes an intermediate goal that helps you in attaining your new primary goal.

Writing Goals

Write primary goals first and use them to write your intermediate and current goals. Keep a list of your goals in a special place so you can read them from time to time. The following discussions explain how to write goals that are positive, measurable, and realistic.

Write Positive and Measurable Goals   Positive goals state a behavior you want, whereas negative goals state a behavior you do not want. Compare the following goals:

I will earn a B average this term.
I will try to stop wasting my time.

The first goal is positive—it states a behavior a student wants; the second goal is negative—it states a behavior she doesn't want. Pursue positive goals; it is more satisfying to spend time and effort working for the worthwhile things you want than to dwell on behaviors you disapprove of. Positive goals will focus your attention on self-improvement rather than on self-defeat.

The first goal is also measurable; it states exactly what will be accomplished in terms that can be measured. If the student keeps records of the grades she receives on tests, quizzes, and assignments, she can easily monitor the degree of success she has in earning a B average. In contrast, the second goal is not measurable; it is worded in a way that makes it virtually impossible to assess when it is achieved.

Write Realistic Goals   A goal is realistic if it is one that you are able and willing to work toward and over which you have reasonable control. Use the following criteria to decide whether a goal is realistic.

Criteria for Realistic Goals

- **You have the abilities that are needed to achieve the goal**. Only a few people have the abilities that are necessary to be a professional football player or to write a best-selling novel, but millions of people have the abilities that are needed to graduate from college and to find a better-paying job. When you lack abilities, you may make it your goal to acquire them. For instance, if you lack the math skills to earn the grade you want in a statistics course, you may make it your goal to improve these skills.

- **You have enough time to achieve the goal.** There are goals for which you may possess the necessary skills but that you are unable to achieve because you don't have enough time. For instance, you may not be able to earn grades of B or higher in all of your courses because work, family, or other responsibilities deprive you of the study time you need to achieve this goal. (See the discussion titled "Balance Your Responsibilities" on pages 107–108.)

- **You are willing to pay the price necessary to achieve the goal**. To achieve an academic goal you may need to spend many hours alone at your desk and away from friends and activities you enjoy. A goal is not realistic for you unless you are willing to make it a priority and pay whatever price is necessary to achieve it.

- **You are in control of the circumstances necessary to achieve the goal.** I once knew an English composition teacher who gave A's only to students who wrote as well as he did. In his first ten years of teaching he gave only four A's! Students with the goal of earning A's in a composition course taught by this teacher seldom succeeded because of his unreasonably strict grading procedures. To be more in control of earning A's, students needed to identify instructors who were more generous in giving A's and study composition with them. Analyze your goals to make certain that you have reasonable control over the circumstances necessary for you to accomplish them.

Think of something you want very much to accomplish, and use these four criteria to evaluate whether it is a realistic goal for you.

Working Toward Goals

To make steady progress toward a primary goal: (1) plan your intermediate and current goals, (2) do not be discouraged by obstacles, (3) monitor and assess your progress, and (4) revise goals when necessary.

Plan Intermediate and Current Goals   A primary goal is achieved by using an effective plan that is expressed in appropriate intermediate and current goals. When the primary goal is to earn a college degree, intermediate goals invariably include satisfactorily completing all courses that lead to the degree. Following is a list of the current goals a student prepared at the beginning of a term to help in earning a grade of at least B in a psychology course:

> I will read required material before each class.
> I will attend all classes and take good notes.
> I will review and revise notes immediately after class.
> I will do library research for the term paper.

The student used suggestions given in Chapter 11 to schedule the exact times he would read his psychology textbook, revise class notes, and do library research for his term paper.

Do Not Be Discouraged by Obstacles   The path to a goal is seldom unobstructed; if you are not prepared for hindrances, you may become discouraged and give up. For instance, an unexpected problem at work or home could take your attention away from studying and prevent you from achieving the grade you want on a test. Temporary setbacks are inevitable; prepare yourself for them so that you will not become discouraged. Discouragement is the enemy of persistence, and you must be persistent to accomplish the things you want.

Monitor and Assess Your Progress   If you have written specific and measurable goals, it will be easy for you to monitor and assess the progress you make toward achieving them. Following are some examples of current goals that are easy to monitor:

> I will have all assignments completed on time.
> I will schedule time to study for all tests.
> I will participate in all class discussions.

Continually monitor your current goals to assess whether you are accomplishing them.

Also monitor your intermediate goals. For example, a student with the intermediate goal of maintaining a B average assessed his progress toward this goal every few weeks. Following are the grades he estimated he had earned as of the fifth week of a term: English, B+; chemistry, B; history, C; speech, A; and psychology, B. After making these estimates, he realized that he was not achieving his goal in his history course and took measures to raise the grade.

Revise Goals When Necessary   The student who wanted to do better in his history course analyzed why he was falling short of his goal. He determined that he had used ineffective methods in studying the course text-book, that he had not paid sufficient attention to his teacher's study suggestions, and that he had not spent enough time reviewing for tests. He developed a strategy for improvement that he expressed in the following revised current goals.

Examples of Revised Current Goals

- I will make complete notes about things to learn in my history textbook (rather than try to learn the information by reading and rereading the textbook).

- I will spend twelve hours (rather than eight hours) reviewing for the next test.

- When I review for my next history test, I will emphasize learning the things the teacher states are important to learn (rather than only the things that interest me most).

These revised goals helped the student earn a B− in his history course.

However, in pursuing a goal you may sometimes find that you were too optimistic about what you could achieve. For instance, in working for a grade of B in a chemistry course, a student found that despite her best efforts she was unable to earn a test grade higher than C+. Because she did not want to delay her progress toward her degree by dropping the course and taking it later, she revised her goal to bring it in line with the C grade that she could realistically earn.

EXERCISE 10.1   **Primary, Intermediate, and Current Goals**

The following list contains a primary goal, two intermediate goals, and three current goals. On the lines provided, write **P** in front of the primary goal, **I** in front of intermediate goals, and **C** in front of current goals.

_____ 1. I will maintain a 3.00 grade point average.

_____ 2. I will attend all my classes.

_____ 3. I will complete all assignments on time.

_____ 4. I will earn a college degree.

_____ 5. I will be thoroughly prepared for all tests.

_____ 6. I will take all courses required in my program.

The following list contains a primary goal, two intermediate goals, and five current goals. On the lines provided, write P in front of the primary goal, I in front of intermediate goals, and C in front of current goals.

_____ 7. I will read books and articles about Mexico.

_____ 8. I will save $50 each month from my wages.

_____ 9. I will learn a great deal about Mexico.

_____ 10. I will save the money I receive as gifts.

_____ 11. I will find a better-paying job.

_____ 12. I will spend one month traveling in Mexico.

_____ 13. I will buy a map and guidebook for Mexico.

_____ 14. I will save enough money to make the trip.

EXERCISE 10.2   **Writing Goals**

Practice writing positive, measurable, and realistic goals.

1. Write your primary goal for your education.

   _____

2. Write two intermediate goals that will help you achieve your primary goal.

   a. _____

   b. _____

3. Write three current goals that will help you achieve each of your intermediate goals.

   a. _____

   b. _____

   c. _____

EXERCISE 10.3   **Monitoring Goals**

Write the answers to the following questions on the lines.

1. What method will you use to monitor and assess the first intermediate goal you wrote in Exercise 10.2?

   _____

   _____

2. What method will you use to monitor and assess the second current goal you wrote in Exercise 10.2?

   _____

   _____

EXERCISE 10.4   **Your Personal Goals**

Use the following questions to stimulate your thinking about your personal goals. Your instructor may conduct a class discussion about this topic.

1. Do you want to live in a big city, a small town, the suburbs, or a rural setting?

2. What kind of apartment or house do you want for your home?

3. What kind of car, furniture, and other possessions do you want to own?

4. Do you want to live with a friend, a spouse, or by yourself?

5. Do you want to be a parent? If so, how many children do you want?

6. What profession or occupation do you want to pursue?

7. What annual income do you want to have five years from now?

8. Are good health and long life important to you?

9. Do you want others to regard you as having an attractive appearance?

10. Is hiking, hunting, fishing, bicycling, boating, or some other outdoor activity important to you?

11. Do you want to travel extensively in foreign countries?

12. Do you want to write a book, invent a machine, or make some other unique contribution to society?

13. Do you want to work to relieve the suffering of others?

14. Do you want to be respected by others?

15. Do you want to be known as a kind and loving person?

16. What are some of your personal goals that are not in this list?

Manage Your Time

As a college student, you will have many demands on your time. In addition to attending classes and studying, you will spend time visiting with your friends and relatives, participating in sports or other activities, and attending to personal matters such as eating, shopping, traveling, and grooming. You may also spend time working at a job.

The problem all college students confront is to find time to attend class, study, and also do all the other things they need or want to do. This is made more difficult by the fact that college study is very demanding—it requires much more time than studying in high school. In a typical term, full-time college students may read five, six, or more textbooks, complete a major project in each course, and take many tests. With a great deal to accomplish in the few weeks of a term, successful college students find it is essential to schedule their time to accomplish everything they must do.

"How to Manage Your Time," below, summarizes the procedures that are explained in detail in this chapter. You will learn how to manage your time by using a weekly study schedule, a list of things to do, an activity calendar, and a weekly assignment sheet like those shown on pages 102–104.

How to Manage Your Time

- **Analyze the demands on your time.** Analyze how you use your time for school, work, friends, and family, caring for yourself, and for other activities.

- **Decide how much to study.** Figure out how much time you need to study to get the grades you want.

- **Determine how much time you have available for studying.** Use your list of things to do, your calendar, and your analysis of times you can't study because you are engaged in other activities.

- **Decide what to study first.** Keep records of assignments on a form of the type illustrated on page 104.

> ■ **Decide when you will study.** Schedule short rather than long study sessions at times you are most alert and not engaged in other activities.

Analyze the Demands on Your Time

Before you try to figure out how to manage your time, you need to analyze the various ways in which you use it.

Some Demands on Your Time

- **School.** In addition to the time you spend in classes, you need time to study for tests and to complete papers and other projects for your courses.
- **Work.** If you have a job, you may need to plan time for traveling to and from your place of employment in addition to the time you actually spend working.
- **Friends and family.** Developing and maintaining good relations with friends and relatives requires spending time with them. You need time for making telephone calls, writing letters, and socializing, and for celebrating birthdays, anniversaries, and holidays.
- **Activities of special interest to you.** If you have a special interest such as acting, gardening, playing a sport, being an active member of church, or participating in school or local politics, you will need time for this activity.
- **Caring for yourself.** You need time for sleeping, eating, grooming, traveling, paying bills, and caring for your clothing. These activities can be very time consuming if you need to shop for groceries, clean your living place, do your own laundry, or travel to school or work.
- **Caring for others.** If you are responsible for the care of a spouse, children, or parents, this may require many hours each week.

In addition to planning time for the things you need and want to do, you must be prepared to deal with the unexpected. One key to successful time management is to be ready to handle emergencies such as the following.

Common Types of Emergencies

- **Mechanical failure.** You could be delayed in your arrival to school because of the breakdown of an automobile or bus, you could be unable to complete an assignment because a computer went down, or you could be prevented from attending classes because of an electrical or plumbing failure in your home.
- **Illness or injury.** An illness or injury could prevent you from going to school and from completing assignments or preparing for tests.
- **Family and friends.** Someone close to you may need your help or attention suddenly, or the illness or death of a family member or friend could make an unexpected demand on your time.

- **Love interest.** A new romance could take a great deal of your time, or a breakup with your boyfriend or girlfriend could upset you and make it impossible for you to concentrate on schoolwork.
- **Miscalculation.** You could have insufficient time to do an assignment because you underestimated how long it would take you to complete it or because you forgot or overlooked when it was due.

Now and then you will need to adjust your schedule because of emergencies such as these.

Decide How Much to Study

If one of your goals is to earn good grades in your college courses, you will need to decide how much time you will spend studying so you can achieve this goal.

Teachers often tell students that they should spend two hours studying outside of class for each hour they spend in the classroom. For instance, when students take a course that meets for three class hours each week, instructors customarily recommend that they study for six hours each week outside of class. Unfortunately, this advice doesn't take into account that some students need to devote more time to studying than others.

There is no way for anybody but you to know how long it will take you to do any particular assignment; you should study for as long as it takes you to achieve the goals you have set for yourself and to learn whatever it is you want to learn. An assignment that takes you two hours may take another student five hours, and an assignment that takes you five hours may take someone else two hours.

One way to find out how much you must study is to keep records of how long it actually takes you to study for your courses. For example, when you read a textbook, write the time in pencil on the page where you begin. After you have finished reading, write the time again. Then count the number of pages you read and figure out the average time it took you to read each page. If you do this a few times with each book you are studying, you will soon be able to estimate very accurately how long it takes you to read ten, twenty-five, or fifty pages in any book you are studying. Use this information to help in deciding how much time you will spend studying.

Determine Time Available for Study

Use the following three steps to determine how many hours each week are available to you for studying.

1. **Enter in your schedule all the times you have specific obligations, such as attending class, working, traveling, or engaging in other activities that you cannot change.** Use one of the study schedules printed on the last pages of this book. In Figure 11.1 on page 103 these types of obligations are shaded in light blue. "Free" indicates time that may be used for exercise, leisure activities, or additional studying.

2. **Keep a list of chores and other things that you have to do each week.** The study schedule in Figure 11.1 includes the items in the following list.

Things to do
Wash the car
Do the laundry
Plan dinner for Sat. (10/14)
Buy birthday present for Mom
Lose five pounds

If you have a personal computer that you use each day, I recommend that you store your list of things to do in a computer document. Divide the list into whatever categories best suit your needs. For instance, it might be organized under headings such as "Today," "Tomorrow," "Next Week," and "Next Month," or "School," "Work," "Home," and "Shopping." Each morning

- Read your list of things to do.
- Delete the items you did the day before.
- Copy the list and select from it the things you will do today.
- Print the list of things you will do today.

Refer to the list throughout the day, crossing off items as you do them.

3. **Prepare a calendar of social activities and other important dates.** Some of the activities shown in the following calendar are included in the study schedule in Figure 11.1.

OCTOBER

Sunday	Monday	Tuesday	Wednesday	Thursday	Friday	Saturday
1	2	3 Psych Quiz	4	5	6	7 Jane's party 9 PM
8 Lunch/movie with George	9	10	11 Photography Club 8 PM	12	13	14 Friends for dinner 7 PM
15	16	17	18 History paper due	19 Football game 2 PM	20	21
22	23 Mom's birthday	24	25	26 Chemistry test	27	28 Rita visits campus
29	30	31 Halloween party 9 PM				

When you analyze how much time you have for studying, you may find that you don't have enough time to study because you devote a great deal of time to work, sports, family responsibilities, or some other activity. If you are so busy with another activity that it interferes with your ability to do well in college, you may need to reduce the number of courses you take each term, or you may need to spend less time engaging in the conflicting activity (see pages 107–108).

FIGURE 11.1

A Weekly Study Schedule

The student cannot study during the hours shaded in blue because she is in class, working, or engaged in other activities.

	SAT	SUN	MON	TUE	WED	THU	FRI
	Oct. 7	Oct. 8	Oct. 9	Oct. 10	Oct. 11	Oct. 12	Oct. 13
8-9	Eng- Revise	Free	Chem-	Psych- Read Ch. 9	Math- Odd	Psych- Read Ch 10	Chem- Ex 12.1,
9-10	Type paper	Free	Ex 11.1-11.5	Prep to discuss ques 1, 4, & 6	problems 1-19, pp 187-188	Prep to discuss ques 1-7	12.3, 12.7-12.9
10-11	Hist- Read	Chem-	X	X	X	X	X
11-12	Ch. 8 pp 231-252	Read Ch. 11	X	X	X	X	X
12-1	X	↓	X	X	X	X	X
1-2	Hist- work on	Lunch and movie	Hist- Read	Math- Prep for	Hist- Answer	Eng- Research	X
2-3	paper (Library)	with George	Ch. 8, pp 253-279	quiz on Ch. 4-6	ques 1-12, pp 280-281	for paper (Library)	Hist- work on
3-4	X	↓	X	Eng- Outline	X	X	paper (Library)
4-5	X	- Do Laundry	Math- Odd	for paper (Library)	X	X	↓
5-6	X	-Wash car	Problems, 20-39 pp. 172-174	Free	X	Free	X
6-7	Free	-Plan dinner	X	Free	X	Free	X
7-8	Free	for Oct. 14	X	X	X	X	Free
8-9	Free	Math- Odd problems	Free	Chem-	↓	Chem- Read	Free
9-10	Free	1-19, pp 171-172	Free	Ex 11.6-11.11	Photography Club	Ch. 12	Free
10-11	Free	X	X	X	↓	X	Free

Set Priorities for What to Study

Students sometimes make the mistake of studying first for the courses for which they prefer to study rather than for the courses for which they need to study. One secret of success is to do now the things that must be done now. Begin each day by looking over your assignments to decide which of them must absolutely, positively be done today, and do those assignments now. This decision is easier to make if you keep your assignments in the format illustrated in Figure 11.2 on page 104.

FIGURE 11.2

A Method for
Keeping
Assignments

COURSE	MON Oct 9	TUE Oct 10	WED Oct 11	THU Oct 12	FRI Oct 13
English	Revise the two-page paper Type neatly		Bring outline for research paper		Bring list of references for research paper (at least 10)
Math	Odd problems 1-19, pp. 171-172	Odd problems 20-39, pp 172-174	Quiz on chapers 4-6	Odd problems 1-19, pp. 187-188	
Chemistry	Read Ch. 11 Do Ex. 11.1-11.5 (Test Oct. 26)		Do Ex. 11.6-11.11		Read Ch. 12 Do Ex. 12.1, 12.3, & 12.7-12.9
History	Read Ch. 8, pp. 231-252 (Paper due Oct. 18)	Read Ch. 8, pp. 253-279		Write answers to questions 1012, pp 280-281	
Psychology		Read Ch. 9 Prepare for discussion questions 1,4,&6		Read Ch. 10 Prepare for discussion questions 1-7	

The record of assignments in Figure 11.2 was used to prepare the study schedule in Figure 11.1 on page 103. For example, compare Figure 11.2 with Figure 11.1 to notice that the student plans to complete Thursday's assignments on Wednesday and Thursday.

At the back of this book, there are forms that you may use to keep records of your assignments. Make photocopies of one of the forms, punch holes in the copies, and put them in the assignment section of your ring binder.

You may sometimes find that you are so busy that it is impossible for you to do all of your assignments as thoroughly as you would like. If this happens, use the following procedure.

Deciding How Much Time to Spend Studying

- **Will the assignment help me master a skill that is important to my long-term goals?** A business student may give priority to English composition assignments because he knows that the ability to write well will be important to his success in business.

- **How will my grade for the assignment or test affect my final course grade?** A student of electrical technology may give priority to written assignments in her electrical technology courses because her instructors use assignment grades to compute final course grades.
- **How important is my grade in the course to help me achieve my goals?** A student at a school in Florida wants high grades in all of her courses so she can transfer credits for the courses she takes in Florida to a school in Illinois.

You probably want to do your best in each course you take. However, when you have insufficient time to study as much as you want, establish your priorities by spending your study time in the ways that will benefit you most in the future.

Decide When to Study

Some students try to study when they are taking a sunbath; when they are watching television; or when they are overly tired, hungry, or under too much stress. Unfortunately, studying at times such as these is not likely to be very effective. Rather, use the following suggestions as a guide in deciding the actual times you will study for your various courses.

Deciding When to Study

- **Study at the time you are most alert.** Observe yourself when you study to determine whether you are most alert early in the morning, in the afternoon, in the evening, or late at night. Use what you learn to schedule study periods at the time of day you concentrate best.
- **Study about lecture topics immediately before class.** By reading about the lecture topic just before class, you will have the material fresh in your mind when you listen to the lecture.
- **Review and correct class notes immediately after class.** If you don't understand your notes right after class, you won't understand them later when you study them to prepare for a test; therefore, review your notes as soon after class as possible.
- **Try learning information just before you go to sleep.** There is evidence that we remember more information when it is learned just before sleep than when it is learned at other times.
- **Schedule many short study sessions rather than a few long ones.** For example, when you schedule six hours to study for a test, plan six one-hour study sessions rather than one six-hour or two three-hour study sessions. Short study sessions are more effective than long ones because it is tiring to study for long periods, and we do not learn well when we are tired.
- **When you must study a subject for several consecutive hours, take a five- or ten-minute break every hour.** You can make these breaks productive by using them to do things you need or want to do—make a short telephone

call, go for a brief walk, shoot a few baskets, read the baby a bedtime story, make a pot of coffee, or put clothes in the washer.

It is necessary to revise study schedules often to accommodate changing school, social, and other obligations. Also, some weeks have holidays that offer uninterrupted stretches of time for working on major projects and preparing for examinations. There are study schedule forms at the back of this book; you may photocopy one of them if you want. You may want to make one copy for each week of the term because no two weeks are exactly alike.

Make Better Use of Time

If you analyze how you spend your time, you may find that you waste time each day that you could use studying and doing other things you need to do. One way you can make better use of your time is to combine activities by doing two things at once, as suggested in the following list.

Some Ways to Do Two Things at Once

- As you drive friends or children from place to place, have them quiz you on material in your notes.
- Write material on 3-by-5-inch cards and study the information while you walk from place to place or ride on a bus.
- Think about what you will do during your next study session while you are walking, driving, or doing routine chores.
- Record material you want to learn on an audiocassette and listen to the cassette while you are driving or doing household chores.
- Study while you wash clothes, while you wait for a favorite television program to start, or while you wait for a friend to arrive.

A second way to accomplish more is to make use of short periods that you now may waste doing nothing of importance. Following are some suggestions.

Some Ways to Use Short Periods

- **Five minutes.** In five minutes, you could review words you are learning, revise your list of things to do, plan your next study session, do some sit-ups or pushups, take out the garbage, put clothes in the washer, or clean the bathroom sink.
- **Fifteen minutes.** In fifteen minutes, you could review notes, survey a chapter, wash dishes, solve a math problem, pick the topic for a paper, balance a checkbook, pay some bills, or work out on exercise equipment.
- **Thirty minutes.** In thirty minutes, you could run an errand, write a letter, locate material in the library, review notes, read five pages in a textbook, buy birthday cards, or jog three miles.

Give some thought to how you might make better use of your time. One of my students saved time by using the telephone. He avoided unnecessary trips to the library by calling first to find out whether books he wanted were available;

he also avoided time-consuming shopping trips by using catalogs and toll-free numbers to do much of his shopping by telephone. Another of my students taught her nine- and ten-year-old children to do laundry and other household chores so that she would have more time to play with them and help them with their homework. The best time-saving strategies are the ones that you devise to suit your particular circumstances.

Balance Your Responsibilities

Some students don't have enough time for studying because they devote much of their time to a job, family responsibilities, a sport or hobby, or some other activity. If you are so busy with another activity that it interferes with your ability to do well in college, you may need to reduce the number of courses you take or you may need to spend less time engaging in the conflicting activity.

Place checks in the boxes in front of any of the statements in the following multiple-choice questions that describe you.

1. I have been absent from classes because of
   - □ a. my job.
   - □ b. family responsibilities or friends.
   - □ c. a sport or hobby.
   - □ d. something else I do.

2. I have been late to classes because of
   - □ a. my job.
   - □ b. family responsibilities or friends.
   - □ c. a sport or hobby.
   - □ d. something else I do.

3. I am sometimes tired in classes because of
   - □ a. my job.
   - □ b. family responsibilities or friends.
   - □ c. a sport or hobby.
   - □ d. something else I do.

4. I have done poor work on assignments because of
   - □ a. my job.
   - □ b. family responsibilities or friends.
   - □ c. a sport or hobby.
   - □ d. something else I do.

5. I have failed to turn in assignments because of
   - □ a. my job.
   - □ b. family responsibilities or friends.
   - □ c. a sport or hobby.
   - □ d. something else I do.

6. I have been poorly prepared for a test or quiz because of
   - □ a. my job.
   - □ b. family responsibilities or friends.
   - □ c. a sport or hobby.
   - □ d. something else I do.

7. I have been absent from a test or quiz because of
   □ a. my job.
   □ b. family responsibilities or friends.
   □ c. a sport or hobby.
   □ d. something else I do.

If you checked any box, your job or some other responsibility or interest is interfering with your ability to do your best in college. You need to figure out how you can balance your desire to do well in college with your other responsibilities or interests. For instance, if you are a full-time student having academic difficulty because of your job, following are some alternatives you might consider.

How to Balance Work and School

- Work a great deal during the summer and very little, or not at all, during the school year.

- If you spend much time traveling to and from work, find a job on campus, near campus, or near where you live (even if it pays less money).

- If the hours that you must work are the problem, find a job with more suitable hours (even if it pays less money).

- If you are working only because you want to enjoy a luxury, such as an expensive automobile, consider doing without the luxury.

- If you are working mainly because you receive more approval from your parents for working than you do for being a student, consider explaining the demands of college study to your parents.

If none of these alternatives is a solution for you, or if you are a part-time student working full-time to support yourself or your family, you may need to enroll in fewer courses next term or to use one of the other suggestions in this chapter.

EXERCISE 11.1   ## Decide How Much to Study

List the courses you are taking, the grade you want for each course, and the number of hours per week you will need to study for each course to earn the grade you want.

Courses	Grades I Want	Hours I Need to Study
_____	_____	_____
_____	_____	_____
_____	_____	_____
_____	_____	_____
_____	_____	_____

What is the total number of hours you will study each week? _____

EXERCISE 11.2   ## Make a Calendar for the Term

Make a calendar for the entire term.

1. Use a calendar of the type illustrated on page 102 (they are sometimes available free in bookstores and card shops).

2. Consult your school's catalog for the dates of holidays, vacations, final examinations, and other important dates in your school's academic calendar.

3. Use syllabuses, outlines, and other materials your instructors give you to find the dates of tests and the dates papers and other course projects are due.

4. Use the school newspaper or other student government publications to find the dates of important athletic and social events you want to attend.

5. Use your personal records as the source of information about the dates of weddings, birthdays, anniversaries, and other important events you will observe with your relatives and friends.

Include these and other important dates in your calendar.

EXERCISE 11.3   ## Prepare a List of Things to Do

Prepare a list of the things you need to do next week. Include chores, social obligations, and other things you want to accomplish. Title your list "Things to Do Next Week."

EXERCISE 11.4   ## Determine Time Available for Study

Referring to your list of things to do, your calendar, and your class schedule, use one of the forms at the back of this book to analyze how many hours you have available next week that you can use for studying. Cross out the times when you cannot study because you are attending class, working, traveling, eating meals, or engaging in other activities. Be certain to cross out enough time for each activity. If it takes you an hour each morning to get dressed and eat breakfast, cross out an hour, not half an hour. Also, be certain to allow enough time for meals and relaxation; they are essential to your enjoyment of life and to your physical and mental well-being.

How many hours do you have available for studying next week?_____

If you have fewer hours than you need for studying, figure out how you can make more time available or consider whether you overestimated the number of hours you will need for studying when you did Exercise 11.1.

EXERCISE 11.5   ## Decide What to Study First

Use one of the assignment forms in the back of this book to list the assignments you must do next week. Also, on the following lines, list days tests will be given and the days reports are due.

Tests and Reports

_____

_____

_____

_____

_____

_____

EXERCISE 11.6   ## Decide When to Study

Referring to the materials you prepared when you did Exercise 11.5, enter in your study schedule the exact times you will study for each of your courses next week.

EXERCISE 11.7   ## Balancing Responsibilities

If a job, family responsibilities, a sport or hobby, or some other activity or interest is preventing you from doing your best work in college, write an explanation of what adjustments you will make to accommodate the conflict.

Increase Concentration

To make the best use of your study time, you must be able to focus your thought and attention on studying during the time you set aside for this purpose. Yet you may find that you are unable to concentrate for long stretches of time. Some students report that their minds begin to wander after as few as five minutes of reading. Others complain that their minds can't concentrate on studying for more than ten or fifteen minutes.

This chapter explains strategies for increasing concentration, which are summarized in "How to Increase Concentration for Studying," below. In addition, when you study Chapters 13 through 20 of *College Study Skills*, you will learn methods that will keep your mind active and less likely to wander when you read and study.

How to Increase Concentration for Studying

Use these strategies to improve your ability to concentrate on studying for longer periods.

- Accommodate your preferences for the conditions under which you study, such as the place, temperature, and presence or absence of music, food, or other people.
- Try to always study in the same place.
- Explain to your friends and relatives that you do not want to be interrupted while you are studying.
- Keep records of how long you concentrate when you study and try to concentrate longer the next time you study.
- Keep your list of things to do handy and add items to it as they come into your mind while you are studying.
- Decide that you want to study rather than do something else.
- Begin study sessions by doing routine or easy tasks.
- Do large tasks a bit at a time.

- Accept that you must do difficult tasks to achieve your goal of getting a college degree.
- Reward yourself for studying.

In addition, use the study methods that are explained in Chapters 13 through 20 of *College Study Skills.*

Accommodate Your Preferences

Use your answers to Exercise 6.5 on page 55 as a guide for providing yourself with a study environment in which you are likely to concentrate best. For instance, study at the time of day you are most alert. Also, take into account your preferences for conditions, such as the place you study, the kind of desk and chair you use, the brightness or dimness of light on your study surface, the temperature of the room, and whether you prefer to study while music is playing or while other people are present.

Select a Specific Place to Study

Try to always study in the same place and avoid using your study place for other purposes, such as watching television or socializing. In this way, when you go to your study place, you will sense your purpose for being there and your mind will prepare itself to concentrate on studying.

Eliminate Interruptions

You will probably find that it is difficult for you to concentrate if you are constantly interrupted. Therefore, if you have roommates, agree with them about the hours that will be devoted to study each day. Also, explain to friends and relatives that you do not want to be disturbed while you are studying because it will interrupt your concentration. You may devise a method to signal that you are studying. One of my students uses a silk rose to indicate that she doesn't want to be disturbed; when her husband and children see her seated at the kitchen table wearing the pink rose, they know that she is studying and they don't bother her.

If you have friends who insist on interrupting you while you are studying, try to replace them with more considerate companions. You deserve friends who respect your study time and who want you to do well in college.

Keep Records of Concentration

When you begin to study, make a note of the time. Then, when you first become aware that your attention is not focused on studying, record the time again. Compare the two times and make a note of how many minutes you studied before you lost your concentration. Next, spend a few minutes doing something other than studying; you might stand up and stretch or look out the window. When you begin to study again, make another note of how long you concentrate.

Continue in this way until you are satisfied with the length of time you are able to concentrate. Many students report that keeping this kind of record helps them to double or triple their attention span very quickly.

Use Your List of Things to Do

Your list of things to do, explained on page 102, provides a handy method for dealing with distracting thoughts, such as "Do the laundry," "Telephone Dad," and "Photocopy the report for history." When you study, keep your list of things to do handy and add items to it as they come into your mind. By writing the things you want to do in the place they belong, you free your mind to concentrate on studying rather than on keeping track of other responsibilities.

Decide That You Want to Study

Once your mind drifts off, you are no longer studying. You might be thinking about something that happened earlier in the day, something that is worrying you, or something that you would rather be doing—but you are not studying!

If you want to make the best use of your study time, decide that you want to study rather than daydream, listen to music, watch television, or do other things you enjoy. If you don't decide that you really want to spend your study time studying, you may become resentful and grow to feel that studying is a punishment. If you feel that you are being punished when you study, your thoughts will be about your suffering. When you think about your suffering, you cannot concentrate on reading or studying.

Do Routine Tasks First

Keep a list of your assignments, arranged in the sequence they must be completed, and start each study session by examining the list; do first what is either most routine or easiest (see Exercise 11.5 on page 110). If it is equally important to proofread a draft of a paper for an English course and to study for a chemistry test, do first whichever of the assignments is easier for you.

Another way to begin a study session is to review material you have studied previously. For instance, before trying to solve a new type of problem for a mathematics course, spend a few minutes solving a kind of problem you already know how to do. You will provide yourself with the review practice you need and you will put yourself in the right frame of mind for learning how to solve the new type of problem.

Do Large Tasks a Bit at a Time

It is sometimes difficult to concentrate on a task that seems impossible to accomplish. For instance, the thought of reading and learning everything in a six-hundred-page textbook can be overwhelming. However, reading and learning the information in a textbook is accomplished one step at a time using methods that are explained in following chapters of *College Study Skills*. Similarly, English handbooks explain how to do the small tasks that make it possible to write long term papers.

Mathematics, science, technology, and foreign language courses are among the ones for which information must be learned a bit at a time. If you do not keep up-to-date with the work in courses such as these, you may find it is extremely difficult to catch up.

Accept Difficult Tasks

When your mind is focused on the thought that a task is difficult or unpleasant, it cannot concentrate on accomplishing the task. Replace the thought "I don't want to do this difficult task" with the thought "To achieve a worthwhile goal, I accept that I must do this and other difficult tasks."

Those who achieve important goals do difficult or unpleasant things they would not do except for the fact that they are intent on attaining their objectives. For example, if you are determined to own an expensive automobile, you may work long hours at a difficult or unpleasant job that you would not work at except that you are determined to have the car you want. In the same way, if your goal is to earn a college degree, you may have to do difficult or unpleasant tasks that you would rather not do except that you are determined to have the benefits of a college education.

Reward Yourself for Studying

You can motivate yourself to concentrate by arranging your schedule so that studying is followed by something pleasant to do. Before you begin to study, plan that after an hour or two you will telephone a friend, read a magazine, go jogging, or engage in some other activity that you enjoy. When you study on a Saturday afternoon, plan that in the evening you will visit a friend, go to a movie, or do something else that entertains you.

Study followed by a reward is usually productive. If you know that you have only three hours to study because you've scheduled some fun for yourself, you may be inspired to make the best use of the three hours that you set aside for studying.

EXERCISE 12.1   **Accommodating Your Environmental Preferences**

Refer to your answers to Exercise 6.5 on page 55 to write a description of the environment in which you prefer to study. Include all ten conditions mentioned in the ten questions in Exercise 6.5.

EXERCISE 12.2   **Keeping Records of Concentration**

When you begin to read for a college course, make a note of the time in pencil at the place where you begin reading. Then, when you detect that your attention is not focused on reading, record the time again. Compare the two times and make a note of how many minutes you read before you lost your concentration. Continue in this way, striving each time to concentrate longer than you did the time before.

Determine how many minutes it now takes you to read ten pages in four textbooks you are studying for courses you are taking this term.

EXERCISE 12.3   **Do Routine Tasks First**

1. Refer to Exercise 11.5 on page 110 and copy on the following lines the first two assignments you will do next week. Then, decide which of these two assignments is easier, more routine, or more interesting, and do it first.

_____

_____

2. Decide for which of your courses it is appropriate to begin a study session by reviewing material you have studied previously.

_____

_____

EXERCISE 12.4   **Unpleasant or Difficult Tasks**

List the most unpleasant or difficult tasks you must do this term.

1. _____

2. _____

3. _____

4. _____

5. _____

Is your education important enough to you that you are willing to do these unpleasant or difficult tasks?

III

Study Effectively

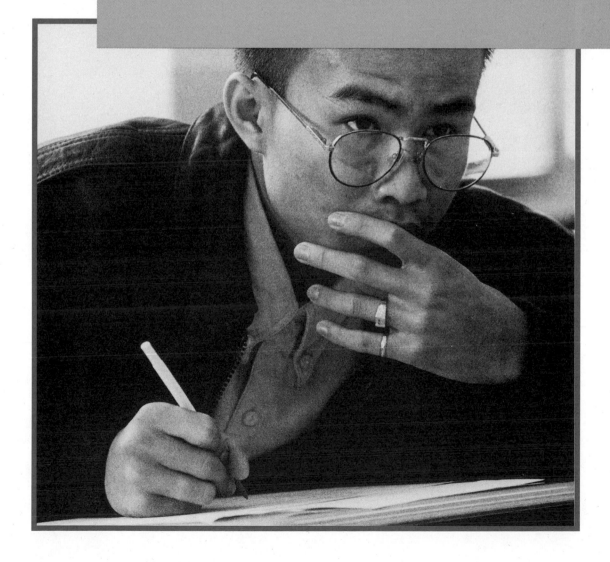

Preview of PART III

Some students have difficulty when they take tests because they prepare for them by reading rather than by studying. **Reading** is the process we use to understand information presented in writing, but **studying** is the process that is used to learn and remember information. Studying calls for using procedures such as the following:

- Listen in class and take good class notes.
- Use study aids provided in textbooks.
- Mark your textbooks.
- Make notes for information in textbooks.
- Anticipate test questions.
- Recite, rehearse, and review from notes.

These and other study procedures are explained in the next eight chapters. Several chapters in Parts I and II of *College Study Skills* explain additional study procedures, especially Chapters 2, 5, 6, 9, 11, and 12.

Use Effective Study Methods

Studying involves identifying the information you want to learn, organizing it for easy learning, and using effective methods to remember and recall it. The procedures for effective study have been stated in a variety of ways, including the well-known SQ3R study formula (see pages 197–198).

This chapter provides an overview of the procedures for effective studying and it includes specific guidelines for studying mathematics and science courses. The procedures that are summarized below are explained in detail in Chapters 14 through 20.

The Study Process

Use the following procedures to learn information and skills for college tests.

1. Listen in class and take good class notes (Chapters 14 and 15).
2. Preview before you read (Chapters 16 and 17).
3. Organize information in textbooks.
   - Mark books (Chapter 18).
   - Make notes for books (Chapter 19).
4. Anticipate test questions (Chapter 13).
   - Use your class notes as a guide.
   - Use helps provided in textbooks.
   - Attend test reviews.
   - Talk with teachers' former students.
   - Examine teachers' past tests.
   - Learn "easy" information.
5. Recite, rehearse, and review (Chapter 20).

Listen and Take Good Class Notes

It is essential for you to have good notes about what your instructors say in your classes. During class meetings, your teachers will explain information in required course reading material that they know is difficult for many students to understand and they will provide important information that is not printed in course textbooks. They will also give hints about what you should study when you prepare for tests. You need records of these kinds of information if you want to do your best in your college courses.

Methods for improving listening skills and taking good notes are explained in Chapters 14 and 15.

Preview Before You Read

For most of your courses, you will need to learn information in textbooks. Textbooks are books that summarize information taught in college courses, such as the books teachers assign for psychology, business, and chemistry courses.

Preview your books when you purchase them at the beginning of each term and preview the chapters in your textbooks before you read them. A **preview of a book** includes reading the preface, introduction, and table of contents to learn how the book is organized and what its major features are. A **preview of a chapter** involves reading the introduction, headings, and closing summary. It takes only a few minutes to preview a chapter, but this is time well spent because it provides background information that increases reading comprehension. The methods for previewing are explained in Chapters 16 and 17.

Mark and Make Notes for Textbooks

One of the best-known facts about human learning is that information is easier to learn when it is organized in a meaningful way. Figures 13.1 and 13.2 on page 121 illustrate how to organize information in a textbook by marking it and summarizing it in well-organized notes. The skills you developed when you studied Chapter 9 will help you learn how to take good class notes, mark books, and make notes for textbooks when you study Chapters 15, 18, and 19.

Anticipate Test Questions

The questions that appear on college tests tend to emphasize the information that is most important for students to know. Therefore, if you anticipate test questions, you will study the things that are most important for you to learn and you will also be more likely to earn good test grades.

Use Class Notes as a Guide   Most college teachers use class time to help students understand the things that are important for them to learn. As a result, the notes you take in class will usually be your best source of

FIGURE 13.1

An Example of Highlighting

Conflict

We encounter conflict when we must choose between two or more alternatives. There are three basic types of conflict: approach-approach, avoidance-avoidance, and approach-avoidance.

The **approach-approach conflict** is the need to choose between two attractive alternatives. The need to choose between vacationing in England or France is an example of an approach-approach conflict. This type of conflict is resolved when one possibility becomes more attractive than the other. If a vacation in England will include visits with friends and the trip to France will not, then England may become the more attractive choice.

The **avoidance-avoidance conflict** exists when you must choose between to *unattractive* alternatives. An example is the need to decide whether you will have a tooth pulled or have root canal work done on it. This type of conflict is resolved when one possibility becomes more *unattractive* than the other. If having a tooth pulled becomes more unattractive, you may choose to have root canal work done on the tooth.

The **approach-avoidance conflict** is present when one possibility or goal is both attractive and unattractive. The pursuit of a college degree is an approach-avoidance conflict for many students. It is attractive because a college degree may lead to better job opportunities in the future. But it is unattractive because it requires students to study hard and to take courses that they may prefer not to take. This type of conflict is often resolved unsatisfactorily. For instance, many students resolve their conflict about college study by dropping out of college. Later many of these people regret that they did not stay in school and earn a college degree.

FIGURE 13.2

Notes for the Passage in Figure 13.1

Types of Conflict

Approach-approach - when I must choose between two attractive alternatives. (Ex) Vacation in England or France. Resolved when one choice becomes more attractive.

Avoidance-avoidance - when I must choose between two unattractive alternatives. (Ex) Have a tooth pulled or have root canal work. Resolved when one choice becomes more unattractive.

Approach-avoidance - when one possibility is both attractive and unattractive. (Ex) College study is attractive and unattractive. Often not satisfactorily resolved (many students drop out of college and later regret it).

information about test questions. When you study your notes, be certain to give special attention to the following.

Information to Give Special Attention When Studying

- Information you copy from the chalkboard
- Information teachers say is important or difficult to learn
- Information teachers state while reading directly from their notes
- Information about topics that are also discussed in required course reading material

Mark these four types of information so that you don't overlook them when you study. You might draw a star or write *Important* in the margin next to the information or you might highlight it in yellow so it will stand out in your notes when you prepare for tests.

Methods for taking class notes are explained in Chapter 15.

Use Textbook Helps   Use learning goals, review questions, lists of terminology, and exercises and problems in your textbooks to help you anticipate test questions.

Textbook Helps for Studying

- **Learning goals** and **review questions** give information about what students are expected to learn in a textbook. Therefore, when a chapter begins with learning goals or ends with review questions, make certain that you have achieved the goals or that you can answer the questions.
- The meaning of course **terminology** is usually tested in many questions on college exams. For this reason, it is essential that you make certain you know all of the terminology that is listed at the end of chapters or that is printed in italics or boldface within chapters.
- When instructors assign you to do **exercises** or solve **problems** in a textbook, they will also usually require you to do similar exercises or to solve similar problems on tests. Therefore, when you take a test, be prepared to do any kind of exercises or to solve any type of problems that are in the course textbook.

These features of textbooks are explained in Chapter 17.

Attend Test Reviews   Some of your instructors will give reviews for tests during class or at special times outside of class. Attend reviews, take complete notes, and learn everything that you are told to learn. Teachers who give reviews want to focus your attention on learning what is most important. When instructors don't give test reviews, ask them what to study; it is reasonable for you to assume that your teachers want you to know what you should learn. Whether or not an instructor sets aside a specific time for a test review, you should learn the answers to all the questions in the following checklist so that you can prepare for the test properly. Write checks in pencil so you can erase them and reuse the checklist before each test you take.

Questions to Answer During Test Reviews

❑   What material will be covered on the test?

❑   Will equal importance be given to information in the textbook, class notes, and handouts, or will greater importance be given to one of these?

❑   What specific suggestions does the teacher have about what you should study in preparation for the test?

❑   Will you be allowed to refer to any books, notes, or handouts during the test?

❑   Will you be allowed to use a calculator or other equipment during the test?

❑   Must you bring any material or equipment to the test?

❑   What kinds of problems, if any, will you be required to solve?

❑   Will you answer true-false, multiple-choice, matching, fill-in, essay, or some other kind of questions?

❑   How many minutes long will the test be?

❑   Where will the test be given?

❑   Will the test be similar to other tests the teacher gave?

Attend all test reviews, take complete notes, and learn everything that you are told to learn. Teachers who give reviews want to help you do your best.

Talk with Teachers' Former Students   If at all possible, ask former students of your teachers how to study for tests. Teachers' testing methods seldom change much from year to year. As a result, students who studied with your teachers in the past have answered test questions very much like the ones you will answer. Students who received good grades for the courses you are taking know things that may be very useful to you. They may be eager to explain the methods that they used to earn good grades.

Examine Teachers' Past Tests   Some teachers give students tests to keep and some schools place tests on file for students to examine. Ask your teachers' former students if they have copies of tests you may examine and, if your teachers' tests are on file, locate them and study them.

Also, analyze the questions on the first test you take for a course; they will give you hints about the types of things to learn for subsequent tests. For instance, if the questions on a first test are mostly about little facts in a textbook, that teacher's other tests are also likely to focus on the same kinds of facts—study them for the next test.

Learn "Easy" Information   Some students believe incorrectly that if information is easy for them to understand, they know it. However, the difference between understanding and knowing is the difference between reading and studying. Reading is done to understand information; studying is done to remember and recall it.

You have no doubt understood everything you have read in *College Study Skills* about how to study. However, you cannot recall most of the information in this book unless you have studied it. For instance, when you read Chapter 12, you understood the methods listed there for increasing your concentration; however, you cannot recall all the methods unless you studied them. Without looking back at Chapter 12, list the methods it suggests you use to concentrate for longer periods. Unless you studied Chapter 12, or looked back at it, you were probably not able to list accurately the ten suggestions it gives for increasing concentration.

When you study for tests, make certain that you learn easy-to-understand information. It is extremely disappointing to lose points on tests for failure to learn information that you could have learned easily.

Remember and Recall

Many students try to learn information in books and notes by reading and rereading it. These students believe incorrectly that reading and studying are the same process.

It is true that books must be read to be studied; however, books may be read without being studied! *Reading* is the process that is used to understand information that is presented in writing. It involves such activities as locating the major thoughts and the details that are related to them. *Studying* is the process that is used to decide what to learn, to organize the information to be learned, and to use effective methods to remember and recall that information.

Most information stays in your memory only about twenty seconds unless you do something to store it there (see Chapter 5). When you want to remember and recall information, you must recite it, rehearse it, and review it.

Recitation, Rehearsal, and Review

- **Recitation** is the act of repeating information silently or aloud until you can recall it without reading it.
- **Rehearsal** is the act of analyzing information and relating it to information that is already stored in memory.
- **Review** is the repetition of recitation and rehearsal that makes it possible to retrieve information quickly when it is needed.

Much of what we learn is difficult to retrieve unless we review it. If you find that you have difficulty recalling information you studied for tests, you probably did not review sufficiently. You will remember best what you review most. Chapter 20 explains how to recite, rehearse, and review.

Guidelines for Mathematics Courses

Most colleges include courses in mathematics as a degree requirement. This often frustrates students who did not receive a good background in math while they were in high school and who prefer to study information-oriented subjects rather than subjects that stress problem solving.

Most college courses have as their main purpose to convey organized bodies of information. Anthropology, astronomy, biology, earth science, education, geography, government, history, law, management, marketing, political science, psychology, and sociology are among the information-oriented subjects taught in college. The following guidelines are provided for students who favor information-oriented subjects such as these and who view the prospect of studying mathematics with apprehension.

If you are one of these students, try studying math using the following guidelines together with the other study methods that have already been summarized in this chapter.

1. **Eliminate deficiencies before enrolling in a math course.** Before you enroll in a math course, learn or review any necessary concepts or skills. If your math background is weak, enroll in a review math course. If you have only minor deficiencies, study with a tutor, work on an appropriate computer-learning program, or review with another student.

    You may also review by auditing a course. To **audit** is to have official permission to attend a course without receiving a grade or academic credit. For instance, if you have forgotten much of what you know about advanced algebra, you may find it helpful to audit an advanced algebra course before you enroll in a trigonometry course. To audit a course, you must first ask for and receive the teacher's permission. Because teachers who give you permission to audit their courses are doing you a favor, show your appreciation by being attentive to instruction, doing assignments, and attending class faithfully.

2. **Keep in mind that learning math is a sequential process.** In elementary school, pupils learn addition before subtraction, subtraction before multiplication, and multiplication before division. Then, in high school and college, students learn basic algebra before geometry, geometry and advanced algebra before trigonometry, and trigonometry before calculus. Because learning mathematics is a sequential process, failing to learn a concept in its proper sequence will create difficulties for you when you attempt to learn other concepts later in the sequence. For instance, if you have not mastered multiplication, you will experience difficulty in learning algebra; if you have not mastered trigonometry, it will be impossible for you to learn calculus. In addition, you are likely to encounter serious difficulties if you fall behind in a math class and fail to master concepts and skills in the appropriate sequence.

3. **Take math courses in long terms rather than short terms.** If you have the choice of taking a math course during a long term or a short term, take the course during the long term. For instance, if your school offers you the option of taking math during a fifteen-week or an eight-week term, enroll in the course during the fifteen-week term. The longer terms will give you more time to master a topic before you have to move on to the next topic.

4. **Take consecutive math courses in consecutive terms.** Enroll in consecutive math courses in consecutive terms that are not separated by a long break. If you take Algebra I in a spring term and Algebra II in a fall term, you may forget much of what you learned in Algebra I during summer vacation. You will not have this problem if you enroll in Algebra I and Algebra II in consecutive terms that are not separated by a long break.

5. **Select good teachers.** Ask students who have already taken the course you will take for their opinions of who the good teachers are. In math courses, you want teachers who explain concepts in an easy-to-understand

manner, who give clear answers to students' questions in class, who help students outside of class, and who give fair tests.

Don't select teachers solely because they are known to be generous when grading. Your goal should be to learn mathematics; if you don't learn the things you need to learn, you will encounter unnecessary difficulty when you take more advanced math classes or science classes that require mathematical knowledge.

6. **Buy the textbook immediately.** Before the first class meeting, buy a new textbook or a used one that is free of highlighting or other markings. The student who wrote in a used book may have made marks that will confuse and frustrate you rather than help you. You want a book that is completely clean of all markings except for the ones you make to help yourself learn.

7. **Read your textbook with the goal of learning how to solve problems.** Learning how to solve problems is at the heart of the study of mathematics. Therefore, read your textbook with the goal of trying to understand the explanations about how to solve problems. Reread an explanation referring to the sample problem, and attempt to understand the exact procedure you must use to solve similar problems. Place a question mark next to material that you do not understand and try to eliminate your confusion by rereading the material or by using one of the methods suggested in guidelines number 12, 17, and 18 in this list.

8. **Learn terms, symbols, and formulas.** If you prefer to study information-oriented subjects, you are likely to find math textbooks difficult to read because they use symbols, formulas, and graphic displays rather than words to convey concepts and procedures. You must learn to translate the information in your textbook into language you understand. Learn terms, symbols, and formulas by using the methods that are explained in Chapters 14 through 20.

9. **Do the problems at the end of chapters in your textbook.** Do the problems your teacher assigns and as many more problems as you need to become able to solve them without looking back at sample solutions in the textbook. When your textbook does not contain enough problems for this purpose, solve additional problems using the method suggested in guideline number 17 in this list.

10. **Attend all classes.** If you are not a whiz at mathematics, you put yourself at a great disadvantage when you miss a class. If you must be unavoidably absent, use the suggestions on page 16 to find out what you missed and to catch up with your classmates.

11. **Take notes of your teacher's explanations.** The basic procedure for learning mathematics is to observe the precise steps in a technique and then, through practice, to become able to perform the steps yourself. Therefore, carefully observe how your teacher solves problems on the chalkboard, copy the problems and their solutions into your notes, and practice solving the problems in the same way your teacher did. See Chapter 15 for suggestions about taking class notes.

12. **Ask questions during class.** Make notes of the questions that occur to you during class or when you study your textbook and ask your questions during the time your teacher sets aside for this purpose. Avoid making

vague statements such as "I don't get it." Rather, formulate specific questions such as "What are some applications of that theorem?" If your question is about a problem you could not solve, you might show your work to the teacher, point to the place where you had difficulty, and say, "I followed everything down to here, and then I couldn't figure out what to do next."

13. **Review your notes soon after class.** Review your notes as soon after class as possible and practice solving problems of the type your teacher did in class (see page 154).

14. **Do homework on time.** The purpose of homework assignments is to help you learn the things you need to learn. Therefore, do all homework assignments on time even if your teacher does not collect and grade them. Be certain you know what the assignment is and record it in the place where you keep a record of all assignments (see pages 17–18 and 103–104).

15. **Review throughout the term.** Review is essential to learning (see Chapter 5 and Chapter 20). Therefore, throughout a term, practice doing problems of the type you did earlier in the term. If you do not do this kind of review, by the tenth week of a term you will have forgotten how to do the problems you learned to do in the second, third, and fourth week of the term.

16. **Find a study partner or form a study group.** You may find it helpful to study with another student or with a group of other students. Find another student in your math class with whom you can practice working problems and prepare for tests. You want somebody who shares your desire to do well and who will be prepared when the two of you get together to study. There are suggestions for forming a study group on page 35.

17. **Purchase a reference book on the same topic.** If you have difficulty understanding your textbook, purchase another book that covers the same topics. In your college bookstore, you may find a course guide, course outline, or another textbook that is easier for you to understand.

    Evaluate a book by comparing its table of contents to the table of contents of your textbook—they will not be identical, but they should be similar. Then, read a portion of the book that corresponds to information that you find difficult to understand in your textbook. After examining the available books in this way, purchase the one that is most understandable and that includes many problems and exercises with step-by-step solutions.

    Then, when you have difficulty understanding a concept in your textbook, find the section in your reference book that deals with the concept. Read the section and work out the problems that are provided.

18. **Get help at the first sign of a problem.** If you fall behind in doing assignments, immediately revise your study schedule to include the additional study time you need to catch up. In addition, if you discover that you do not understand concepts or cannot solve problems, don't delay in using the services of a tutor, learning center, math lab, or whatever other source of help is available to you on your campus. You may be able to overcome your difficulties if you seek help immediately; however, you may fall hopelessly behind if you do not get help at the first sign of difficulty. Also see Chapter 4.

Don't become discouraged if you have difficulty in studying mathematics. The math courses at your college are geared to the average ability of the students who study there; if they were not, most students wouldn't pass them. If other students just like you have succeeded in studying math, you can too!

Guidelines for Science Courses

The guidelines in this section are intended especially for students who would not take a science course except that they are required to take one to fulfill a degree requirement.

The following suggestions may benefit *any* student, but they are *not* intended as definitive advice for students who are majoring in science or in disciplines such as medicine, engineering, and nursing to which the study of science is fundamental. Students who major in college subjects such as these should possess a special aptitude for science and they should have done well in their high school science and mathematics courses. If you are weak in math or science and have enrolled in a program of study in which these subjects are fundamental, please discuss with your adviser or a counselor what your options are in case you discover that you have enrolled in a curriculum that is inappropriate for you.

Use the following guidelines together with the other study methods that have already been summarized in this chapter.

1. **If you favor studying information-oriented subjects, take an information-oriented science course.** Science courses such as astronomy, biology, and earth science emphasize learning a body of information, whereas chemistry and physics stress problem solving. If you are strong in math, you may have a rewarding experience studying physics or chemistry. However, if you are weak in math, you will probably find the study of some other science more to your liking.

2. **Ask other students for suggestions about what science course to take.** When you talk with students who have completed their science requirement, ask them what course they took, who taught the course, and whether they recommend the course and the teacher.

    You should also request advice from your adviser or counselor. However, I emphasize seeking advice from fellow students because as a student I found that my classmates' advice about courses and teachers was invariably more useful to me than the advice I received from faculty members. I was never disappointed by a course or teacher recommended to me by a classmate, but I was displeased and annoyed on several occasions by taking courses that were "sold" to me by a faculty adviser. After all, my classmates had actually taken the courses they recommended to me, whereas faculty members had not. You may find, as I did, that your fellow students are often better informed about some important matters than are faculty members.

    Keep in mind, though, that not all students have good judgment, keen powers of observation, or useful advice about courses and teachers. Therefore, solicit advice *only* from those students whom you respect and whose opinions you trust. Use what you learn by talking with faculty and classmates to undertake the analysis suggested in the following guideline.

3. **Study course descriptions and prerequisites in your catalog and examine textbooks before you enroll in a science course.** Though a science course may be oriented toward learning information, it may also assume specific abilities in math and basic knowledge of chemistry or physics. For instance, biology textbooks usually include something about the chemistry of living organisms. However, a biology course for students who are not majoring in science may place little emphasis on the chemistry of biology.

   Therefore, study the descriptions of science courses in your college catalog paying special attention to any math or science prerequisites. When you have identified two or three science courses you might take, visit your college bookstore to examine the textbooks that are used in the courses. Preview the books using the procedure explained in Chapter 16, keeping in mind that those who teach the course may not all assign the same textbook. If you are weak in math and chemistry, avoid taking a course in which the textbook is filled with mathematical equations and chemical formulas.

4. **Use the guidelines for studying mathematics.** Most of the guidelines for studying mathematics pertain when you study science or any other subject that is difficult for you. Give special attention to guidelines 3 through 18 on pages 125–127.

5. **Learn the vocabulary of the science you study.** Each college subject has its own *terminology*—words or phrases that have specific meanings in that subject. As many as 75 percent of the questions on some science tests cannot be answered without knowing terminology learned as a result of studying the science. Learn terminology by making notes on index cards or notebook paper (see pages 221 and 231–232).

   Be alert to three problems in learning scientific terminology. First, correct pronunciation is important, and terminology may be difficult to pronounce—*cephalochordata* and *reticuloendothelial*, for instance. Second, some words have similar spellings but very different meanings—*intermolecular* and *intramolecular*, for example. In addition, identical words often have different meanings in different disciplines. For instance, the word *nucleus* has different meanings in biology, botany, anatomy, physics, chemistry, astronomy, and meteorology! For instance, in botany, *nucleus* refers to the central kernel of a nut or seed; and in astronomy it refers to the central portion of the head of a comet.

6. **Don't be put off by scientific terminology when you preview chapters.** A science textbook chapter is likely to be filled with terminology that you will learn as a result of studying the chapter; this terminology may be used in the learning goals at the beginning of the chapter and in the summary and exercises at the end of the chapter. Because it is impossible to understand the meaning of written material that is loaded with unfamiliar scientific terminology, you may need to modify the suggestions for previewing textbook chapters that are explained in Chapter 17.

   For instance, you may decide not to read the summaries at the end of chapters as part of your preview because you find they include too many technical words the meanings of which you will not know until you read the chapter (see page 184).

7. **Read assigned material *before* class.** Many science professors lecture with the assumption that students have already read about the material they discuss in class. If you cannot follow your teacher's classroom explanations, the problem may be that you did not prepare properly for class.

8. **Plan plenty of time for reading.** Science textbooks tend to be dense. The sentences in them are often long and complex, and one paragraph may contain several concepts that must be understood in a specific sequence in order to be able to grasp a general principle that is being explained. As a result, you will probably find that it is necessary for you to read your science textbook sentence by sentence, stopping frequently to make certain you understand what you have read.

   Therefore, schedule more time for reading your science textbook than you do for other textbooks. Read each chapter a section at a time and reread each section as many times as you need to understand it. When you find yourself reading slowly and having difficulty understanding, keep in mind that the fault is not with you. It is inherent in the nature of scientific writing that it must be read slowly because it is complex and difficult to understand.

9. **As you read, relate the text to accompanying illustrations.** Most science textbooks are filled with diagrams, charts, graphs, and other kinds of illustrations. Whereas illustrations in a history or psychology textbook may usually be examined and understood very quickly, this is seldom the case with illustrations in science textbooks. One illustration in a science textbook may require an hour of careful study, which involves relating the illustration to a detailed explanation in the text.

   If you have difficulty relating information in the text to an accompanying illustration, your fingers will help you. Use the fingers of one hand to keep your place in the text that refers to the illustration and use the fingers of the other hand to point at the places in the illustration to which the text refers.

10. **Take well-organized class notes.** When you take notes, keep in mind that the purpose of a science lecture is to complement the text. Your science teacher will probably give a logical overview of the material, present related material that is not in your required textbook, and give examples of the applications of concepts explained in the text.

    Make well-organized notes of the points your teacher emphasizes and the steps your instructor uses to illustrate an idea or prove a statement. Use your notes to further your understanding of the textbook and to guide you in studying and preparing for tests (see Chapters 15 and 20).

11. **Give special attention to any appendixes in your textbook.** An **appendix**, which contains supplementary material, is usually located immediately after the last chapter. The appendixes of your science textbook are very likely to include useful information.

    For instance, the appendixes of a chemistry textbook in my library include (1) a summary of basic math for chemistry, (2) chemical tables, and (3) suggestions for learning chemistry. The appendixes of one of my biology textbooks include (1) answers to self-quiz questions, (2) a classification of living things, (3) a summary of the metric system, and (4) an explanation of a learning technique.

12. **Benefit from lab.** It is virtually impossible to make general statements about science laboratories—they differ first because of the differences in the content and methodology of the various sciences. In addition, they range in format from the cookbook approach, in which every step in a procedure is spelled out and demonstrated, to the open-ended lab, in which students are provided with equipment and materials and instructed to plan and carry out experiments with a minimum of supervision.

    However, labs generally have as their primary purposes to give students experience with equipment, to teach them about scientific methodology, to help them relate course content to the physical world, and to give them experience with scientific equipment.

    To benefit from a lab session, start by reading the purpose of the experiment. Study the experiment procedures in advance and try to estimate its likely outcome. Make data tables before lab so that you won't have to waste time preparing them in lab where you could better spend your time concentrating on your experiment. Don't let your lab partner handle the equipment while you record data—take an active part in experiments. If there are calculations to perform or graphs to plot, do them before you leave the laboratory so you can spot and correct any obvious mistakes. Before you turn in your report, carefully reread the experiment directions to make certain that you have completed all the requirements.

13. **Study to learn and enjoy rather than to earn a specific grade.** If you are accustomed to earning A's and B's in your area of specialization, don't put yourself under the pressure of insisting that you also earn an A or B in your required science course. Rather, study your chosen science to learn as much as you can about it. If you assume this attitude, you will be more relaxed and enjoy the study of science more. As a result, you will be more likely to earn the kind of grade for science that you usually earn for other courses. However, a passing grade is probably all you need to fulfill your science requirement.

The crucial step in completing a science requirement without undue difficulty is to enroll in the right course taught by the right teacher. If you are successful in using guidelines 1, 2, and 3, you are likely to have a very good experience studying science.

EXERCISE 13.1

Your Study Procedures

Write a description of the study procedures you use. Compare your strategies to the study suggestions in this chapter and to the SQ3R study method, which is described on pages 197–198.

EXERCISE 13.2

Anticipating Test Questions

Do this exercise in pencil so you can erase your marks and use it for each course you are taking. Write the name of the most difficult course you are taking on the line.

_____

Check the items in the following list that are sources of help for you in anticipating test questions for this course.

☐ The teacher writes important information on the chalkboard.

☐ The teacher sometimes mentions that specific information is important or difficult to learn.

☐ The teacher covers topics in class that are also discussed in the textbook.

☐ Learning goals appear at the beginning of textbook chapters.

☐ Terminology is listed at the end of textbook chapters or it is printed in italics or boldface in the chapters.

☐ Review questions or problems appear at the end of textbook chapters.

☐ The teacher gives test reviews.

☐ Some of the teacher's former students can tell me how to study for the teacher's tests.

☐ Tests the teacher gave in the past are available for me to examine.

☐ I have already taken one of the teacher's tests and examined it to figure out what kinds of questions might be on the teacher's next test.

EXERCISE 13.3   Studying Mathematics

If you are taking a math course, use the following checklist to evaluate your study methods. Each item in the checklist corresponds to one of the guidelines for math courses on pages 125–127. Read a statement and check **yes** if it is true or **no** if it is false. Reread a guideline for which you check **no,** and consider whether you can use the suggestions given in the guidelines to do better in your math course.

Yes No

☐ ☐ 1. I eliminated deficiencies before I enrolled in the course.

☐ ☐ 2. I keep up-to-date with course work; I do *not* let myself fall behind.

☐ ☐ 3. I am taking math in long terms, not short terms.

☐ ☐ 4. If I am taking consecutive math courses, I am taking them in consecutive terms.

☐ ☐ 5. I have a good teacher.

☐ ☐ 6. I bought the textbook before the first class meeting.

☐ ☐ 7. I read the textbook with the goal of learning how to solve problems.

☐ ☐ 8. I have an effective system for learning terms, symbols, and formulas.

☐ ☐ 9. I do all the problems at the ends of chapters and when there aren't enough problems in my textbook I supplement them with additional problems in a reference book that I purchased.

☐ ☐ 10. I attend all classes.

☐ ☐ 11. I make accurate notes of the procedure my teacher uses to solve problems on the chalkboard.

☐ ☐ 12. I ask questions and receive answers to my questions during class.

☐ ☐ 13. Soon after each class, I review my class notes and practice solving problems of the type my teacher demonstrated in class.

☐ ☐ 14. I do homework on time, even if my teacher does not collect it.

☐ ☐ 15. Throughout the term, I practice doing problems of the type I did earlier in the term.

☐ ☐ 16. I have a study partner, or I am a member of a study group.

☐ ☐ 17. I purchased a reference book to supplement my textbook.

☐ ☐ 18. I am getting help from a tutor or at a learning center or math lab.

EXERCISE 13.4   Studying Science

If you are taking a science course, use the following checklist to evaluate your study methods. Each item in the checklist corresponds to one of the guidelines for science courses on pages 128–131. Read a statement and check **yes** if it is true or **no** if it is false. Reread a guideline for which you check **no,** and consider whether you can use the suggestions given in the guidelines to do better in your math course.

Yes No

☐ ☐ 1. I am taking an information-oriented science rather than chemistry or physics.

☐ ☐ 2. I asked other students which science courses they recommend.

☐ ☐ 3. I selected the science course in which I enrolled after studying course descriptions in the catalog and evaluating textbooks in the bookstore.

☐ ☐ 4. I study science using guidelines 3 through 18 for math courses on pages 125–127.

☐ ☐ 5. I am up-to-date in learning the terminology in my science course.

☐ ☐ 6. I preview chapters in my science book before I read them.

☐ ☐ 7. I always read assigned material *before* class.

☐ ☐ 8. I schedule sufficient time for reading my science textbook.

☐ ☐ 9. I carefully study the diagrams, charts, graphs, and other illustrations in my science textbook.

☐ ☐ 10. I take well-organized class notes.

☐ ☐ 11. I know what is in the appendixes of my science book.

☐ ☐ 12. I benefit from my science lab.

☐ ☐ 13. I study science with the goal of learning as much as I can rather than worrying unduly about the grade I will receive.

Listen in Class

Researchers have discovered that far more communication time is spent listening than reading, speaking, or writing. One study, for instance, reported that college students spend 53 percent of their communication time listening, compared to 17 percent reading, 16 percent speaking, and 14 percent writing.* When you think about it, this finding is not surprising. Virtually every college course requires students to attend class meetings during which information and ideas are communicated to them through the spoken word.

Considering the central role listening plays in learning, it is somewhat of a mystery why few schools offer listening instruction. Whereas schools invariably teach students how to improve their reading and writing, few offer instruction especially designed to help them improve their listening skills. However, you can improve your listening in the same way that you can improve any other skill.

Be an Active Listener

In the college classroom, **active listeners** are students who, when necessary, verify their understanding by asking appropriate questions and who demonstrate their understanding of what teachers say by making accurate notes of lecture content. This kind of listening requires expending effort and energy in the ways explained in this chapter and summarized in the following list.

How to Improve Classroom Listening

1. **Prepare to listen.** Read assigned material, review your class notes, and do assigned problems or exercises before class.

* Larry Barker, "An Investigation of Proportional Time Spent in Various Communication Activities by College Students," *Journal of Applied Communication Research* 8 (1980): 101–109.

2. **Eliminate physical distractions**. Don't let hunger, an annoying classmate, or some other physical distraction interfere with your ability to listen.

3. **Eliminate mental distractions.** Develop the ability to set aside worries and concerns so that you can focus your attention on what happens in class.

4. **Do not prejudge a teacher.** Give every teacher a fair chance; don't tune out what a teacher has to say simply because there is something about him or her that doesn't appeal to you.

5. **Focus on the teacher's message.**

   - **Listen to opening comments**—they may provide essential background information.

   - **Listen for major thoughts**—they are the topics that provide the basic structure for a lecture.

   - **Listen for details**—they explain and support the major thoughts.

   - **Listen for examples**—they help in understanding information and concepts.

   - **Listen for study hints**—they guide you in deciding what is most important to learn.

6. **Watch the chalkboard.** Many teachers use the chalkboard to provide study hints; others (such as mathematics teachers) use it as the basic means for helping students understand how to solve problems.

7. **Attend to nonverbal clues.** Sit where you can clearly see your teachers' gestures and facial expressions—they may convey important information.

8. **Ask questions.** When you are in doubt about what a teacher said, it is your responsibility to ask questions that help you verify whether you understood correctly.

Prepare to Listen

Use the procedures explained on pages 145–146 to prepare for each of your college classes.

- Read assigned material before class.
- Review your notes from the previous session before class.
- Do assigned problems or exercises before class.

In addition, don't rush into a class at the last minute. Arrive a few minutes early and spend the time trying to put yourself in a frame of mind that will help you benefit as much as possible from the session.

Eliminate Distractions

The second step in good classroom listening is to eliminate any physical or mental distractions that may interfere with your ability to focus your attention on a teacher's message.

Physical Distractions Before you go to a class, take care of any physical needs that may become sources of discomfort and interfere with your concentration. You may need to use the rest room, have a drink of water, or eat something. In addition, consider the following.

- Sit where you have a good view of the teacher but where you cannot be distracted by what happens outside the classroom. You might find, for instance, that an attractive person walking in the hallway or on campus grounds is more interesting to you than whatever your teacher has to say. Sit where your attention is focused on the class rather than events outside of it.

- Select a seat away from students who distract you. Don't let classmates who want your attention prevent you from your main purpose in attending college—to learn and earn a degree. Socialize with the people you like before or after class.

- Dress so you can remove clothes if a classroom is too warm or put on clothes if it is too cold. If you wear a shirt or blouse under a sweater or jacket, you can take off the sweater if you become too warm or put on the jacket if you become too cold.

When a classroom is small, a seat in the last row may provide the best view of the teacher. However, when a classroom is very large, don't sit in the back away from the action.

Mental Distractions You will sometimes arrive at a class with your mind preoccupied with concerns or worries of various kinds.

- You may be thinking about things you will do after class, such as go to work, shop for groceries, meet a friend, or make a telephone call.

- You may be worrying about something such as a car that needs an expensive repair, a disagreement at work, or an exam you will take later in the day.

- You may be preoccupied with thoughts about a spouse, boyfriend, girlfriend, parent, child, or other loved one.

- You may be trying to solve a problem, such as how to resolve a disagreement with an employer.

If your mind is filled with thoughts such as these during class, it will be impossible for you to listen to the lecture. You must learn to temporarily put other concerns out of your mind and redirect your attention to what your teacher is saying. One of the following strategies may help.

- If you are thinking about something you want to remember to do, write it on your list of things to do. For instance, if you want to remember to shop for specific items later in the day, write them on your list of things to do.

Knowing that you have a record of what you want to remember, you should find it easy to redirect your attention to the lecture.

- If you are thinking of something about which you can do nothing, accept that fact and try to put it out of your mind. For instance, if you are worrying about a relative who is in the hospital, remind yourself that you can do nothing for your relative while you are in a college classroom. If you feel your relative is receiving good medical attention or if you are going to visit him or her soon, try to comfort yourself with these thoughts. Then do your best to redirect your thoughts to the lecture.

- If you are trying to solve a problem, remind yourself that you cannot solve the problem and also give full attention to a lecture. For instance, if you are trying to figure out how to resolve a disagreement with your employer, remind yourself that you cannot work on the solution to that problem *and* listen to a lecture. Then, decide to listen to the lecture *now* and to work on the solution to your problem *later*.

It will be a great benefit to you throughout your life if you can learn now to set aside your concerns to effectively deal with study, work, or whatever other tasks you set for yourself.

Do Not Prejudge a Teacher

Don't be put off by teachers because there is something about them that you don't like. Give each of your instructors a chance to show you whether they have something worthwhile to offer you before you decide they don't.

When I was in college, I took a sociology course with a classroom full of other students who were extremely disappointed that it was taught by somebody other than the professor who was supposed to teach it. The scheduled teacher was a distinguished professor—an elegant, charming, articulate man. However, when he became unavailable, he was replaced by a rumpled and somewhat arrogant man who spent the entire term seated behind his desk smoking a pipe. This man never stood up, he never raised his voice above a mumble, and he refused to teach the course the way my classmates thought he should.

To my surprise, I soon discovered that this replacement teacher was one of the best professors I had ever had! Those who were willing to listen had a good time in his class and learned a great deal. However, most of my classmates didn't give him a chance; instead of listening to what he had to offer, they spent the entire term arguing with him and being resentful that he was not the teacher they wanted.

Try not to be put off by teachers because there is something about them that annoys you or is unappealing to you. If you give them a chance, you may find that they are sometimes better teachers than the ones in which you find no obvious flaws.

Focus on the Teacher's Message

You think much more rapidly than your teachers can speak. Your mind processes words at the rate of about 500 words per minute, but your teachers speak at the rate of only about 125 to 150 words per minute. Thus, you have somewhere between 300 to 400 words of thinking time for each minute you spend listening to your teachers in class.

If you don't put your thinking time to good use during lectures, you will likely find your mind drifting off to think about something else. To zero in on what your teachers are saying, especially listen for

- Opening comments
- Major thoughts
- Details
- Examples
- Study hints

The following discussions explain how listening for these components of lectures will help you focus on a teacher's message.

Listen to Opening Comments   Begin listening from the moment a teacher starts talking. It is important for you to focus your attention on your teachers' comments from the first moment they begin to speak. At the beginning of classes, teachers often summarize previous instruction, review important concepts, or provide an overview of the day's lecture. You do not want to miss any important information such as this—it is the background you need to better understand that which will follow.

Listen for Major Thoughts   During lectures, make it your goal to find your teachers' major thoughts—they are going to form the basic structure for your class notes (see Chapter 15). There are three strategies teachers commonly use to indicate they are stating a major point.

- **Direct statement.** They may directly state important thoughts by using phrases such as "Now I'm going to discuss . . . " and "My next point is . . .".
- **Pause.** They pause while lecturing as a clue that they stated a major point just before the pause or that they will state it after the pause.
- **Repetition.** When teachers repeat statements, this is usually a hint that the statements are of particular importance.

Use these three hints to help you zero in on your teachers' major points.

Listen for Details   In addition to listening for major thoughts, develop skill in listening for the significant details teachers give to support their major thoughts. Many lecturers make it clear how many details to list under major thoughts by making statements such as the following.

- Sociologists identify *four* types of families.
- There are *five* steps in the selling process.
- Let's examine *three* tragic effects of the Civil War.

When instructors make statements such as these, it is clear exactly how many details should follow.

In other instances, teachers make it clear that they are about to state details, but not the number of details they will give. For instance, an instructor may say, "I'm going to talk about some of the problems involved in starting a small business." In this case, students know that "Problems with starting a small business" is the major thought; however, they will not know how many problems there are until the teacher states them. Very often, a list in a lecture is about the following kinds of information:

causes	kinds	theories	characteristics
effects	types	criteria	advantages
results	categories	parts	disadvantages
reasons	purposes	stages	differences
factors	functions	steps	similarities

When teachers use these and similar words during lectures, they are providing hints about the major thoughts *and* the kinds of details they will give. For instance, if a teacher states "There are six *factors* to consider when enrolling in a science course," you know that the major thought under discussion is "enrolling in a science course" and that six details will follow—they will be "factors to consider."

Listen for Examples   Many of your teachers will give examples to help you understand information and concepts. For instance, during a lecture for a business course, a teacher explained that one way to make an ethical decision is to decide what is the greatest good for the greatest number. She gave the following example to help students grasp a problem in using this method for making decisions.

> *Imagine that you are driving eight people in a van with faulty brakes down a mountain road. Suddenly you come upon a baby lying in the middle of the road. What should you do? Should you drive off the road to spare the baby's life? Or, should you risk killing the baby in order to spare your life and the lives of the other people in the van?*

Some students became so engrossed in the dilemma posed by this example they did not grasp that its purpose was to develop understanding rather than simply to entertain.

Listen for your teachers' examples and try to understand how they are intended to help you better understand course content.

Listen for Study Hints   Instructors often inform students about what is especially important to learn by making statements such as the following:

- This is very important.
- I'll probably ask a test question about this.
- You must be able to do these kinds of problems.
- This confuses some students—don't let it confuse you.

When teachers make such statements, write them in your notes and mark the information to which they pertain for special attention in the same way you mark the information you copy from chalkboards.

Watch the Chalkboard

All of your teachers have been students, and as students they learned that the information their teachers wrote on chalkboards was very often used as the basis for test questions. Many of your teachers assume that you also have figured out that you should give special attention to anything written on the board. Many of them believe that they are announcing a test question to you whenever they write on a chalkboard.

Therefore, when you use the suggestions in Chapter 15 to take class notes, include in them everything that your teachers write on the chalkboard and mark it for special attention when you study. You might draw a star or write *Important* in the margin next to the information, or you can mark it with yellow or pink highlighting ink so you will not overlook it when you study for a test.

Following are some of the types of information that instructors write on chalkboards:

- Tables, charts, and diagrams
- Mathematical formulas
- Solutions to mathematical, scientific, or engineering problems
- Important terminology
- Names and dates

Give special attention to these kinds of information when you study.

Attend to Nonverbal Clues

The main reason you should sit where you can see your teachers clearly is that their gestures, facial expressions, and eye movements may often convey important information.

- **A gesture may supplement words.** For instance, an instructor may point at the chalkboard to emphasize something written there that she wants you to understand or know. Or, she may use her hands to indicate the size of something, such as the height of a stack of students' papers she graded over the weekend.

- **A facial expression may contradict words.** An instructor may say, "This is easy," but a playful expression on his face may suggest that he is teasing and wants you to understand the opposite—"This is very difficult."

- **A gesture or facial expression may suggest what you are to do.** A teacher may stop talking and raise her eyebrows, suggesting that she is ready to answer your questions, or she may purse her lips or give some other signal when opening a book of poetry to indicate that she wants complete silence before she reads aloud from the book.

- **Eye movements may indicate important information is being given.** When instructors glance at their notes as they make a statement, this often indicates that the point is especially important.

Take care not to be hasty in drawing conclusions about your teachers' emotional responses. They may show less or more emotion than they are actually feeling! For instance, a teacher who is truly angry and disappointed that some students are not doing homework may not show his anger; however, his pent up hostility may reveal itself when he assigns final grades. Or a teacher may make an emotionally charged fuss over students who are not doing homework, not because she is angry but because she wants to motivate students to avoid the embarrassment of her tirades by doing homework.

Ask Questions

When you are in conversation with friends who say something you don't understand, you ask questions to let them know what you don't understand and to give them the opportunity to give you more information or a fuller explanation. Similarly, when you are unclear about something a teacher says, it is your responsibility to seek the clarification you need. Skillful teachers view the classroom as a place for dialog with students—they depend on students' questions to know what is not clear in their lectures.

Guidelines for Asking Questions

- **Be patient.** When teachers have complicated or detailed information to convey, you may find yourself formulating questions that they will eventually answer. Therefore, don't ask a question until it becomes clear to you that the teacher is not going to provide the information you want.
- **Ask questions at the times instructors indicate they want to answer them.** Some teachers prefer to answer questions at the beginning or end of class, whereas others stop from time to time and ask, "Are there any questions?" Reserve your questions for these times.
- **Be specific in wording questions.** "Will you please give more examples of palindromes?" is specific, but "I don't get it" is not. Formulate your questions in a manner that will make it clear to your teacher the kind of answer you are seeking.
- **If you still don't understand, ask for an example.** If you are confused about an answer to a question, ask your teacher for an example. An example may clear up your confusion.
- **Be polite.** Use a sincere, questioning tone; avoid a critical, sarcastic, or whining tone. "Is this important?" is a reasonable question when it's asked sincerely, but it is rude when it is asked in a sarcastic or whining voice.
- **Ask only questions that may also benefit other students.** Requesting an explanation about course content may benefit other students who are also interested in the answer. However, a question such as "May I have another copy of the syllabus to replace the one I lost?" benefits only you. Ask this sort of question before or after class.

It is *not* a good idea to ask a question if (1) the question reveals that you have not done required reading, (2) the question makes it obvious you did not do homework, or (3) your teacher does not welcome questions. In these instances, it is best to find out what you need to know by waiting until after class to talk with a fellow student or study the course textbook.

EXERCISE 14.1   ## Time You Spend Listening

With your classmates, agree on a specific school day during which you will all keep records of the amount of time you spend listening.

1. Using the following table, check each fifteen-minute segment that you spend listening in class that day. For instance, if you listen to a lecture from 9:00–10:00 A.M., place checks next to 9:00, 9:15, 9:30, and 9:45. How many hours did you spend listening in class?

   _____

2. Place an X through each fifteen-minute segment you spend listening in situations other than class. For instance, if you are with friends from 1:00–2:30 spending half the time talking and half the time listening, x out three of the six fifteen-minute segments during that time period. Don't forget to include the time you spend in such activities as talking on the telephone, listening to the radio, and watching television. How many hours did you spend listening in situations other than in class?

   _____

3. In class, compare the time you spent listening with the time your classmates spent listening.

Morning				Evening			
5:00	5:15	5:30	5:45	5:00	5:15	5:30	5:45
6:00	6:15	6:30	6:45	6:00	6:15	6:30	6:45
7:00	7:15	7:30	7:45	7:00	7:15	7:30	7:45
8:00	8:15	8:30	8:45	8:00	8:15	8:30	8:45
9:00	9:15	9:30	9:45	9:00	9:15	9:30	9:45
10:00	10:15	10:30	10:45	10:00	10:15	10:30	10:45
11:00	11:15	11:30	11:45	11:00	11:15	11:30	11:45
12:00	12:15	12:30	12:45	12:00	12:15	12:30	12:45
1:00	1:15	1:30	1:45	1:00	1:15	1:30	1:45
2:00	2:15	2:30	2:45	2:00	2:15	2:30	2:45
3:00	3:15	3:30	3:45	3:00	3:15	3:30	3:45
4:00	4:15	4:30	4:45	4:00	4:15	4:30	4:45

EXERCISE 14.2   ## Your Classroom Listening Skills

Check **yes** for statements that describe you and **no** for the ones that do not describe you. Use the items you checked **no** as a guide for improving your classroom listening strategies.

Yes No

☐ ☐ 1. I prepare myself for listening by reading assigned material, reviewing class notes, and doing assigned problems or exercises before class.

☐ ☐ 2. I plan ahead so that I do not become hungry or thirsty during class.

☐ ☐ 3. I select seats that give me good views of teachers but from which I cannot be distracted by events outside the classroom.

☐ ☐ 4. I select seats away from students who distract me.

☐ ☐ 5. I dress in layers so I can remove clothes if a room is too warm or put on clothes if it is too cold.

☐ ☐ 6. If I am distracted by thoughts about things I must do after class, I write them on my list of things to do and redirect my attention to the lecture.

☐ ☐ 7. If I am distracted by thoughts about a personal problem, I remind myself that I cannot think about the problem *and* listen to the lecture, and I redirect my attention to the lecture.

☐ ☐ 8. I try to ignore anything about teachers' appearance or manner that displeases me and focus my attention on what they have to say.

☐ ☐ 9. I listen to teachers' opening comments to learn if they are reviewing previous instruction or providing an overview of the day's lecture.

☐ ☐ 10. I listen for teachers to directly state their major thoughts using phrases such as "Now I'm going to discuss . . .".

☐ ☐ 11. When teachers don't directly state major thoughts, I use their pauses and repetitions as clues to major thoughts.

☐ ☐ 12. I listen for teachers to state the number of details they will give.

☐ ☐ 13. I listen for examples and try to understand how they are intended to help me better understand course content.

☐ ☐ 14. I watch how teachers use the chalkboard to indicate what they believe is important to know and learn.

☐ ☐ 15. I listen for teachers' statements about what is important or difficult to learn.

☐ ☐ 16. I watch my teachers' gestures, facial expressions, and eye movements and try to understand what they communicate.

☐ ☐ 17. When I am in doubt about something teachers say, I ask questions to help clear up my confusion.

☐ ☐ 18. When I ask questions, I do so at the times teachers indicate they want to answer them.

EXERCISE 14.3   **Focusing on the Teacher's Message**

In each of your classes, keep records of how long you are able to concentrate on the lecture before your mind wanders or before you tune out what the teacher is saying.

- Record the time you start listening.
- When you detect that your attention is not focused on listening to the teacher, record the time again.
- Compare the two times and make a note of how many minutes you listened before you lost your concentration.

Continue in this way for two weeks, using suggestions in this chapter to strive each time to concentrate longer than you did the time before.

At the end of two weeks, write a report about whether you were successful in increasing the length of time you can focus on lectures.

Take Good Class Notes

Within two days after a lecture you will have forgotten about three-fourths of what you heard, and within a week you will have forgotten virtually all that was said during the lecture. If you don't have written records of what your teachers say in class, you will not be able to prepare for tests by studying what they taught you during class meetings.

Class notes usually include explanations about complicated course material, important facts that are not stated in required reading material, methods for solving problems, and hints about what to study for tests. Thus, they are usually the best source of help for understanding course subject matter and for deciding what to study for tests. Attend classes faithfully to take complete and well-organized notes about the explanations, facts, methods, and hints you will need when you take examinations.

Prepare for Each Lecture

A shockingly high proportion of college students attend classes for which they are totally unprepared. They schedule classes without breaks between them so they must rush from one class to another or they wander into classes at the last minute still thinking about conversations or other entertaining activities they were engaged in before class. These are not the strategies of successful college students. To prepare for classes, use the following strategies.

How to Prepare for Classes

- **Read assigned material.** Instructors assign material for students to read before class because they know that they are going to give lectures that students cannot fully understand without having first read about lecture topics. When you have difficulty understanding lectures, it may be because you didn't prepare by reading required material. Do this reading as near to class time as possible so that the information will be fresh in your mind during lectures.

- **Preview assigned material.** When you do not have time to read assigned material, at least preview it before class using the strategies that are explained in Chapter 17. It is better to have a little information about a lecture topic than to have no information at all. Again, preview material as near to class time as possible.

- **Review class notes.** Before class, also review the notes you took during the previous class meeting. When you look over your notes, you provide yourself with necessary review and you prepare your mind to listen to information that likely progresses logically from information given in the preceding class. In addition, while reviewing your notes you may identify questions that you want to ask during the upcoming class.

- **Do assigned problems or exercises.** Teachers assign problems and exercises to provide students with practice they need. For instance, mathematics instructors assign problems for students to solve and foreign language teachers assign exercises in translation because students will be graded on their abilities in these skills. When you do assigned problems or exercises, you prepare yourself properly for class and you increase the likelihood that you will learn course content.

When you have difficulty in a college course, analyze whether you are using these strategies to prepare for class. If you are not, consider that your problem may be lessened by using them.

Use Good Listening Strategies

Use the suggestions given in Chapter 14 to improve your listening comprehension. If you do not use effective listening strategies, you cannot take good notes; if you do not take good class notes, you will not have a record of what you need to learn. Good listening is essential to your success in college.

The following strategies explained in Chapter 14 are basic for taking good class notes:

- Listen for opening statements that provide an overview of a lecture.
- Listen for major thoughts and use them as the basic structure for your notes.
- Listen for details and list them under major thoughts.
- Listen for examples and include them in your notes (perhaps marking them with the circled letters *ex*, as in Figure 15.1 on page 150).
- Listen for study hints and record them in your notes.

If you improve your listening, you will reap benefits at school, at work, and in all your relations with others. Think for a moment. Do you choose as friends people who are interested in the things you have to say or people who look at you blankly when you speak? If you were a teacher, would you be more favorably disposed toward students who show they are listening in class or to the ones who seem to be bored or disinterested? If you were an employer, would you hire workers who understand what you tell them, or would you pick the ones who don't seem to grasp what you say? The answers to these questions are obvious—we all value good listening in our friends and associates.

Use an Appropriate Notebook

It is essential that you have a notebook that makes it easy for you to keep notes for each class completely separate from the notes for your other classes. For example, notes for a biology course, a math course, and an English course should be kept in three notebooks or in three separate sections of a notebook. If you mix your notes for one class with your notes for another class, your notes will not be properly organized when you study them to prepare for tests.

There are additional suggestions for selecting a notebook on pages 17–18.

Take Well-organized Class Notes

Take well-organized class notes by using the traditional format illustrated in Figure 15.1 on page 150, the Cornell system shown in Figure 15.2 on page 151, or in any of the note-taking formats displayed on pages 219–224. The following suggestions for organizing class notes apply no matter what note-taking method you use.

How to Organize Class Notes

- Take notes on 8½-by-11-inch notebook paper so that all the information about topics is usually on one page rather than on two or three pages.
- Write your name, address, and telephone number in the front of your notebook so it can be easily returned to you if you lose it.
- Keep assignments for all classes in a special assignment section of your notebook so when you study you'll be less likely to overlook assignments buried in notes.
- Start each day's notes on a new sheet of paper and begin them with a heading that includes the date and course name or course number. The date is essential for putting notes back in correct sequence when they become mixed up, for verifying that notes are complete, and for finding where to begin studying when teachers announce that tests cover material beginning on a particular date.
- Leave at least one blank line before each main idea. Make diagrams and other drawings large, and skip lines before and after them.
- Punch holes in papers instructors hand out and insert them in your ring binder for safekeeping.

- Number each page so you can easily put notes back in correct order if you remove them from your ring binder.

Also, consider writing only on one side of each piece of paper so you can see all your notes when you spread them out on a desk to study them.

The Traditional Note-taking Format

Notice in Figure 15.1 on page 150 that notes in the traditional format emphasize the relations between major thoughts and details:

- **Major thoughts stand out clearly**. In Figure 15.1, major thoughts are preceded by a line with no writing on it, they are written to the left side of the page, and they are underlined.
- **Details are listed under major thoughts in an orderly fashion**. In Figure 15.1, some details are preceded by numbers and others are preceded by stars.

Of course, the notes you take under pressure during a class are not likely to be as neatly written and tidy as the notes in Figure 15.1.

The Cornell Note-taking System

Many experienced students favor the Cornell note-taking system, developed by Walter Pauk at Cornell University.* To use this procedure, divide each sheet of notebook paper into the three areas illustrated in Figure 15.2 on page 151 and Figure 15.3 on page 157.

1. **Summary area.** Create the 2-by-8½-inch area at the bottom of the page by drawing a horizontal line two inches from the bottom of each page. Use this area to write a one- or two-sentence summary of the notes on the page. In writing summaries, you analyze the details in your notes to understand their overall meaning.

2. **Cue column.** Create the 2½-by-9-inch area on the left side of the page by drawing a vertical line two-and-a-half inches from the left side of each page; extend the line from the top of the page to the line that separates the summary area. Use this column to write questions that you anticipate may be asked about the information in the notes. According to Professor Pauk, "Writing questions helps clarify meanings, reveal relationships, establish continuity, and strengthen memory."

3. **Note-taking area.** Record your notes in the 6-by-9-inch area on the right side of each page.

*Walter Pauk, *How to Study in College*, 5th ed. (Boston: Houghton Mifflin Company, 1993), pp. 110–114.

This innovative note-taking system is widely used by successful students and business people. Study the sample notes in Figure 15.2 on page 151 to understand how the cue column and summary area are used.

Other Note-taking Formats

When you take class notes, you may also use any of the note-taking formats that are illustrated on pages 219–224:

- Paragraph summaries are useful when lectures do not emphasize major and minor details (see page 220).
- Notes for definitions of terminology facilitate the learning of new vocabulary (see page 221).
- The classification chart format is a good way to record information about two or more persons, places, or things that are alike or different in two or more ways (see page 222).
- Time lines are ideal for notes when a lecturer gives a chronological sequence of events (see page 223).
- Use maps to show the relations between ideas, information, and concepts (see page 224).

Develop your own distinctive note-taking style by experimenting with a variety of note-taking formats.

Summarize What Teachers Say

When you take class notes, summarize what teachers say; do not attempt to write down what they say word for word. It is impossible to record teachers' words exactly because they usually speak at the rate of about 125 to 150 words per minute, but you can probably write no more than 25 to 30 words a minute. Therefore, you must learn to summarize and paraphrase what teachers say in your own words.

A summary of a lecture is a greatly condensed version of what an instructor said that includes the main points and details as they were stated in the instructor's original words. In contrast, a **paraphrase** is a statement of your understanding of what somebody said. When you paraphrase, you restate what lecturers' say using your own words, phrases, and sentence structures. Summaries are brief versions of lectures, whereas paraphrases are reworded versions of statements that consist of about the same amount of detail and the same number of words as the originals.

Your accurate paraphrases of what your teachers say provide proof that you understand their lectures. However, take care that in changing your teachers' words you do not also change their meaning. Skillful teachers often state important concepts so succinctly and precisely that it is impossible for students to improve on them. For instance, if your English professor states, "A *morpheme* is the smallest meaningful unit in a language," you should record this definition as it is stated because your spur-of-the-moment paraphrase will not improve it.

FIGURE 15.1   **Class Notes in the Traditional Format**

Study Skills 101, 9/14   Shepherd

Taking Good Class Notes

○ <u>Five characteristics of good notes</u>
1. Written on 8½-by-11-inch notebook paper.
2. Heading includes name or number of course, teacher's name,
    date, and lecture topic.
3. Major details stand out clearly.
4. Minor details are listed neatly under major details.
5. They summarize what teachers say.

<u>How to improve listening</u>
★ Eliminate environmental distractions. Ⓔx Don't sit near windows
    or annoying classmates.
★ Eliminate physical distractions.
    1. Visit rest room before class.
○ 2. Eat before class so you won't get hungry.
    3. Dress so you won't be too warm or cold.
★ Eliminate internal distractions. Ⓔx Don't think about
    what you'll do after class.

<u>Hints for taking and studying notes</u>
★ Read about lecture topics before classes.
★ Mark things written on chalkboards and about which
    teachers give study hints for special attention
    when studying.
★ Review notes as soon after class as possible.
○ ★ Study notes thoroughly before tests.

FIGURE 15.2 **Class Notes in the Cornell Note-taking Format**

Psych. 105 – Prof. Martin — Sept. 14 (Mon.)

<u>MEMORY</u>

Memory tricky – Can recall instantly many trivial things of childhood; yet, forget thins recently worked hard to learn & retain.

Memory Trace
— Fact that we retain information means that some change was made in the brain.
— Change called "memory trace."
— "Trace" probably a molecular arrangement similar to molecular changes in a magnetic recording tape.

Three memory systems: sensory, short-term, long-term.
— <u>Sensory</u> (lasts one second)
    Ex. Words or numbers sent to brain by sight (visual image) start to disintegrate within a few tenths of a second & gone in one full second, unless quickly transferred to S-T memory by verbal repetition.
— Short-term memory [STM] (lasts 30 seconds)
    • Experiments show: a syllable of 3 letters remembered 50% of the time after 3 seconds. Totally forgotten end of 30 seconds.
    • S-T memory-limited capacity=holds average of 7 items.
    • More than 7 items - - jettisons some to make room.
    • To hold items in STM, must rehearse - - must hear <u>sound</u> of words internally or externally.
— Long-Term memory [LTM] (lasts a lifetime or short time).
    • Transfer fact or idea by:
      (1) <u>Associating</u> w/ information already in LTM
      (2) <u>Organizing</u> information into meaningful units
      (3) <u>Understanding</u> by comparing & making relationships.
      (4) <u>Frameworking</u> - fit pieces in like in a jigsaw puzzle.
      (5) <u>Reorganizing</u> - combining new & old into a new unit.
      (6) <u>Rehearsing</u> - aloud to keep memory trace strong

Cue column questions:

How do psychologists account for remembering?

What's a "memory trace"?

What are the three memory systems?

How long does sensory memory retain information?

How is information transferred to STM?

What are the retention times of STM?

What's the capacity of the STM?

How to hold information in STM?

What are the retention times of LTM?

What are the six ways to transfer information from STM to LTM?

Summary:

Three kinds of memory systems are sensory, which retains information for about one second; short-term, which retains for a maximum of thirty seconds; and long-term, which varies from a lifetime of retention to a relatively short time.

The six ways (activities) to transfer information to the long-term memory are: associating, organizing, understanding, frameworking, reorganizing, and rehearsing.

Adapt to Subject Matter

Because the lectures you hear in college will differ in many ways, you must be able to adapt your note-taking methods to those differences. For one thing, subject matter will determine the nature of lectures and, thus, the appearance of lecture notes. For example, notes about how to solve algebraic problems in a mathematics course will appear quite different from notes about historical events in a history course. In addition, subject matter may to some extent determine how many pages of notes you will take during a class meeting. In mathematics, foreign language, and speech courses, brief lectures may be followed by practice solving problems, translating a foreign language, or listening to speeches. In other courses, you may spend entire class periods taking notes on lectures or discussions.

Adapt your note-taking strategies to be appropriate for each subject you study and to the style of each of your teachers.

Adjust to Each Teacher

College teachers are trained to be specialists in the subjects they teach; they are *not* taught how to teach or how to give lectures. Biology teachers earn degrees in biology, sociology professors are trained to be sociologists, English instructors study English literature, and so on. Therefore, when you have teachers who you believe are good teachers and lecturers, this is usually either because they have natural talent for these activities or because they have worked hard to develop skill in them.

In my experience, most teachers make a sincere effort to give well-organized notes; however, some of them give disorganized lectures, some ramble from topic to topic, and some refer to the course textbook while they lecture.

- When you have teachers who give disorganized lectures, use the Cornell note-taking system. There is no point in trying to take notes in the traditional format when teachers give disorganized lectures.
- When you have teachers who ramble from topic to topic without explaining how the topics are related, take the most complete notes you can about each topic they discuss. Paragraph summary notes may be useful in this situation (see page 220).
- When you have teachers who read from the course textbook, follow along in your copy of the textbook; mark the points they emphasize and cross out the information they tell you is not important.

It is your responsibility as a student to adjust to the instructional methods each of your teachers use.

Take Complete Notes

When you are aware that you have missed information during a lecture, leave a blank space in your notes. Also, place a question mark (?) or some other symbol in the margin next to information that you do not understand or that you believe you may have recorded incorrectly. When the time is appropriate, raise your hand and ask the question that will help you to make your notes complete or accurate. Do not be reluctant to ask questions—skillful instructors depend on students' questions to know what is not clear. You can also improve your notes after class by talking with the teacher, by talking with a classmate who takes good notes, or by studying required reading material.

The following list summarizes what you can do to ensure that you have complete class notes.

How to Take Complete Class Notes

- Attend *all* classes.
- Be ready to take notes the minute class begins.
- Include everything that teachers write on the board and mark it for special attention when you study.
- Include everything that teachers say after glancing at their notes; they often refer to notes to make certain they state precisely information they intend to include in a test.
- Mark for special attention material in notes teachers say is important or difficult to learn.
- Record examples in such a way that you will recognize them if they show up in test questions.
- Include all definitions of terminology; in many subjects, a large portion of test questions directly or indirectly test students' knowledge of terminology.
- When you miss information, leave a blank space for it in your notes. After class, find out what you missed and write it in your notes where it belongs.
- Take notes until the very end of class. Instructors often rush to cover a great deal of information during the last few minutes of a class session.
- Build note-taking speed by using simplified handwriting and abbreviations.
- Avoid recopying your notes; it is easy to make errors and lose information when recopying notes.
- Copy notes from a classmate if you must be absent.

Attend All Classes

It is extremely important for you to attend all of your classes so you will have a complete set of notes. If you are absent from a class, you have no alternative but to copy the notes taken by one of your classmates. Unfortunately, though, the notes that are useful to your fellow students may not be very helpful to you. Therefore, when you copy notes, make certain you completely understand them by having the person who took them carefully explain what they mean.

Copy notes before or after class, not during it. Students who copy notes during class miss two lectures—the one they are copying and the one their teacher gives while they are copying.

Review Notes After Class

Notes taken in September may contain information that you need to learn for a test in November. If you don't understand your notes in September, you won't understand them in November when you study for a test. Therefore, during the first free time you have following a lecture, reread your notes to make certain that you understand them and that they are complete.

Change your notes in any way that makes them easier to understand. Correct misspelled words, fill in missing information, and make other changes that improve them.

Build Note-taking Speed

Because lecturers speak much faster than students can write, good class notes are summaries rather than word-for-word records of teachers' statements.

Note-taking requires the ability to write quickly and neatly, but there are very few first-year college students who use a fast, neat method for writing class notes. If you want to write notes more quickly and neatly, you may benefit from an experience reported by Walter Pauk in *How to Study in College*:

> The breakthrough in my own note-taking came when I saw an instructor write on a blackboard using a modified printing style. Her writing was not only surprisingly rapid, but also amazingly clear. I immediately began to write in a similar style—without needing practice at all. I believe anyone can adopt this style, and use it to write neatly and clearly.

Here is how the individual letters are formed in this modified printing style:

a b c d e f g h i j k l m n o p q r s t u v w x y z

And here is the style as used in two paragraphs:

There are four advantages to using this modified printing style. First, it is faster than cursive writing; second, it is far neater, permitting easy and direct comprehension; third, it saves time by precluding rewriting or typing; and fourth, it permits easy and clear reforming of letters that are ill-formed due to haste.

Even today, I almost always write this way because the style is the easiest, swiftest, and neatest of any I've tried.

Practice writing class notes more neatly and rapidly by using Professor Pauk's simplified method of handwriting. You may also write faster by using abbreviations of the following kinds.

Common Abbreviations

- **Standard abbreviations:** *pp.* (pages), *etc.* (and so on), *e.g.* (for example), *i.e.* (that is)
- **Standard abbreviations without periods:** *NY* (New York), *ex* (example), *mph* (miles per hour), *p* (page)
- **First letters of words:** *subj* (subject), *psy* (psychology), *chap* (chapter), *ques* (question)
- **Omitted vowels:** *bldg* (building), *hdbk* (handbook), *wk* (week), *yr* (year)
- **The letter *s* added to abbreviations to form the plural:** *subjs* (subjects), *hdbks* (handbooks), *chaps* (chapters), *yrs* (years)
- **Arabic numerals:** *7/4/1776* (July 4, 1776), *2* (two), *4th* (fourth), *$15 million* (fifteen million dollars)

The best abbreviations for you to use in class notes are the ones you understand. Be careful not to use an abbreviation such as *comp* and later find yourself unable to remember whether it stands for *companion, comparative, compensation, complete, compose, composition, compound, comprehensive,* or one of the many other words that begin with *comp.*

Another way to build note-taking speed is to abbreviate in class notes using symbols such as the following.

Symbols for Building Note-taking Speed

Symbol	Meaning	Example of Its Use
&	and	Bring a pen & pencil.
#	number	He gave his SS #.
%	percent	Only 41% voted for the candidate.
$	money	She earns a lot of $.
@	at	He bought 2 shirts @ $20 each.
?	question	The ? was never answered.
'	feet	There are 5,280' in a mile.
"	inches	She is 6'7" tall.
×	by	The room is 10' × 14'.
=	equals	A kilo = 2.2 pounds.
≠	not equal to	He is ≠ the task.
∴	therefore	I think, ∴ I am.
∵	because	She smiles ∵ she is happy.
…	and so on	We ate, sang, danced …
>	greater than	His taxes are > than hers.
<	less than	His income is < than hers.
w/	with	Red wine improves w/age.
w/o	without	He is never w/o a kind word.

Finally, do not slow yourself down by worrying a great deal about spelling when you take class notes. You are the only one who reads your notes. When you are uncertain about the spelling of a word, write "sp" in the margin next to the word and locate the correct spelling after class.

You Need Not Share Your Notes

When I was a college student, classmates sometimes glanced at my notebook during lectures because my class notes were usually complete and accurate. This embarrassed me because my notes invariably contained misspelled words that I would not correct until after class. I did not realize then, but I know now that it was rude of other students to look at my notes without asking for my permission.

If you are ever annoyed by a student looking at your notes without your permission, do what I should have done. Say to him or her, "Please don't read my notes. Thank you."

EXERCISE 15.1   ## The Cornell Note-taking System

Practice using the Cornell note-taking system by first preparing a few sheets of notebook paper in the way illustrated in Figure 15.3 on page 157:

1. Create the summary area by drawing a horizontal line 2 inches from the bottom of each page.
2. Create the cue column by drawing a vertical line 2½ inches from the left edge of each page.

Use the 6-by-9-inch area to take class notes and use the cue column and summary area in the ways explained on page 148.

EXERCISE 15.2   ## Abbreviations and Symbols

Rewrite the following sentences using abbreviations and symbols for the words printed in boldface. If you do not know the standard abbreviation, make up an abbreviation of your own.

1. **Seventy-five percent** of the students earned **less than one hundred dollars** last **month**.

    _____

2. He **could not answer** the **professor's question**.

    _____

3. She is **five feet four and one-half inches** tall.

    _____

FIGURE 15.3

The Cornell Note Sheet

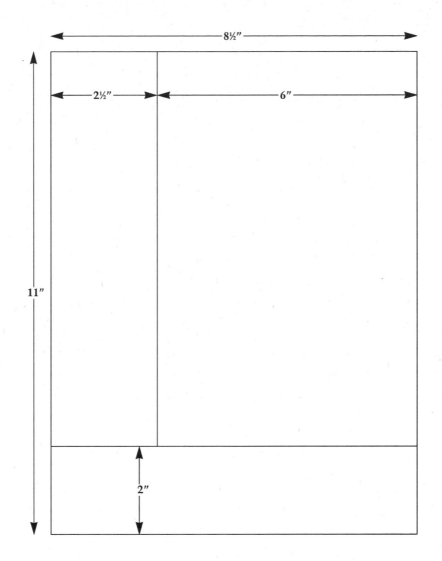

4. They lived **two thousand years before the birth of Christ**.

_____

5. We drove **fifteen miles north** of **New York City**.

_____

6. Read the **first twenty pages** of **Chapter Ten**.

_____

7. His acting was **without equal**.

_____

8. Our debts are **greater than** our income.

_____

9. The dance floor measures **twenty feet by forty-five feet**.

_____

10. The **United States of America** entered **World War II** on **December 8, 1941**.

_____

EXERCISE 15.3   **Abbreviations**

Write abbreviations for the following common words. If you do not know a standard abbreviation, make up an abbreviation of your own.

1. Mister _____   11. following _____

2. miles per hour _____   12. company _____

3. Senior _____   13. incorporated _____

4. Junior _____   14. corporation _____

5. Doctor _____   15. chapter _____

6. Professor _____   16. without _____

7. pages _____   17. equal _____

8. for example _____   18. number _____

9. page _____   19. money _____

10. handbook _____   20. second _____

EXERCISE 15.4   **Summarizing and Paraphrasing**

Write summaries of the following statements. For instance, you might summarize the first problem in the following way: "Write notes on 8½" x 11" paper."

1. Write class notes on paper that measures 8½ by 11 inches rather than on paper of a smaller size, such as 5-by-8-inch paper.

   _____

   _____

2. Major thoughts should stand out clearly in notes, and details should be listed neatly under them; however, they need not be labeled with Roman numerals, capital letters, and Arabic numerals in the traditional outline format.

   _____

   _____

3. Each day's notes should have a heading that includes the name or number of the course, the date, the teacher's name, and the lecture topic. For example, a heading might include the following: Introduction to Psychology; September 22, 1996; Professor Martin; Freud's Theory of Personality.

   _____

   _____

4. All your teachers have been students and, as students, they learned that the information their teachers wrote on chalkboards was very often used as the basis for test questions. Many of your teachers assume that you also have figured out that you should copy and learn anything written on the board. Many of them believe that they are announcing a test question whenever they write on a chalkboard. Therefore, include in class notes everything that your teachers write on chalkboards and mark it for special attention when you study.

   _____

   _____

5. If you believe you write too slowly, you can increase the speed with which you take class notes by using fewer lines, curves, and flourishes in your writing and by using abbreviations (such as *eq* for equation) and symbols (such as % for percent).

   _____

   _____

EXERCISE 15.5   **Summarizing and Paraphrasing**

Write summaries of the following statements, as you did for Exercise 15.4.

1. Teachers ordinarily explain course requirements during the first few days of classes. When course requirements are presented orally, take accurate and complete notes; when they are distributed on printed pages, keep them in a safe place. In either case, understand them completely and follow them exactly.

   _____

   _____

2. Be certain that you arrive at your classes on time. When students arrive late to class, they interrupt their teacher and classmates and they create the impression that they are disorganized or irresponsible. Don't be rude or create an unfavorable impression of yourself; arrive at your classes on time.

   _____

   _____

3. College terms start out slowly. They gradually get busier and busier, reaching a peak of activity at final examination time. If you fall behind in the work for a course, you will find yourself trying to catch up at the time when you are very busy with all of your other courses. Don't fall behind— keep up-to-date with course work.

   _____

   _____

4. Always keep photocopies of papers you write for college credit so you will have accurate records of what you wrote in case a teacher loses or misplaces one of your papers. In addition, you may find that the photocopy of a paper you wrote for one of your courses contains references or other information that will be helpful to you in the future.

   _____

   _____

5. If you have difficulty with a course, turn to a teacher, counselor, or adviser for help. These people usually know if study groups, tutors, or other sources of help are available. If they do not, they can suggest where to look further for help. They may advise visiting the office of the department that offers the course that is giving you a problem. Or they may suggest visiting an office of academic skills, a learning center, a tutorial service, or some other department or service on campus.

   _____

   _____

EXERCISE 15.6   **Rating Lectures**

Write the names of two of your lecture courses above the columns on the right. Then rate lecturers in each category, using 100 (perfect), 90–99 (excellent), 80–89 (good), 70–79 (satisfactory), 60–69 (poor), 0–59 (unacceptable).

1. _____   2. _____

1. Gives well-organized lectures.   _____   _____

2. States main ideas clearly.   _____   _____

3. Usually identifies the number of minor details to include in a list.   _____   _____

4. Pauses to give me time to write.   _____   _____

5. Repeats important statements so I can get them in my notes.   _____   _____

6. Makes me feel free to ask questions so my notes will be complete.   _____   _____

7. Makes good use of the chalkboard.   _____   _____

8. Informs me what is most important to learn.   _____   _____

9. Seems very interested in the subject matter of the course.   _____   _____

10. Explains difficult ideas and concepts so they are easy for me to understand.   _____   _____

Totals   _____   _____

Divide totals by 10 to find averages.

Averages   _____   _____

EXERCISE 15.7   Rating Class Notes

Write the names of the same lecture courses you wrote in Exercise 15.6 above the columns on the right. Then rate your notes for the courses in each category, using 100 (perfect), 90–99 (excellent), 80–89 (good), 70–79 (satisfactory), 60–69 (poor), 0–59 (unacceptable).

1. _____   2. _____

1. I read about lecture topics before class when lectures are difficult to understand.

    _____   _____

2. I begin each day's notes with a complete heading.

    _____   _____

3. Main ideas stand out clearly.

    _____   _____

4. Minor details are listed under main ideas, and they are often numbered.

5. My notes summarize rather than repeat word for word what the teacher said.

    _____   _____

6. My notes include everything written on the chalkboard, marked for special attention when I study for tests.

    _____   _____

7. My notes include study hints and the information to which they pertain is marked for special attention when I study for tests.

    _____   _____

8. I ask questions when I need to make my notes complete.

    _____   _____

9. I practice new ways to write faster when I take notes.

    _____   _____

10. I review my notes as soon after class as possible.

    _____   _____

Totals   _____   _____

Divide totals by 10 to find averages.

Averages   _____   _____

Compare your ratings for lecturers in Exercise 15.6 with those for your class notes to determine whether there are relationships between them. For instance, if you rated a lecturer for a course high, did you rate your class notes for the course high also?

Preview Textbooks

If you are a full-time college student, you will usually need to read, study, and learn the information in five or more textbooks each term. This may seem to be an impossible task, but it isn't—thousands of college students do it every year. The first step in studying your textbooks is to preview them soon after you purchase them using the procedures summarized below.

> ## How to Preview a Textbook
>
> Before you read a textbook, examine the features in the front and back of the book.
>
> 1. Preview the front of the book.
>   - Read the **title page** to learn the title, author (or authors), and publisher of the book.
>   - Read the **copyright page** to find out the year the book was published.
>   - Read the **table of contents** to get an overview of the organization of the book and the major topics discussed in it.
> 2. Preview the back of the book.
>   - Determine whether the last chapter is followed by an **appendix**; if it is, find out what is in the appendix.
>   - Check to see if there is a **glossary** at the end of the book or if there are short glossaries in each chapter.
>   - Determine whether **references** are listed at the end of the book or at the end of each chapter.
>   - Determine whether there is an **index** at the end of the book or if the book has a subject index *and* a name index.

Examine Exercises 16.1 through 16.9 on pages 166–174 before you read the following explanations.

163

The Title Page

Begin a preview by reading the **title page**. It gives exact information about the title of a book, the author or authors, the publisher, and the city in which the book was published. The title page is usually the second or third page in a book. When the title of a book is not followed by an edition number, it is the first edition; and when more than one city is listed on a title page, the book was published in the first city listed. There is a title page in Exercise 16.1 on page 166.

The Copyright Page

After you have read the title page, read the page that follows it—the copyright page. A **copyright page** tells when a book was published. When more than one year is listed in the copyright information, the book was published in the most recent year listed. For example, if the years 1998, 1994, and 1990 are listed, the book was published in 1998. The years 1994 and 1990 refer to earlier editions of the book.

The copyright year tells you whether the information in a book is sufficiently up-to-date for your purposes. For instance, if you want to learn about the current tax laws of the United States, you will want to read a book with a very recent copyright date. However, if you want to learn how to give a speech, a book published ten years ago may give information that is sufficiently up-to-date for this purpose. There is information from a copyright page in Exercise 16.2 on page 167.

The Table of Contents

Continue your preview by reading the **table of contents,** which provides an overview of the organization of a book and the major topics discussed in it. When a table of contents does not follow the copyright page, look for it following the preface or introduction. Part of a table of contents is shown in Exercise 16.3 on page 168.

The Preface or Introduction

A **preface** or an **introduction** explains why a book was written; it usually presents information about the purpose, philosophy, or contents of a book, and it often describes special features that are provided to help students learn information in the book. These opening remarks are usually located on pages following the table of contents, but sometimes they appear before the table of contents. Most books have either a preface or an introduction; some books have both. Part of a preface appears in Exercise 16.4 on page 169.

The Appendix

An appendix, which contains supplementary material, is usually located immediately after the last chapter. An appendix in a chemistry textbook may present an overview of the mathematics that is important to know in chemistry and an appendix in an English textbook may explain how to punctuate and capitalize when writing. However, many textbooks have no appendix. There is part of an appendix in Exercise 16.5 on page 170.

The Glossary

A **glossary** is an alphabetically arranged list of important words and their definitions. When a glossary is included in a book, it is usually located after the last chapter or after the appendix. A textbook that has no glossary at the end may have short glossaries at the end of each chapter. There is part of a glossary in Exercise 16.6 on page 171.

The References

The **references**, a **bibliography**, or **notes** are lists of publications and other sources that an author quotes or refers to in a book. References are usually listed at the end of a textbook, following the glossary or last chapter. When they are not at the end of a book, they may be listed at the end of each chapter. Textbooks for subjects such as English, speech, and mathematics usually have no references. There are references in Exercise 16.7 on page 172.

The Index

An *index* is an alphabetically arranged list of subjects and the numbers of the pages on which the subjects are discussed in a book. When an index is included in a book, it is on the very last pages.

Some books have two indexes: a **subject index** and a **name index**, or author index. When a name index (or author index) is included in a book, it is located before the subject index. If you do not find the name of a person in an index, look to see if the book has a name index. For instance, if you do not find Sigmund Freud listed in the index of a psychology textbook, look for his name in the name index or author index. There is a part of a name index in Exercise 16.8 on page 173 and a part of a subject index in Exercise 16.9 on page 174.

EXERCISE 16.1   **Title Page**

Answer the questions that follow the title page.

BUSINESS
3rd Edition

WILLIAM M. PRIDE
Texas A & M University

ROBERT J. HUGHES
Dallas County Community College

JACK R. KAPOOR
College of DuPage

Houghton Mifflin Company   Boston

Dallas   Geneva, Illinois   Palo Alto   Princeton, New Jersey

1. How many authors wrote the book? _____

2. At what school does Robert J. Hughes teach? _____

3. Who is the publisher? _____

4. In what city was the book published? _____

EXERCISE 16.2 **Copyright Page**

Answer the questions that follow the copyright information from *Business*.

Copyright © 1998 by Houghton Mifflin Company. All rights reserved.

No part of this work may be reproduced or transmitted in any form or by any means, electronic or mechanical, including photocopying and recording, or by any information storage or retrieval system without the prior written permission of Houghton Mifflin Company unless such copying is expressly permitted by federal copyright law. Address inquiries to College Permissions, Houghton Mifflin Company, 222 Berkeley Street, Boston, MA 02116.

Printed in the U.S.A.

Library of Congress Catalog Card Number: 90-83039

ISBN: 0-395-47308-X

1. In what year was the book published? _____

2. If people want permission to reproduce passages in *Business*, to what address should they write to request the permission?

_____

_____

_____

_____

EXERCISE 16.3   Table of Contents

Answer the questions that follow part of the table of contents from *Business*.

CONTENTS

1. What is the title of the first chapter? _____

_____

2. On what page is there a summary of Chapter 1? _____

<u>**EXERCISE 16.4**</u>   **Preface**

Answer the questions that follow part of the preface of *Business*.

PREFACE

The American system of business is no mere abstraction. It's a network of real people—millions of individuals seeking challenges, opportunities, and excitement through participation in business. Professors and students of business are an important part of this network. The time they invest jointly in examining the business system today bears directly on the success of the business system tomorrow.

Accordingly, we believe that professors and students deserve the best textbook available, one that is current, dynamic, and interesting—just like business itself. We have developed *Business, Third Edition*, to meet this challenge. Along with its comprehensive instructional package, *Business* provides instructors with the opportunity to present business fundamentals effectively and efficiently. For their part, students will enjoy the *Business* experience and will be well prepared for further study in a variety of business fields.

The third edition of *Business* covers new topics, presents expanded coverage of important issues, focuses on small as well as large businesses, provides thorough career information, and contains numerous pedagogical aids. The comprehensive ancillary package includes a computerized study guide and the *Video Resource Manual*, which accompanies *Business Video File*, a free series of twenty-four videos—one for each chapter and the Appendix. Here are several distinctive features of *Business, Third Edition*, and the instructional package that accompanies it.

1. What challenge was the book developed to meet? _____

_____

2. List three of the five features of the third edition of *Business* that are stated in the third paragraph.

_____

_____

_____

EXERCISE 16.5   Appendix

Answer the questions that follow part of the appendix from *Business*.

APPENDIX

As you look ahead to your own career, you should consider the effects that the trends described below will have on employment and employment opportunities.

▶ Jobs in service industries will account for an increasing proportion of total employment.

▶ Training—and retraining—will become increasingly important, as firms require their employees to understand and utilize the latest technology. Good jobs will require strong educational qualifications.

▶ Automation of factories and offices will create new types of jobs. Many of these will be computer-related. In some cases, employees will be able to complete assignments at home on remote computer terminals.

▶ The number of women in the work force, of two-income families, and of older workers will increase. There will be a greater emphasis on job sharing, flexible hours, and other innovative work practices to accommodate employees' special circumstances.

Where will the jobs be? A 1989 survey by *Monthly Labor Review* indicates that paralegals will be in greatest demand, followed closely by medical assistants. Those college graduates with majors in computer science, accounting, business, marketing, and economics will also be in high demand, according to human resources experts. There will be fewer manufacturing jobs, and those that remain will require high-tech skills.

---

1. Why will the retraining of employees become increasingly important?

_____

_____

2. Which two occupations are expected to be in greatest demand in the future?

_____

_____

EXERCISE 16.6   Glossary

Answer the questions that follow part of the glossary from *Business*.

GLOSSARY

absolute advantage   the ability to produce a specific product more efficiently than any other nation (23)

accessory equipment   standardized equipment used in a variety of ways in a firm's production or office activities (12)

account executive (or **stock broker**)   an individual who buys or sells securities for clients (19)

accountability   the obligation of a subordinate to accomplish an assigned job or task (6)

accounting equation   the basis for the accounting process: Assets = liabilities + owners' equity (16)

accounting   the process of systematically collecting, analyzing, and reporting financial information (16)

accounts payable   short-term obligations that arise as a result of making credit purchases (16)

accounts receivable turnover   a financial ratio that is calculated by dividing net sales by accounts receivable; measures the number of times a firm collects its accounts receivable in one year (16)

accounts receivable   amounts that are owed to a firm by its customers (18)

acid-test ratio   a financial ratio that is calculated by dividing the sum of cash, marketable securities, accounts receivable, and notes receivable by current liabilities (16)

Active Corps of Executives (ACE)   a group of active managers who counsel small-business owners on a volunteer basis (4)

ad hoc committee   a committee created for a specific short-term purpose (6)

administrative law   the regulations created by government agencies that have been established by legislative bodies (21)

administrative manager   a manager who is not associated with any specific functional area but who provides overall administrative guidance and leadership (5)

advertising media   the various forms of communication through which advertising reaches its audience (14)

affirmative action program   a plan designed to increase the number of minority employees at all levels within an organization (2)

agency   a business relationship in which one party (called the principal) appoints a second party (called the agent) to act on behalf of the principal (21)

agency shop   a workplace in which employees can choose not to join the union but must pay dues to the union anyway (10)

agent   a middleman that facilitates exchanges, represents a buyer or a seller, and often is hired permanently on a commission basis (13)

1. What term has the same meaning as *account executive?*

_____

2. What is an *ad hoc committee?* _____

_____

3. Must the employees of an *agency shop* join a union?

_____

EXERCISE 16.7   References

Answer the questions that follow the notes from *Business.*

NOTES

CHAPTER 1

[1] Based on information from Christopher Knowlton, "How Disney Keeps the Magic Going," *Fortune*, December 4, 1989, pp. 111–112, 114, 116, 120, 124, 128, 132; Susan Spillman, "Animation Draws on its Storied Past," *USA Today*, November 15, 1989, pp. 1D, 2D; Richard Turner, "Kermit the Frog Jumps to Walt Disney as Company Buys Henson Associates," *Wall Street Journal*, August 29, 1989, p. 1B. [2] *Fortune*, September 29, 1986, p. 7. [3] Adapted from "The Origins of Enterprise in America," Exxon U.S.A., third quarter 1976, pp. 8–11.

CHAPTER 2

[1] Based on information from Sharon Begley, "Smothering the Waters," *Newsweek*, April 10, 1989, pp. 54–57; Geoffrey Cowley, "Dead Otters, Silent Ducks," *Newsweek*, April 24, 1989, p. 70; Claudia H. Deutsch, "The Giant with a Black Eye," *New York Times*, April 2, 1989, pp. 3–1, 3–8; Stuart Elliot, "Public Angry at Slow Action on Oil Spill," *USA Today*, pp. B1–B2; Philip Shabecoff, "Ship Runs Aground Off Alaska, Causing Largest U.S. Tanker Spill," *New York Times*, March 25, 1989, pp. 1, 19; Michael Satchell, "Tug of War Over Oil Drilling," *U.S. News & World Report*, April 10, 1989, pp. 47–48; Kenneth R. Sheets, "Would You Believe $16.67 an Hour to Scrub Rocks?" *U.S. News & World Report*, April 17, 1989, p. 48; and Rae Tyson, " 'We've Done All We Can Do' On Spill," *USA Today*, April 24, 1989, pp. 1A–2A. [2] CNN poll conducted by the Roper Center of Public Opinion Research, *U.S. News & World Report*, February 23, 1987. [3] O. C. Ferrell and Larry G. Gresham, "A Contingency Framework for Understanding Ethical Decision Making in Marketing," *Journal of Marketing*, Summer 1985, pp. 87–96.

[4] "Engineers' Duty to Speak Out," The Nation, June 28, 1986, p. 880. [5] "Ozone Standards," *Environment*, March 1989, p. 24; and Merrill McLoughlin, "Our Dirty Air," *U.S. News & World Report*, June 12, 1989, pp. 48–54. [6] Merrill McLoughlin, "Our Dirty Air," *U.S. News & World Report*, June 12, 1989, pp. 48–54. [7] Dan Morse, "What's Wrong with the Superfund?," *Civil Engineering*, April 1989, pp. 40–43. [8] "Acid Rain Affects Coastal Waters Too," *Environment*, June 1988, p. 22. [9] Merrill McLoughlin, "Our Dirty Air," *U.S. News & World Report*, June 12, 1989, p. 54. [10] "A Biodegradable Recyclable Future," *The Economist*, January 7, 1989, pp. 61–62. [11] Faye Rice, "Where Will We Put All That Garbage?" *Fortune*, April 11, 1988, pp. 96–100. [12] "A Biodegradable Recyclable Future," *The Economist*, January 7, 1989, pp. 61–62. [13] "A Biodegradable Recyclable Future," *The Economist*, January 7, 1989, pp. 61–62. [14] David Landis, "Tighter Rules Put Squeeze on Firms," *USA Today*, May 26, 1989, pp. B-1, B-2.

CHAPTER 3

[1] Based on information from "The Kitchens that Don't Miss a Beat," *Business Week*, June 1989, pp. 45, 49; Erik Larson, "The Man with the Golden Touch," *Inc.*, October 1988, pp. 66–68, 70, 75–76; Stephen Michaelides, "Rich Melman Wears Gym Shoes," *Restaurant Hospitality*, May 1987, pp. 97–102. [2] "The Top 100 Industrial/Service Companies," *Black Entrepreneur*, June 1988, p. 121. [3] Cindy Skrzycki, "Why Nonprofit Businesses Are Booming," *U.S. News & World Report*, January 16, 1984, p. 65. [4] John DuMont, "Swallowing Competition," *Maclean's*, November 7, 1988, p. 42. [5] Ibid. [6] Frank Lichtenberg, "Productivity Improvements from Changes in Ownership," *Mergers and Acquisitions*, September/October 1988, pp. 48–50.

1. Who published the article referred to in the third note for Chapter 1?

   _____

2. What are the titles of the first three publications referred to in the first note

   for Chapter 2? _____

   _____

3. Who wrote the article referred to in the sixth note for Chapter 3?

   _____

EXERCISE 16.8   Name Index

Answer the questions that follow part of the name index of *Business.*

NAME INDEX

AAMCO Transmissions, 117, 120
ABC, 155, 158
Abraham & Straus, 656
Adelante Advertising Inc., 416
Adolph Coors Company, 206
Aetna Life and Casualty, 194, 240, 274
Agri-Tech, 57
Aiken, Howard, 457
Akers, Fred, 452, 453
Allied-Signal, 265
Allied Stores Corporation, 656, 657
A.M. Best Company, 629
AMC. *See* American Motors Corporation
Amerco, 96
American Airlines, 195
American Business Conference, 93
American Can Company, 241
American College, 593
American Continental Corporation, 522
American Dairy Association, 420
American Express Company, 55, 245, 380, 416, 417, 438, 483
American Express Foundation, 241
American Football Conference, 19
American Motors Corporation (AMC), 20, 218–219

American Photographic Group, 19
American Red Cross, 135
American Telephone & Telegraph (AT&T), 81, 168, 420, 438, 483, 683, 688
American Tobacco Company, 687
Amman, Robert J., 187–188
Amstead Industries, 300
Anderson, Warren M., 63
Andretti, Mario, 398
Anheuser-Busch, Inc., 363, 424
Antonini, Joseph, 398
Apple Computer, Inc., 102, 107, 108, 136, 157, 241, 323, 453, 460, 482
A&P supermarkets, 399
Artex, 19
Arthur Andersen Worldwide Organization, 486, 487
Arthur Young, 486
Arts & Entertainment Network, 158
Association of American Railroads, 420
Atlantic Richfield, 264
AT&T. *See* American Telephone & Telegraph
Audi, 736
Aug, J. Vincent, Jr., 657

Au Printemps, 397
Avia, 97
Avis, Inc., 120, 300
Avon Products, Inc., 339, 385, 400, 416

Babbage, Charles, 457
Baltimore Gas and Electric Company, 575
BankAmerica Corporation, 241, 274
Baskin-Robbins, 117, 122
Bayer, 17
Beatrice Foods, 554
Bechtel Group, 85
Beijing Animal Husbandry Bureau, 724
Beijing Kentucky Company, 724
Beijing Tourist Bureau, 724
Bell Telephone, 307
Bell Telephone Laboratories, 259
Ben Franklin, 126
Ben Franklin five-and-dime stores, 104
Denton, Phillip E., 323
Bergdorf Goodman, 327
Bernheim, Alain, 662
Best Products, 398
Bethlehem Steel Corporation, 167, 228, 229

1. On what pages are there references to the Avis car rental company? _____

   _____

2. On what page is there a reference to Howard Aiken? _____

3. On what pages are there references to AT&T? _____

   _____

EXERCISE 16.9   Subject Index

Answer the questions that follow part of the subject index of *Business*.

SUBJECT INDEX

Abacus, 457
Absolute advantage, 711–712
Acceptance, contracts and, 663
Accessory equipment, 352
Account(s), 493
   bank, *see* Bank accounts
   doubtful, 497
Accountability, creating, as a step in
   delegation, 172
Accountants, 488(table), 488–489
   nonpublic, 488
   private, 488
   public, 488–489
Account executives, *see* Stockbrokers
Accounting, 485–511
   accounting cycle and, 493–495
   accounting equation and, 492
   balance sheet and, 495–498, 496(fig.)
   bookkeeping compared with, 487–488
   defensive, 491
   defined, 487
   double-entry bookkeeping system
      and, 492–493, 493(fig.)
   financial ratios and, 504–511,
      510(table)
   financial statement analysis and, 503,
      504(fig.)

Activities, PERT and, 211
Activity ratios, 508–509
Actuaries, 628
Adaptations, of products, 358
Ad hoc committee, defined, 178
Administered vertical marketing system, 389
Administration, of insurance, careers
   in, 634
Administrative expenses, 501
Administrative law, 658–659
Administrative manager, 142
Advertising, 419–428, 420(fig.)
   brand, 419
   comparative, 419
   cooperative, 421
   defined, 418
   developing campaign for, 424–426
   direct-mail, 422–423
   ethics and, 38
   evaluating effectiveness of, 426
   immediate-response, 419
   institutional, 420
   outdoor, 423
   primary-demand, 420
   reminder, 419
   selective, 419

Agency law, 672–673
Agency shop, 303
Agent, 672
   commission and, 388
   distribution channels and, 388
   export/import, 724
   manufacturer's, 394
   sales, 394
Agricultural businesses, small, 101
Airplanes, physical distribution and,
   408
Air pollution, 58
Alien corporation, 82
Alliance(s), strategic, 93
Alliance for Labor Action, 290
Allowance for doubtful accounts, 497
All-salaried work force, 240
American College, 593
American Federation of Labor (AFL),
   287. *See also* AFL-CIO
American Institute of Certified Public
   Accountants (AICPA), 487, 489
American Stock Exchange, 588
Analytical engine, 457
Analytic skill, of managers, 144
ANI, *see* Automatic number identifica-
   tion

1. On what page is *ad hoc committee* explained? _____

2. On what page is *manufacturer's agent* discussed? _____

3. On what page is *outdoor advertising* mentioned? _____

EXERCISE 16.10 Preview of a Textbook

When you do this exercise, use a textbook you are studying for another course; however, if you have no other textbook, answer the questions referring to *College Study Skills.*

1. Title _____

2. Author(s) _____

3. Publisher _____

4. Date of publication _____

Check the items that pertain to the textbook you are previewing.

Table of Contents

☐ It provides an outline of the topics in the textbook.

☐ It shows that the book is divided into parts or sections.

Preface or Introduction

☐ It states for whom the book is intended.

☐ It describes special features that are provided to help students learn.

Appendix

☐ It contains useful or interesting information.

☐ There is no appendix.

Glossary

☐ It is at the end of the book.

☐ There is a short glossary in each chapter.

☐ There is no glossary.

References, Bibliography, or Notes

☐ They are listed at the end of the book.

☐ They are listed at the end of each chapter.

☐ There are no references, bibliography, or notes.

Index

☐ There is a subject index and a name (or author) index.

☐ There is only one index.

☐ There is no index.

Preview Chapters

Most students read a chapter in a textbook by turning to the first page and reading the chapter through to the last page. This is not an efficient way to read and study the chapters in textbooks. Experienced students know that it is more effective to preview a chapter before reading it. When you preview a chapter, you learn things that make it possible for you to read the chapter with greater understanding. The following is a summary of the suggestions about how to preview a chapter that are explained in this chapter.

How to Preview a Chapter

Use the following steps to preview a chapter before you read and study it.

1. Survey the beginning of the chapter.
   - Read the **title** and **introduction** to learn the topic and purpose of the chapter.
   - If there are **learning goals** at the beginning of the chapter, read them to find out what you are supposed to learn when you study the chapter.
2. Survey the body of the chapter.
   - Read the **headings** throughout the chapter to find out what topics are discussed in it.
   - Examine **graphs**, **diagrams**, photographs, **cartoons**, and other illustrations in the chapter.
   - Scan any **inserts** or **marginal notes.**
3. Survey the end of the chapter.
   - If there is an easy-to-understand **summary** at the end of the chapter, read it to get a quick overview of the important information or ideas discussed in the chapter.

- If **terminology** is listed at the end of the chapter, read it to find out what new words you are supposed to learn when you study the chapter.
- If there are **review questions** at the end of the chapter, read them to get an idea of the types of questions you may have to answer about chapter content when you take a test.
- If there are **exercises** or **problems** at the end of the chapter, read them to understand what skills you are expected to learn when you study the chapter.

Scan the sample textbook chapter on pages 299–319 of the appendix before you read the discussions that follow.

Title and Introduction

Begin a preview by reading the chapter title and the introduction to the chapter. The title and introduction should summarize what the chapter is about, and an introduction may state the main purpose of the chapter. Whether an introduction to a chapter is short or long, read it carefully as part of your preview.

Learning Goals

Textbook chapters sometimes begin with a list that explains what you should learn as you read and study them. The list may have a heading such as "Learning Goals," "Learning Objectives," "Performance Goals," "Study Guides," or "Chapter Preview." When a chapter begins with learning goals, read them as part of your preview, and make certain you have achieved the goals in the list before you take a test on the chapter. When you study chapters using learning goals as a guide, your attention will be focused on learning what you are supposed to learn.

Headings

Continue a chapter preview by reading the headings to learn what topics are discussed in the chapter. Textbook designers use a variety of methods to show the relationships between headings.

Relationships Between Headings

- The size of a heading indicates its importance; the larger the heading, the more important it is.

- A heading in boldface or a special color (such as red) is more important than a heading of the same size that is not in boldface or a special color.
- A heading printed above a paragraph is more important than a heading printed on the first line of a paragraph.

Textbooks often have headings in addition to major headings and subheadings. The hints in this list will help you to understand the relative importance of headings in books that have three or four types of headings.

Figures

A **figure** is a photograph, diagram, graph, or other illustration in a textbook; figures are usually assigned numbers so they can be referred to in the text and easily located by readers. Following is a list of the six types of illustrations that appear most often in textbooks and the purposes that they serve.

Type of Illustration	Purpose
Photograph	To illustrate a point, show what things look like, or arouse an emotional response
Cartoon	To make an amusing comment or provoke thought
Diagram	To show what things look like and provide organization for recall
Bar graph	To condense information and show differences in amounts
Line graph	To condense information and show increases, decreases, or trends
Circle graph	To condense information and show the sizes of the parts that make up a whole

This chapter includes examples of these six types of illustrations. For instance, Figure 17.1 on page 179 shows a photograph and Figure 17.4 on page 181 shows a bar graph. Study these figures, and study figures whenever you preview a textbook chapter. They illustrate and usually summarize, organize, or condense material presented in the text.

Photographs

Photographs are usually included in textbooks to illustrate a point in the text, to show the characteristics of something, or to arouse an emotional response. Interpret a photograph by studying it to understand what it depicts. Then, read the caption to learn additional information about whatever is depicted in the photograph or to learn why the photograph was included in your book.

What is depicted by the photograph in Figure 17.1 on page 179? What suggestions in this book are illustrated by the photograph?

FIGURE 17.1

A Student at His Computer

Computers facilitate research, writing, time management, and other college tasks.

(Courtesy Microsoft Corporation)

Cartoons

A **cartoon** is a drawing depicting a humorous situation, often accompanied by a caption. Textbook authors sometimes use cartoons to make amusing comments or to provoke thought about topics in their books. Interpret a cartoon by studying the drawing and reading the caption to decide whether it is amusing to you. Then try to figure out how the cartoon is related to a topic in the text. Is the cartoon below amusing to you? How is the cartoon related to the topic of this text?

FIGURE 17.2

A Cartoon

(Courtesy Earl Emil Kemppainen)

I was thinking to myself, "Professor Picky, you don't make the rules." But then I remembered—I do make the rules.

Diagrams

A diagram is a drawing that explains something by depicting its characteristics or by outlining its parts and showing the relations between them. Very often a diagram is provided to illustrate information provided in the text.

The diagram in Figure 17.3 below illustrates how water is recycled through the processes of transpiration, evaporation, condensation, and precipitation. The diagram provides an easy-to-understand summary of a long and rather complicated explanation in a meteorology textbook.

FIGURE 17.3

The Hydrologic Cycle

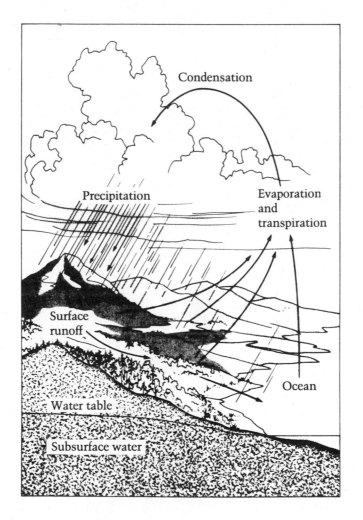

Bar Graphs

A **bar graph** is a drawing in which the lengths of parallel bars are used to show differences in amounts. The information from top to bottom of a bar graph is on the vertical axis, and the information from left to right is on the horizontal axis. Use the following steps to interpret the information in the bar graph in Figure 17.4 on page 181.

1. **Read the title.** What information is presented in the graph?

2. **Study the vertical axis.** What information is presented from top to bottom on the left side of the graph?

3. **Study the horizontal axis.** What information is presented from left to right across the bottom of the graph?

4. **Compare the data.** How much greater is the median income for families in which the head of household has thirteen to fifteen years of education than for families in which the head of household has nine to eleven years of education?

5. **Decide the important point.** What is the important point made by the data in the bar graph?

The answers to the questions are (1) median income of families by education of the head of household, (2) amount of education, (3) income in thousands of dollars, (4) about $8,000, and (5) median family income is related to the number of years of education of the head of household.

FIGURE 17.4

Median Income of Families, by Years of Education of Head of Household (*in thousands of dollars*)

Source: U.S. Bureau of the Census, *Statistical Abstract of the United States, 1986* (Washington, D.C.: U.S. Government Printing Office, 1986).

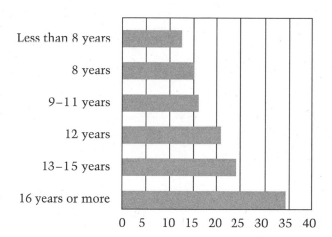

Line Graphs

A **line graph** is a drawing in which lines are used to show increases or decreases in amounts. The information from top to bottom is on the vertical axis, and the information from left to right is on the horizontal axis. Use the following steps to interpret the information in the line graph in Figure 17.5 on page 182.

1. **Read the title.** What information is presented in the graph?

2. **Study the vertical axis.** What information is on the vertical axis (top to bottom)?

3. **Study the horizontal axis.** What information is on the horizontal axis (left to right)?

4. **Read the key.** What is represented by the dotted line?

5. **Compare the data.** What percentages of females were in the labor force in 1960 and 1995?

6. **Decide the important point.** What is the most important point made by the graph?

The answers to the questions are (1) percentages of males and females in the labor force, (2) percentages, (3) years from 1960 to 1995, (4) males, (5) 38 percent and 62 percent, and (6) from 1960 until 1995 the percentage of women in the labor force increased dramatically while the percentage of men in the labor force decreased somewhat

FIGURE 17.5

Percentages of Males and Females in the Labor Force

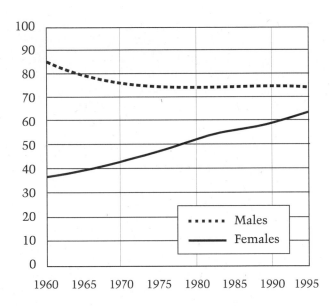

Circle Graphs

A **circle graph** is a drawing in which a circle is divided into segments to show the sizes of the parts that make up a whole. Circle graphs are also sometimes called pie graphs or pie charts. The segments of the circle (or pieces of the pie) are usually given different colors or designs. There is a circle graph in Figure 17.6 on page 183.

Use the following procedure to interpret the data in the circle graph.

1. **Read the title.** What information is presented in the graph?

2. **Read the key.** What is represented by the five segments of the graph?

3. **Compare the data.** (a) What percentage of income is earned by the richest 20 percent of households? (b) What percentage of income is earned by the poorest 20 percent of households?

4. **Decide the important point.** What is the most important point made by the data in the circle graph?

The answers to the questions are (1) distribution of income in the United States, (2) 20-percent segments of households from richest to poorest, (3a) 44.6 percent, (3b) 4.4 percent, and (4) the richest 20 percent of households have 40 percent more income than the poorest 20 percent of households.

FIGURE 17.6

Distribution of Income in the United States

Source: U.S. Bureau of the Census, 1993.

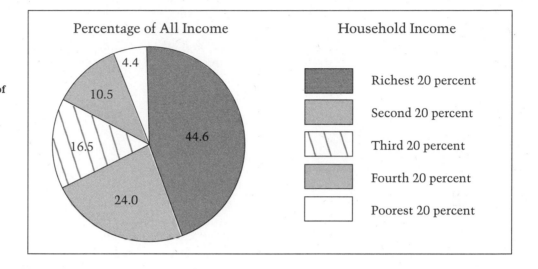

Tables

A **table** is a systematic listing of statistical information that is presented in orderly columns and rows to facilitate comparisons among data. The following table has three columns and eight rows. The columns read from top to bottom and the rows read from left to right beginning with "Five or more years of college."

Median Income by Sex and Years of Schooling*

Years of Schooling	Men	Women
Five or more years of college	$ 49,093	$ 33,771
Four years of college	39,115	28,042
One to three years of college	31,566	22,227
Four years of high school	26,515	18,323
Nine to eleven years of school	20,905	14,429
Eight years of school	20,050	13,322
Five to seven years of school	16,960	11,850
Zero to four years of school	15,192	12,161

*People twenty-five years old and older in 1991
SOURCE: U.S. Bureau of the Census (1992).

Use the following procedure to interpret the data in the table:

1. **Read the title.** What information is presented in the table?

2. **Read the column headings.** What information is presented in the first, second, and third columns?

3. **Compare the data.** (a) What is the median income for men with four years of high school and four years of college? (b) What is the median income for women with four years of high school and four years of college?

4. **Decide the important point.** What is the important point made by the data in the table?

The answers to the questions are (1) median income for various years of schooling; (2) years of schooling, men, and women; (3a) $26,515 and $39,115, (3b) $18,323 and $28,042; and (4) the more years of schooling people have, the higher their median income, *and* men have higher median incomes than women at all educational levels.

Inserts

An **insert** is material set off from the rest of the information in a textbook by lines or by a shaded background of light blue, yellow, gray, or some other color. Inserts serve a variety of purposes; for example, they may discuss timely issues, explain ways information in a text may be put to practical use, or provide students with opportunities to test themselves. "How to Preview a Chapter" on pages 176–177 is an example of an insert.

Summaries

A chapter summary provides a quick overview of the information that is explained in the chapter; therefore, when a textbook chapter ends with a summary, read the summary before you read the chapter. The only time it is not helpful to read a summary before reading a chapter is when it is difficult to understand because it includes many technical words whose meanings you will not know until you read the chapter.

Terminology

At the end of chapters, there is often a list of the important terminology, or words, used in the chapter. Terminology may be listed under a heading such as "Key Terms," "Important Words," "Key Concepts," or "Terms Used in This Chapter." When there is a list of terminology at the end of a chapter, study it before you read the chapter. Also, learn the meanings of all the words in the list before you take a test on the chapter; in many college courses, a majority of test questions directly or indirectly test students' understanding of subject terminology.

If there is no list of terms at the beginning or end of a chapter, scan the pages of the chapter to locate important words introduced in it; they are likely to be printed in italics, boldface, or a special color (such as red). In *College Study Skills*, terminology is printed in boldface and defined in a glossary at the back of the book.

Review Questions

A chapter may end with a list of questions that summarize what you should learn in the chapter. This list may have a heading such as "Questions," "Exercises," "Discussion Questions," or "Review Questions." When there are review questions at the end of a chapter, read them before you read the chapter. Also, make certain that you can answer the questions before you take a test on the chapter.

Exercises and Problems

Some textbooks provide exercises or problems to help in learning skills, which are abilities acquired through practice. Writing error-free prose, solving mathematical problems, speaking foreign languages, and performing scientific experiments are a few of the skills taught in colleges.

It is often necessary to do more exercises or problems than a teacher requests. For instance, when a mathematics textbook provides forty problems of a specific type, a teacher may assign only twenty of them. However, some students may need to do twenty-five, thirty, or all forty problems.

If you are an accomplished athlete, musician, dancer, or writer, you know that long hours of practice are necessary to acquire a skill. Do the exercises and problems in your textbooks to give yourself the practice you need to develop the abilities taught in mathematics, science, foreign languages, and other courses that teach skills.

EXERCISE 17.1   **Previewing a Chapter in Your Textbook**

When you do this exercise, use a textbook you are studying for another course you are taking or have taken.

1. Textbook title _____

2. Chapter title _____

3. Number of pages in the chapter _____

4. Check the statements that are true about the chapter.

   ☐ The **title** states what the chapter is about.

   ☐ The **introduction** states the purpose of the chapter.

   ☐ There are **learning goals** at the beginning of the chapter.

   ☐ **Headings** summarize the topics that are discussed in the chapter.

   ☐ There are **photographs** in the chapter.

   ☐ There are **diagrams**, **cartoons**, or other drawings in the chapter.

☐ There is a bar **graph**, line graph, or circle graph in the chapter.

☐ There is a **table** in the chapter.

☐ There is a **summary** at the end of the chapter.

☐ The summary is easy to read and understand.

☐ There is a list of **terminology** at the end of the chapter.

☐ Terminology is printed in boldface, italics, or a special color in the chapter.

☐ There are **review questions** at the end of the chapter.

☐ There are **exercises** or **problems** at the end of the chapter.

EXERCISE 17.2   **"Developing a Professional Presence"**

This is the first of five exercises for applying study skills to the sample textbook chapter on pages 299–319 of the appendix. The other exercises are for marking books (Exercise 18.9), making notes (Exercise 19.9), reciting and rehearsing (Exercise 20.4), and test taking (Exercise 21.3).

Previewing a Chapter

Preview the sample textbook chapter on pages 299–319 of the appendix by removing this page from the book and answering the following questions.

1. What is the **title** of the chapter?

   _____

2. **Learning goals** are listed under the heading "Chapter Preview." What is the sixth learning goal?

   _____

3. According to the introduction on page 301, what are two important goals of the chapter?

   a. _____

   b. _____

4. There are two major headings in the chapter. The first major heading is "Making a Good Impression." What is the other major heading in the chapter?

   _____

5. "Professional Presence" is the first subheading following "Making a Good Impression" (page 302). Beginning on page 302, check the headings in the list that have the same level of importance as "Professional Presence."

   ☐ "The Primacy Effect"
   ☐ "The First Few Minutes"
   ☐ "Thinking/Learning Starters"
   ☐ "First Impressions in a Work Setting"
   ☐ "Total Person Insight"
   ☐ "Assumptions Versus Facts"
   ☐ "The Image You Project"
   ☐ "Surface Language"
   ☐ "Thinking/Learning Starter"
   ☐ "Selecting Your Career Apparel"
   ☐ "Wardrobe Engineering"
   ☐ "Thinking/Learning Starter"
   ☐ "Your Facial Expression"
   ☐ "The Business Casual Look"
   ☐ "Your Facial Expression"
   ☐ "Your Entrance and Carriage"
   ☐ "Your Voice"
   ☐ "Your Handshake"
   ☐ "Your Manners"
   ☐ "Total Person Insight"
   ☐ "Assessing Your Professional Presence"

6. Write an answer to the "Thinking/Learning Starter" insert on page 308.

   _____

   _____

   _____

   _____

7. In the photograph on page 303, what impression is conveyed about the personality of the woman on the left?

   _____

   _____

8. How is the cartoon on page 310 related to the topic discussed on pages 311–312?

   _____

   _____

9. Read the summary on pages 317–318. Does it provide an easy-to-understand overview of the content of the chapter?

   _____

10. How many key terms are listed on page 319? _____

11. What is the definition of *wardrobe engineering* given on page 311?

    _____

    _____

12. Read the review questions on page 319 and answer the ninth question.

    _____

    _____

    _____

    _____

    _____

Mark Your Books

As you learned when you read about memory in Chapter 5, it is easier to store information in memory when it is well organized. Most successful college students mark information they want to learn in their textbooks and then use their marks as a guide for summarizing the information into organized study notes.

Figure 18.1 on page 190 shows a marked passage and Figure 18.2 on page 191 illustrates how the markings were used as a guide in making notes. This chapter explains how to mark books.

How to Mark Books

- **Read a section before you mark it.** If you mark as you read, you may mark information that you later decide is not especially important.

- **Do not mark too much.** If almost everything on a page is marked, it is the same as if nothing were marked. As a general rule, don't underline more than 20 percent of the information on a page. For instance, if there are 40 lines of print on the pages of a book, don't underline more than about 8 lines on a page. Avoid excessive underlining by numbering details and by using vertical lines to mark information that you might otherwise underline.

- **Mark information that will help you make notes.** The purpose of marking a book is to make a permanent record that will help you later make notes for learning information.

- **Make major details stand out.** You use major details to make well-organized notes, and it is almost always important to learn them.

- **Mark definitions of terminology.** On many college tests, up to 70 percent of questions directly or indirectly test students' knowledge of terminology.

- **Mark examples.** Learn the examples included in your book so you will recognize them if they are used in test questions.

Reasons for Marking Books

If you were told in high school that you must not write in books, you may wonder why marking textbooks is an essential skill for efficient college study. The main reason is that when you mark a book in the way explained in this chapter, you make a permanent record of the information you want to learn. When you do not mark a book as you read it, you must reread it to find the information you need to learn.

Some students resist writing in their books because they cannot, or fear they cannot, resell marked books. This is a foolish way to economize. Textbooks are expensive, but they are a small part of the cost of attending college in comparison to tuition, housing, food, transportation, and other expenses. Virtually all successful students mark their books because it saves them valuable study time.

The only students who do not need to mark their books are the ones who make good notes as they read. If you make well-organized summaries of the information in your books as you read, you do not need to underline, highlight, or write in your books.

FIGURE 18.1

A Highlighted
Textbook Passage

More Ways to Improve Learning

The foundations for learning are good organization, reciting, and reviewing. However, learning is further enhanced by scheduling plenty of study time, overlearning, dealing with the effects of interference, and carefully selecting what to learn.

Begin by scheduling more time for studying than you believe is necessary. One of the best established facts about learning is that the more time students spend studying the more they learn.

Second, overlearn! Many studies have shown that learning is greatly improved when study is continued well beyond the point where material is simply learned well enough to recall it once correctly. Master material rather than barely learn it. Overlearning is your best way to ensure you won't freeze up during a test due to nervousness or anxiety.

In addition, keep in mind that the material you learn for one course can interfere with what you must learn for other courses. Protect against this interference by setting aside uninterrupted periods for studying each of your courses. For instance, if you are going to study for three hours on Sunday afternoon, study one subject for the entire three hours rather than study three different subjects for one hour each. In addition, when you prepare for a test, study right before sleep and review the material right before the test.

Finally, be selective in what you learn. Mark your textbooks sparingly. (You know you aren't being selective when you mark most everything in a book.) If you use the Cornell note-taking format, write summaries at the bottom of each page of your class notes. By being selective, you will remember more than you would if you tried to learn everything.

Underline or Highlight

To **underline** is simply to draw lines under words; it is usually done with a pen, using a ruler as a guide. Many students prefer to highlight rather than underline because highlighting can be done neatly without using a ruler. To **highlight** is to mark words using a felt-tipped pen that contains watercolor ink. Yellow and pink are the most popular colors. In this book, I use *underline* to mean "underline" or "highlight." Light blue is used to indicate highlighting in Figure 18.1.

When you use the guidelines that are summarized in "How to Mark Books" on page 189, you may find that it sometimes seems impossible to follow the second guideline: "Do not mark too much." However, there are at least three ways to avoid excessive underlining. First, it is sometimes better to underline only key words that identify major details than to underline information about major details. For instance, if a page in a human anatomy textbook describes all the bones in the hand and arm, underline the names of the bones but not the information about them. Later, use the underlining as a guide for making notes, such as those in Figure 18.2. You may also use numbers and vertical lines to reduce the of underlining in your books.

FIGURE 18.2

Notes for the
Passage in Figure
18.1

WAYS TO IMPROVE LEARNING

1. Schedule more study time — the more you study, the more you learn.
2. Overlearn — master material rather than barely learn it.
3. Protect against the interference of other learning.
   • Study each subject for long, uninterrupted periods.
   • Study for tests right before sleep.
   • Review test material right before the test.
4. Be selective in what you learn.
   • Mark books sparingly.
   • Write summaries at the bottom of each page of class notes.

Numbers and Vertical Lines

It is often more appropriate to number details than to underline them. For example:

Legalization of Marijuana

Should marijuana be legalized so that it could be commercially manufactured and sold like alcohol and tobacco? Because of the extent of marijuana use, the issue has become a serious one for politicians. Although arrest for possession seldom leads to jail, proponents* of legalization argue that (1) inconsistency of enforcement leads to disrespect for the law. In addition, (2) the problems of enforcement become enormous, diverting police efforts from other kinds of crime, and (3) the government is unable to collect taxes on the drug as it can on alcohol and tobacco. Furthermore, (4) buyers are not protected from overpriced, low-quality marijuana.

If the four details in this passage were underlined, the entire last half of the paragraph would be underlined.

Vertical lines are useful for a variety of purposes, including marking definitions and examples.

Prejudice and Discrimination

Prejudice and discrimination are found in any situation of hostility and inequality between racial and ethnic groups. The two words are often used interchangeably in ordinary speech, but in fact they refer to two different, though related, phenomena: attitudes and behavior.

Def. | **Prejudice** is an irrational, inflexible attitude toward an entire category of people. (The word literally means "prejudged.") Although it is possible to be prejudiced in favor of a group, "prejudice" ususally implies negative feelings—antipathy, hostility, even fear. The key feature of prejudice is that it is always rooted in generalizations and so ignores the differences among individuals. Thus, someone who is prejudiced against Arabs will

Ex | tend to have a negative attitude toward any Arab, in the belief that all Arabs share the same supposed traits.

Def. | **Discrimination** is unequal treatment of people on the grounds of their group membership. Again, although it is possible to discriminate in favor of any specific group, "discrimination" usually implies negative actions. In particular, discrimination involves the refusal to give members of one group the opportunities that would be granted to similarly qualified members of another group. Discrimination occurs, for example, if an

Ex | employer refuses to hire or promote someone solely because of that person's racial or ethnic background.

Def is used above as an abbreviation for *definition*, and *Ex* is an abbreviation for *Examples*.

*Words underscored in blue are defined in the vocabulary list on pages 320–326.

In the following example, *Imp't* is used as an abbreviation for *Important* to draw attention to information a reader decided is especially important.

The Family

Imp't

The family is without doubt the most significant single agent of socialization in all societies. One reason for the importance of the family is that it has the main responsibility for socializing children in the crucial early years of life. The family is where children establish their first emotional ties, learn language, and begin to internalize cultural norms and values.

Some students write asterisks (*) next to information they decide is especially important and question marks (?) next to material that is unclear to them. Write any symbols or words in your books that help you to learn the information in them.

Many scholars write comments in the margins of books as they study them. For example, if, while reading a statement written by Carl Jung, students of psychology recall that Sigmund Freud expressed a similar point of view, they may write "Freud agrees" in the margin. You, too, may interact with the authors of your books by writing whatever comments you want in the margins of the books you own.

Helps for Finding Details

Authors and editors provide five helps for locating details to mark in textbooks: (1) subheadings, (2) words in italics or boldface, (3) numbers, (4) bullets, and (5) statements in introductions.

Subheadings   Subheadings may name details. Use the subheadings to locate the major details in the following passage.

Importance of Romantic Love

Romantic love is a noble ideal, and it can certainly help provide a basis for the spouses to "live happily ever after." But since marriage can equally well be founded on much more practical considerations, why is romantic love of such importance in the modern world? The reason seems to be that it has the following basic functions in maintaining the institution of the nuclear family (Goode, 1959):

Transfer of Loyalties   Romantic love helps the young partners to loosen their bonds with their family of orientation, a step that is essential if they are to establish an independent nuclear family. Their total absorption in one another facilitates a transfer of commitment from existing family and kin to a new family of procreation.

Emotional Support   Romantic love provides the couple with emotional support in the difficulties that they face in establishing a new life on their own. This love would not be so necessary in an extended family, where the relatives are able to confront problems cooperatively.

Incentive to Marriage   Romantic love serves as bait to lure people into marriage. In the modern world, people have considerable choice over whether they will get married or not. A contract to form a lifelong commitment to another person is not necessarily a very tempting <u>proposition,</u> however; to some, the <u>prospect</u> may look more like a noose than like a bed of roses. Without feelings of romantic love, many people might have no <u>incentive</u> to marry.

Reference
Goode, William J. 1959. "The theoretical importance of love." *American Sociological Review*, 24, pp. 38-47.

Notice that the subheadings make it clear that there are three reasons for the importance of romantic love.

Words Printed in Italics or Boldface   Words printed in italics or boldface may name the details in a passage. Use the words printed in boldface to locate the major details in the following passage.

Communication Distances

Hall suggests that there are four distinct zones of private space. The first is **intimate distance** (up to 18 inches), which is reserved for intimate personal contacts. The second is **personal distance** (18 inches to 4 feet), which is reserved for friends and acquaintances; there is some intimacy within this zone but there are definite limits. The third is **social distance** (4 feet to 12 feet), which is maintained in relatively formal situations, such as interviews. The fourth is **public distance,** (12 feet and beyond), which is maintained by people wishing to distinguish themselves from the general public, particularly speakers addressing audiences. Invasion of intimate or personal space always excites some reaction on the part of the person whose space is being invaded.

Reference
Edward T. Hall, *The Hidden Dimension* (Garden City, NY: Doubleday, 1969), pp. 116–125.

Notice that the four types of communication distances are printed in boldface.

Numbers   Arabic numerals, such as *1*, *2*, and *3*, or number words, such as *first*, *second*, and *third*, may indicate details. A combination of numerals and italics is used to indicate details in the following passage.

Asking for Criticism

Although asking for <u>constructive</u> criticism is the most direct way of finding out whether our behavior is effective, we are often <u>reluctant</u> to do so because we feel threatened by criticism. Instead, we rely entirely on others' nonverbal cues. Yet even when we interpret nonverbal cues accurately, they fail to help us understand why our behavior missed the mark. Nor will such cues help us decide what changes are needed in order for us to improve. By employing the verbal skill of asking for criticism, we accomplish these two objectives.

The following guidelines can help you ask for constructive criticism.

1. *Ask for criticism so that you will avoid surprises.* Taking the intiative in asking for criticism prepares you psychologically to deal with the criticism.

2. *Think of criticism as being in your best interest.* No one likes to be criticized, but through valid criticism we often learn and grow. When you receive a negative appraisal—even when you expected a positive one—try to look on it not as critical of you personally but as a statement that reveals something about your behavior that you did not know. Whether you will do anything about the criticism is up to you, but you cannot make such a decision if you do not know that the behavior exists or how it affects others.

3. *Specify the kind of criticism you are seeking.* Rather than asking very general questions about ideas, feelings, or behavior, ask specific questions. If you say, "Colleen, is there anything you don't like about my ideas?" Colleen is likely to consider this a loaded question. But if you say, "Colleen, do you think I've given enough emphasis to the marketing possibilities?" you will encourage Colleen to speak openly to the specific issue.

4. *Ask for criticism only when you really want an honest response.* If you ask a friend "How do you like this coat?" but actually want the friend to agree that the coat is attractive on you, you are not being honest. Once others realize that when you request an appraisal you are actually fishing for a compliment, valuable appraisals will not be forthcoming.

5. *Try to avoid contradiction between your verbal and nonverbal cues.* If you say, "How do you like my paper?" but your tone of voice indicates that you do not really want to know, the other person may be reluctant to be honest with you.

6. *Give reinforcement to those who take your requests for criticism as honest requests.* Suppose you ask your colleagues how they like your ideas for the ad campaign, and you get the response "The ideas seem a little understated." If you then get annoyed and say, "Well, if you can do any better, you can take over," your colleagues will learn not to give you criticism even when you ask for it. Instead, reward people for their constructive criticism. Perhaps you could say, "Thanks for the opinion—I'd like to hear what led you to that conclusion." In this way, you encourage honest appraisal.

7. *Be sure you understand the criticism.* Before you react to what you've heard, paraphrase your understanding to make sure it is what the person meant.

Asking for criticism does not require that you always act on every comment. You may decide against making a change in what you've said or done for other good reasons. But asking for criticism does enable you to make a conscious, rational choice about whether or not you will change your behavior.

Numbers such as *first* and *second* are used to help you locate the details in the following passage. Underline the numbers in the passage to emphasize how many characteristics of professions are stated.

Professions

Professions are distinguished from other occupations by several characteristics. First, the skill of professionals is based on systematic, <u>theoretical</u> knowledge, not merely on training in particular techniques. Second, professionals have considerable <u>autonomy</u> over their work. Their clients are presumed to be <u>incompetent</u> to make judgments about the problems with which the profession is concerned; you can give instructions to your hairdresser or tailor but cannot advise a doctor or lawyer on matters of medicine or law. Third, professionals form associations that regulate their profession's internal affairs and represent its interests to outside bodies. Fourth, admission to a profession is carefully controlled by the existing members. Anyone can claim to be a salesperson or a carpenter, but someone who claims to be a surgeon or a professor without having the necessary credentials is an impostor. Becoming a professional involves taking an examination, receiving a license, and acquiring a title, and this process is usually regulated by the professional association concerned. Fifth, professions have a code of <u>ethics</u> that all their members are expected to <u>adhere</u> to.

You should have underlined the words *first*, *second*, *third*, *fourth*, and *fifth*.

Bullets   Bullets are dots or squares that are used to draw attention to items in a list. Bullets indicate the details in the following passage:

Conflict Resolution

Although there are many theories on and approaches to conflict resolution, there are some basic strategies that are generally useful in successfully <u>negotiating</u> with a partner.

- Clarify the issue. Take responsibility for thinking through your feelings and discovering what is really bothering you. Agree that one partner will speak first and have the chance to speak fully while the other listens. Then reverse the roles. Try to understand the other's position fully by repeating what you've heard and asking questions to clarify or <u>elicit</u> more information. Agree to talk only about the topic at hand and not get distracted by other issues. Sum up what your partner has said.

- Find out what each person wants. Ask your partner to express his or her desires. Don't assume you know what your partner wants and speak for him or her. Clarify and summarize.

- Identify various <u>alternatives</u> for getting each person what he or she wants. Practice <u>brainstorming</u> to generate a variety of options.

- Decide how to negotiate. Work out some agreements or plans for change, such as agreeing that if one partner will do one task, the other will do another task or that a partner will do a task in exchange for being able to do something else he or she wants.

- <u>Solidify</u> the agreements. Go over the plan verbally and write it down if necessary to ensure that you both understand and agree to it.

- Review and renegotiate. Decide on a time frame for trying out the new plan and set a time to discuss how it's working. Make adjustments as needed.

To resolve conflicts, partners have to feel safe in voicing disagreements. They have to trust that the decision won't get out of control, that they won't be abandoned by the other, and that the partner won't take advantage of their <u>vulnerability.</u> Partners should follow some basic ground rules when they argue, such as avoiding <u>ultimatums,</u> resisting the urge to give the silent treatment, refusing to "hit below the belt," and not using sex to smooth over disagreements.

Notice that bullets give prominent emphasis to six strategies for negotiating the resolution to a conflict with a partner.

Introductory Statements   Introductory statements often give information about details. An introduction may state the number of details in a passage or it may name the details. The introduction to "The SQ3R Study Method" in Exercise 18.1 below states that there are *five* steps in the process and it names them. It is very common for textbook passages to begin with specific information about the details in them.

EXERCISE 18.1   **"The SQ3R Study Method"**

Use the *subheadings* to guide you in marking the following passage.

The SQ3R Study Method

An excellent set of suggestions for effective studying is to be found in the *SQ3R Study Method* designed by Francis Robinson at Ohio State University. The five steps are *Survey, Question, Read, Recite,* and *Review.* Each is described briefly here.

Survey   To survey a chapter, begin by reading the various headings and subheadings. In this way, you learn generally what the chapter is about and you know what to expect. Skim some of the first sentences and look at any pictures, tables, or graphs. If there is a summary, read it as part of your survey because it will give you the important points of the chapter. The survey technique increases your ability to understand and learn new material.

Question   Some textbooks have lists of questions at the beginning or end of each chapter. If a book has them, use them and try to answer them. Try to think about the material and ask yourself questions about it. Asking questions is a way of actively taking part in the learning process.

Active participation is a key to learning. Questions also are ways of testing yourself to see what you have learned.

Read   The next step is to read. Read carefully and try to answer the questions that you have asked yourself. Make sure that you read everything—tables, graphs, and captions as well as the main text. Students often say, "I forget what I read as soon as I put the book down." So read to remember by telling yourself to remember. Notice particularly any words or phrases that are italicized because authors use italics to point out important terms, concepts, and principles.

Recite   Recitation is an important part of effective studying. Recite, not just in class periods, but to yourself by recalling what you have read. Recitation takes a lot of effort, for it is easy just to read and put the book away. Try to recall main headings and main ideas. For example, what does SQ3R stand for? As you read, stop several times and recite to yourself the major points that are being presented in the text. Recitation is important because it helps prevent forgetting by forcing you to keep your attention on the task.

Review   The fifth step in the SQ3R technique is to review. Review is important for remembering. The best times for review are right after first studying and again just before a test. Most good students try to get one or two reviews in between. These reviews include rereading and recitation.

EXERCISE 18.2   **"A Healthy Lifestyle"**

Use the *headings* and *subheadings* to guide you in marking the following passage.

A Healthy Lifestyle

A healthy lifestyle can provide a higher energy level, a greater sense of self-confidence, and generally a more positive outlook on life. People who maintain good health usually have more endurance, spend less time feeling tired or ill, and miss less work than persons who are not physically fit. Good health is receiving greater attention today because many Americans are investing more time and energy in their work. They are being asked to work longer hours and do more in less time. Good health can help combat stress and tension at work and at home.

There is another important reason to adopt a healthy lifestyle. The cost of health care is steadily increasing. The old saying "I can't afford to get sick" will be on the minds of many workers in the future.

The first step toward adopting a healthy lifestyle is to become well informed—to read, study, and learn what can be done to maintain your current level of health or improve your health. In this section, we offer guidelines that form the framework for a good diet and a good exercise program. The second step is to determine what changes you need to make in your lifestyle and then make those changes. For many people, step one does not automatically lead to step two. Present-day Americans have access to more information about nutrition and exercise than any previous generation, but many have refused to give up poor eating habits and adopt an exercise program. When Ruth Lahmayer was hired to help IBM managers improve their eating habits, she discovered that they "don't focus on their diet because they're so focused on their jobs."[1]

Guidelines for a Healthy Diet

Eating the right foods can improve your health, boost your energy level, and, in some cases, extend your life. The link between health and diet is quite clear. Although we do not know enough about nutrition to identify the "ideal diet" for every person (food needs differ depending on age, body size, gender, physical activity, and other conditions), we can rely on dietary guidelines that are suitable for most Americans.[2]

Eat a Variety of Foods   Eating a variety of foods is important because you need more than forty different nutrients for good health: vitamins and minerals, amino acids (from proteins), essential fatty acids (from fats and oils), and sources of energy (calories from carbohydrates, fats, and proteins).[3] If you eat a variety of foods, you are more likely to maintain a well-balanced diet because most foods contain more than one nutrient (see Figure 18.3).

FIGURE 18.3

Recommended Food Groups and Amounts Necessary for a Healthy Diet

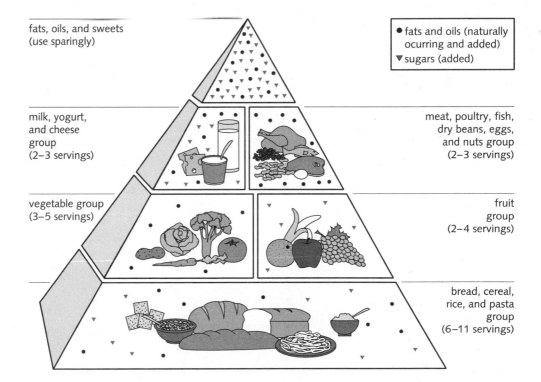

fats, oils, and sweets (use sparingly)

• fats and oils (naturally ocurring and added)
▼ sugars (added)

milk, yogurt, and cheese group (2–3 servings)

meat, poultry, fish, dry beans, eggs, and nuts group (2–3 servings)

vegetable group (3–5 servings)

fruit group (2–4 servings)

bread, cereal, rice, and pasta group (6–11 servings)

Cut Down on Fatty Foods The foods that are popular with many Americans are relatively high in fat, especially saturated fat, which contributes to high blood cholesterol levels. Many restaurant foods are high in fat because it gives menu items the flavor people often seek when eating out. Heart disease and certain kinds of cancer are by-products of a fatty diet.

Although diet is the most important factor in lowering cholesterol, exercise can help. About ninety minutes of aerobic exercise per week along with dietary changes has been found to lower total cholesterol.

Eat Foods with Adequate Starch and Fiber Foods high in starch, such as breads made with whole grains, dry beans and peas, and potatoes, contain many essential nutrients. Many starches also add dietary fiber to your diet. A growing number of scientists believe that high-fiber diets can help reduce the odds of getting cancer of the colon. Some cereals and most fruits and vegetables are good sources of fiber. The National Research Council recommends eating six or more servings of fruits and vegetables as well as six servings of breads or cereals each day to obtain the necessary amounts of fiber.[4]

Maintain Desirable Weight A growing number of Americans are overweight and the problem seems to be getting worse. In 1992–93 the National Institutes of Health found that the average weight of adults, ages 25 to 30, was 171 pounds. In 1985–86, the average weight was 161 pounds for people in that age group.[5] The ten-pound weight gain over the seven-year period appears to be due to consumption of more calories and a decline in physical activity. Being overweight is associated with increases in blood pressure, blood sugar, cholesterol, and blood fats (triglycerides). To lose weight, you must take in fewer calories than you burn. To do this, you must either choose foods with fewer calories, become more active, or both.[6] Ideally, you should combine a low-calorie diet with appropriate exercise. Also, control overeating by eating slowly, taking smaller portions, and avoiding "seconds."

Avoid Too Much Sodium A common by-product of excess sodium is high blood pressure. In the United States, where sodium-rich diets are very common, about one in four adults has elevated blood pressure. In populations with low sodium intakes, high blood pressure is very uncommon.[7] The recommended daily intake of sodium is 1,100 to 3,300 milligrams. It is difficult to avoid too much sodium in our diets because it is present in so many of the foods we eat and the beverages we drink. In fact, most of the sodium we consume comes from processed foods, not from salt shakers on our tables.

If You Drink Alcohol, Do So in Moderation Alcoholic beverages are high in calories and low in nutrients and cause serious health risks when used in excess. When alcohol is consumed in excess of one or two drinks per day, there tends to be a strong relationship between alcohol intake and high blood pressure. Excessive alcohol consumption has been linked to liver damage and certain types of cancers.[8]

With the help of these healthy diet guidelines, you can develop your own plan for achieving a healthful diet. Keep in mind that good nutrition is a balancing act. You want to select foods with enough vitamins, minerals, protein, and fiber but avoid too much fat and sodium. You want to consume enough calories to maintain the energy level required in your life but avoid weight gain. Prior to developing your own diet plan, consider getting advice from a medical doctor or someone with expertise in nutrition.

Improving Your Physical Fitness

In terms of exercise, people often choose one of two extreme positions. Some adopt the point of view that only high-intensity activities (marathon running, high-impact aerobics) increase physical fitness. These people believe in the "no-pain, no-gain" fitness approach. The other extreme position is to become a "couch potato" and avoid all forms of exercise. Both positions should be avoided.

Physical fitness can be defined as the ability to perform daily tasks vigorously with enough energy left over to enjoy leisure activities. Is is the ability to endure difficult and stressful experiences and still carry on. Physical fitness involves the performance of the lungs, heart, and muscles. Physical fitness can also have a positive influence on mental alertness and emotional stability.[9] Research indicates that we can achieve and maintain physical fitness with a moderate exercise program. For most people, a program that involves regular physical activity at least three times a week and includes sustained physical exertion for twenty to thirty minutes is adequate.[10] This modest investment of time and energy will give you a longer and healthier life.

You do not need to become an obsessive fitness fanatic to achieve lifesaving benefits from exercise. Start slowly with an activity you feel you will enjoy, such as those that follow.

Walking   In recent years, walking has become the nation's leading form of exercise. It is a safe, inexpensive way to make your heart stronger, decrease body fat, and give your mood an "uplift." When you feel tense, unable to think clearly, or depressed, take a walk. The calories burned per mile during a brisk walk are 100 (about the same as running), and you will use more than half the body's 650 muscles.[11]

Swimming   Many people swim for fitness and fun. If you swim at the proper intensity for at least twenty to thirty minutes, three times a week, you will develop a stronger heart and increase your resistance to fatigue. Swimming will also help you control your weight and reduce your muscle tension and stress level. You can burn from 150 to 400 calories during a half-hour swim.[12]

Jogging   Some people begin a walking program and then start jogging. Jogging will usually get your heart rate up to the prescribed level quicker than walking. But jogging without proper conditioning and warmups can put too much stress on your joints and may result in injuries. Some people do their jogging on a treadmill.

Walking, swimming, and jogging provide examples of aerobic exercise. When we engage in aerobic exercise, the body is required to improve its ability to handle oxygen.[13] These exercises strengthen the heart, burn up calories, increase <u>stamina,</u> and help release tension. Other examples of aerobic exercise are running, cross-country skiing, rope skipping, skating, rowing, and bicycling. Some people find it easier to stay with an exercise program that includes a variety of fitness activities, such as swimming, walking, and weight training. This approach helps exercise the whole body and avoid the boredom that sometimes comes with the same exercise.[14]

If you are younger than thirty-five and in good health, you probably do not need to see a doctor before beginning an exercise program. If you are older than thirty-five and have been inactive for several years, consult your doctor before engaging in vigorous exercise.[15]

References

1. Russell Mitchell, "Sure, You're Busy. That's No Reason Not to Eat Right," *Business Week*, October 9, 1989, p. 122.
2. *Dietary Guidelines for Americans*, 2nd ed. (Washington, D.C.: U.S. Department of Health and Human Services, 1985), pp. 3–21.
3. *Dietary Guidelines for Americans*, p. 6.
4. "The Straight Facts About Fiber," *AIRC Newsletter*, Fall 1990, p. 4.
5. "Weight of Average Young U.S. Adult Rose 10 Pounds in Seven-Year Period," *Wall Street Journal*, March 18, 1994, p. 5B.
6. *Dietary Guidelines for Americans*, p. 9.
7. *Dietary Guidelines for Americans*, p. 21.
8. *Dietary Guidelines for Americans*, p. 23.
9. *Fitness Fundamentals* (Washington, D.C.: Department of Health and Human Services, 1988), pp. 2-3.
10. "One Small Step . . .," *University of California at Berkeley Wellness Letter*, January, 1991, p. 1; Kenneth Blanchard, D. W. Edington, and Marjorie Blanchard, *The One Minute Manager Gets Fit* (New York: Morrow, 1986), p. 36.
11. Jane E. Brody, "Enjoy the Health Benefits of Walking," *Roanoke Times & World-News*, March 18, 1991, p. E-4.
12. "An Exercise Program You Can Stick With," *Johns Hopkins Medical Letter*, August 1990, p. 7.
13. Robert A. Gleser, *The Healthmark Program for Life* (New York: McGraw-Hill, 1988), p. 147.
14. Gleser, *The Healthmark Program for Life*, p. 143.
15. *Fitness Fundamentals*, p. 2.

EXERCISE 18.3   ## "Maslow's Hierarchy of Needs"

Use the *introduction*, *subheadings*, and Figure 18.4 to guide you in marking the following passage.

Maslow's Hierarchy of Needs

Abraham Maslow, a noted psychologist, found that people tend to satisfy their needs in a particular order—a theory he called the "<u>hierarchy</u> of needs."[1] Maslow's theory rests on two <u>assumptions:</u> (1) people have a number of needs that require some measure of satisfaction, and only unsatisfied needs <u>motivate</u> behavior; and (2) the needs of people are arranged in a hierarchy of prepotency, which means that as each lower-level need is satisfied, the need at the next level demands attention.[2] Basically, human beings are motivated to satisfy physiological needs first (food, clothing, shelter), then the need for safety and security, and then social and esteem needs. Finally, they seek to realize their potential, what Maslow called "self-actualization." Maslow's theory is illustrated in Figure 18.4. It is not difficult to see how this theory can be applied to motivation on the job.

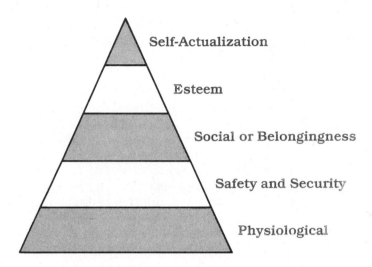

FIGURE 18.4

Maslow's
Hierarchy of Needs

Physiological Needs The needs for food, clothing, sleep, and shelter, or *physiological needs*, were described by Maslow as survival or lower-order needs. In most work environments, these basic needs rarely dominate because they are reasonably well satisfied. During the Great Depression, however, many people worked solely to ensure their own and their families' survival. In most cases, they were not concerned with the type of work they did or whether they liked it.

Safety and Security Needs People's desire for some sort of order and predictability in the world is reflected in *safety and security needs*. In general, people tend to look for security in the known and familiar and avoid what they don't know or understand. They like to know that they won't lose their jobs, that they can provide for their families, and that they will have enough money and resources to take care of themselves in sickness or old age. During the recession in the early 1980s, massive layoffs put employees in a state of limbo. Even those not laid off wondered from day to day if they would have a job the next week. In the late 1980s, it was the heavy volume of mergers, buy-outs, and business closings due to the movement of production facilities to other countries that created a feeling of insecurity among many workers. Even the oldest and largest of organizations were not immune to the economic volatility that spread across America. This insecurity often affected productivity and strained human relations at home and at work.

Organizations recognize the need for security by offering employees pensions, profit sharing, stock option plans, and insurance plans.

Workers are not simply earning a paycheck but protecting themselves against injury and laying aside money for retirement. Several American companies have made a major effort to avoid layoffs. Job security is given a very high priority at such companies as Hallmark Cards Inc., Johnson Wax, Federal Express Corp., and Worthington Industries.

Safety needs usually focus on protection from physical harm. On the job, this means a guarantee of safe working conditions. Unions or employee groups can make sure employers maintain safety standards and reduce the risk of accidents or injuries resulting from environmental hazards. Congress established the Occupational Safety and Health Act (OSHA) to help reduce deaths and injuries on the job.

Safety needs are also satisfied in other ways outside work. Advertisements for additional life or medical insurance, smoke detectors or burglar alarms, or guaranteed savings programs all appeal to people's need for safety and security.

Social or Belongingness Needs   Whereas the first two types of needs deal with aspects of physical survival, *social* or *belongingness needs* deal with emotional and mental well-being. Ron Parks, manager of manufacturing operations and human resources at the Dana Corp. plant in Columbia, South Carolina, can use his computer to contact any of his fifty-one employees. With a few keystrokes he can send a message to the video-display terminals at their work stations. However, he does not rely on this modern technology for all of his communication with the workers. Every Monday morning he goes to the plant with the plant manager to meet with the workers over coffee. These informal meetings not only improve communication, but also meet the social needs of many workers.[3]

Research has shown that fulfillment of people's needs for affection, a sense of belonging, and identification with a group are as important to their health as are food and safety.

Although social needs are felt throughout childhood, they may become more intense during adolescence, when the need to belong to a group becomes more important than family ties or what parents think. As adults, the need for belonging may take the form of joining various organizations—professional associations, church groups, amateur sports teams, or social clubs. Special uniforms or membership privileges reflect the desire to feel part of a group in which individuals share the same interests, values, and goals.

Many people's social needs are also satisfied on the job. People form attachments with coworkers and may join the company sports teams, take part in company picnics or outings, and get together after work. A growing number of business firms are sponsoring softball teams made up of their employees. Employers who are eager to see teamwork develop at the plant or office often pay for all or part of the bill for jerseys, equipment, and postgame refreshments. David Abramis, an organizational psychologist at California State University at Long Beach, says, "People who play company-sponsored softball tend to think of work as being more fun."[4] In many cases, friendships developed at work may function like a "second family." This is not surprising when you consider that many employees spend more time with people on the job than they do with their own family members. Many people are more highly motivated when they work as members of a team. Managers have found that when employees have a strong sense of being a part of the team, they are likely to be more productive.

Esteem Needs   Self-esteem is a term that describes how you feel about yourself. Self-esteem influences work behaviors and attitudes in two fundamental ways. First, employees bring to their work settings different levels of self-esteem, which in turn influence how they act, feel, and think while on the job. Second, individuals need to feel good about themselves; thus, much of what workers do and believe serves to enhance, preserve, or restore their self-esteem.[5]

Esteem needs relate to one's self-respect and to the recognition and respect one receives from others. Arthur Witkin, chief psychologist for the Personnel Sciences Center, believes that: "Perhaps the single most important thing is to be aware of a worker's need for self-esteem. Everyone needs to feel good about himself; if he doesn't, he'll not only turn in a poor job performance, he'll keep others from doing their best."[6]

Esteem needs can be satisfied in many ways. You may set your sights on winning the top-salesperson-of-the-year award, work to build a reputation as a highly skilled and reliable employee, or volunteer to <u>chair</u> a committee for the annual charity drive. Often, managers miss opportunities to reinforce the self-esteem of their workers. For most people, a word of appreciation or praise is a strong motivator. One employee stated, "It's such a simple thing, but hearing the boss say I did a great job makes me feel that all the work I put into a project was worth it. I go away wanting to work even harder on the next one."

Self-actualization Needs   The four needs just described motivate people by their absence, that is, when people feel a lack of food, security, social relationships, or esteem. *Self-actualization needs*, on the other hand, represent the need for growth and motivate people by their *presence*. Self-actualization is fulfilling one's potential or realizing one's fullest capacities as a human being.

Maslow used *self-actualization* in a very specialized sense to describe a rarely attained state of human achievement. Because of the uniqueness of each person, the form or content of self-actualization is a very individual thing.[7] Most of us will probably not reach self-actualization in Maslow's sense of the term, but we do make steps toward it by seeking to expand ourselves through setting new goals and finding new means of expression. The achievement of one goal stimulates the search for new challenges. It is like being on a fascinating journey where the goal is not the end of the road but the journey itself.

Each person's journey toward self-actualization will be individual and unique. It may be difficult to satisfy this need on the job, since most jobs are limited in scope and have their duties fairly clearly defined. However, this is not to say that people haven't found ways to change their jobs, create new positions for themselves, or set new goals year after year. George Guzewicz took a $15,000 pay cut to leave Xerox Corporation, the company where he had worked for seventeen years, to enter a sales job.[8] (He had never sold a product or service before.) Feeling that his job at Xerox was not challenging enough, he went to work for Lambda Semiconductors. After only a few months in the new position,

Mr. Guzewicz was achieving success and feeling a new sense of accomplishment. He was already setting his sights on another position within the company that would offer an even greater challenge. The self-actualizing person may not only create his or her own job, but may have two or three careers in one lifetime. A retired elementary school teacher learned Braille at age sixty-five and taught blind children for fifteen years. In another case, a printer turned his carpentering skills into a side business and began manufacturing grandfather clocks. He kept at his "hobby" until well into his eighties.

References
1. A. H. Maslow, *Motivation and Personality* (New York: Harper & Row, 1954).
2. H. C. Kazanas, *Effective Work Competencies for Vocational Education* (Columbus, Ohio: National Center for Research in Vocational Education, 1978), p. 12.
3. Stephen A. Stromp, "The Art of Corporate Communicating," *U.S. Air*, January 1989, p. 34.
4. James Cox, "Business Playing Softball," *USA Today*, July 8, 1988, p. B-1.
5. Joel Brockner, *Self-Esteem at Work* (Lexington, Mass.: Lexington Books, 1988), p. xi.
6. "How Bosses Get People to Work Harder," *U.S. News and World Report*, January 29, 1979, p. 63.
7. "Maslow's Term and Themes," *Training*, March 1977, p. 48.
8. "Eight Who Switched to Selling—Thanks to Hard Times," *Sales and Marketing Management*, September 13, 1982.

EXERCISE 18.4   "Defense Mechanisms"

Use the *bullets* and the words printed in *boldface* to guide you in marking the following passage.

Defense Mechanisms

To help minimize the anxiety that results from the clash between our wishes, morals, and reality, the ego uses powerful weapons—unconscious **defense mechanisms** that deny and distort our self-perceptions. Here are some common defense mechanisms described by Freud. See if you recognize any of them:

- **Repression** occurs when anxiety-provoking thoughts and memories are "forgotten" and pushed out of awareness. Freud believed that people repress unacceptable sexual and aggressive urges, traumas, and guilt feelings. In the 1990 case of the Central Park jogger who was stripped, raped, beaten, and left for dead by a gang of teenagers, the victim testified that she could barely remember the attack—a possible sign of repression. According to Freud, this mechanism of defense is a necessary prerequisite for all the others, but is seldom a final solution.

- **Denial** is a primitive form of repression in which anxiety-filled external events are not only forgotten but barred from awareness in the first place (see no evil, hear no evil). Denial is common among terminally ill patients and in families who sometimes refuse to admit that a loved one is dying. It is also a characteristic of smokers who refuse to recognize the health risks of their habit, husbands and wives who ignore signs of marital conflict, and politicians who manage to overlook corruption that takes place right under their noses.

- **Projection** occurs when people attribute or "project" their own unacceptable impulses onto others. In Freud's view, a person who is sexually attracted to a friend's spouse, or to anyone else who is "off limits," might repress those feelings and consciously come to believe that the friend's spouse is attracted to him or her. In this way, "I lust for this person" is transformed into "this person lusts after me." Similarly, people who are prejudiced against certain racial or ethnic groups are quick to attribute their own hostile impulses to "them."

- **Reaction formation** involves converting an unacceptable feeling into its opposite. Someone who brags may be masking feelings of inadequacy. Similarly, hatred can be transformed into love, and sadness into joy. Compared to "true" feelings, reaction formations often appear exaggerated. Examples include the mother who smothers with affection an unwanted child she secretly resents, the schoolboy who goes out of his way to taunt a girl he really likes, the antipornography crusader who deep down inside is aroused by sexually explicit material, and the vocal antigay activist who fights to cover up his own homosexual impulses.

- **Rationalization** involves making excuses for one's failures and shortcomings. The fox in Aesop's fable who refused the grapes he could not reach "because they were sour" used rationalization. So do failing students who say they don't really care about grades, gamblers who justify their massive losses as entertainment costs, and scorned lovers who find fault with those who reject them.

- **Sublimation** is the channeling of the id's repressed urges into socially acceptable substitute outlets. Freud saw this as the healthiest defense mechanism because it represents a genuine compromise among the id, ego, and superego. Thus, a person with pent-up hostile impulses may derive satisfaction by becoming a surgeon, football player, or critic. Similarly, a person may sublimate sexual needs by listening to others talk about sex, or through music, art, dance, and other activities. Freud believed that civilization's greatest achievements spring from the wells of sexual and aggressive energy. He suggested, for example, that Leonardo da Vinci painted the famous *Mona Lisa* as a sublimation of his need for intimacy with a mother from whom he was separated at an early age. As for other men, the lyrics of an old song hint at how substitute gratification for repressed Oedipal urges can be achieved: "I want a girl just like the girl that married dear old dad!"

EXERCISE 18.5   **"Learning to Think"**

Use the *introduction*, *numbers* (1, 2, and so on), and words printed in *italics* to guide you in marking the following passage.

Learning to Think

One of the most important achievements of socialization is the development of cognitive abilities—intellectual capacities such as perceiving, remembering, reasoning, calculating, believing. Our knowledge of this process is based largely on the work of Jean Piaget (1896–1980), who emphasized that "social life is necessary for the individual to become conscious of his own mind."

Piaget's many experiments with children suggest that human beings gradually pass through four basic stages of cognitive development, with the attainment of new skills at each stage requiring successful completion of the previous stage. Each stage is characterized by the particular kinds of "operations," or intellectual processes, that a person at that stage can perform (1950, 1954).

1. *The Sensorimotor Stage.* In this stage, which lasts from birth until about the age of two, children's thinking is limited to their immediate sensory and physical experience with the environment. Infants cannot "think" about the world unless they are acting on it directly. In fact, until the age of four months or so, infants cannot even differentiate themselves from their environment. They are thus unaware of the results of their actions; they do not realize, for example, that their own movements cause a rattle to make a sound. Similarly, children under the age of eight months do not understand that objects have a permanent existence: if a toy is removed from their sight, or if a parent leaves the room, they react as though the toy or parent has ceased to exist. By the end of the sensorimotor stage, however, the child realizes that objects exist even when they are not in view. Indeed, the child is able to create mental images of things and events that he or she has experienced in the past.

2. *The Preoperational Stage.* This stage lasts from around the age of two to seven. Piaget called this stage "preoperational" because, during this period, children are unable to do many simple mental operations, largely because they have no real understanding of such concepts as speed, weight, number, quantity, or causality. Particularly during the early years of this stage, for example, children invariably assume that the larger of two objects must be the heavier. (They will typically state that a pound of feathers weighs more than a pound of lead.) They likewise assume that the taller of two containers holds more, even if the taller container is much narrower than the shorter one. They have a limited understanding of cause and effect—often believing, for example, that trees waving in the wind are actually making the wind. And they often attribute life to inanimate objects, such as the sun and moon, and may believe that a table is "hurt" when it is bumped.

3. *The Concrete Operational Stage.* In this stage, which lasts from about seven to twelve, children can reason about concrete situations, but not about abstract or purely hypothetical ones. If children of this age are asked to talk about abstract concepts, such as death or justice, they have great difficulty in doing so without referring to actual events or images, such as the death of a pet or the physical appearance of police officers. Children at this stage, however, are able to handle the concrete world with much the same cognitive skill as an adult. They can perform the various mental operations related to weight, speed, number, quantity, or causality that were not possible in the previous stage. They can also see other people's viewpoint and can thus take the roles of others. This new ability enables them to participate effectively in games and other organized social relationships.

4. *The Formal Operational Stage.* In this stage, which usually begins at the onset of <u>adolescence,</u> people are able to achieve formal, abstract thought. They can think in terms of theories and <u>hypotheses</u> and can manipulate complex mathematical, moral, and other concepts that are not tied to the immediate environment. They are able to use general rules to solve whole classes of problems, and they can reason logically from premises to conclusions with a sophistication that would not be possible in earlier stages. They can think about abstract personal goals and even <u>utopian</u> social conditions. Philosophic brooding may appear on <u>perennially</u> favored topics of youth. (If sex is pleasant, why is it wrong? If God is good and all-powerful, why is there evil in the world and suffering among the innocent? If parents know best, why do they often make mistakes?)

It seems that the *process* of cognitive socialization is universal: in all societies, people advance through the same sequence of development. But the *content* is culturally variable: what and how much we learn depend on our social environment. If our culture believes the earth is flat, or that cause and effect are related to magic, then it is through these concepts that we will interpret the world. Moreover, not everyone reaches the final stage of formal operations; many adults have great difficulty in understanding abstract concepts, particularly if they have little exposure to formal thinking in their own socialization. In fact, more than half the people in the world today cannot read or write, for they live in societies that lacked the resources to make formal education available to them. Even within a given society, too, social and cultural factors encourage different categories of the population to think in different ways about different subjects. American men, for example, are socialized to be more likely than women to think in mathematical or engineering terms.

References

Piaget, Jean. 1950. *The Psychology of Intelligence.* London: Routledge & Kegan Paul.
Piaget, Jean. 1954. *The Construction of Reality in the Child.* New York: Basic Books.

EXERCISE 18.6   **"Women and Reform"**

Use *dates* (such as 1910, 1914, and 1916) to guide you in marking the following passage.

Women and Reform

Organizations formed by or dominated by women burst upon politics during the Progressive era. By 1900 or so, a new ideal for women had emerged from women's colleges and clubs and from discussions on national lecture <u>circuits</u> and in the press. The New Woman stood for self-determination rather than unthinking acceptance of roles prescribed by the <u>cult</u> of <u>domesticity</u> and separate spheres. By 1910, this fresh attitude, sometimes called **feminism,** was accelerating the <u>transition</u> from the nineteenth-century women's movement for <u>suffrage,</u> to the twentieth-century struggle for equality and individualism.

Women's increasing control over one aspect of their lives is evidenced in the birthrate, which fell steadily throughout the nineteenth and early twentieth century as couples chose (or, perhaps, women alone chose) to have fewer children. In the early nineteenth century, many women used abortion to end unwanted pregnancies, but that option became illegal after midcentury. By the end of the century, state and federal laws also banned information about contraception. As a result, women or couples seeking to prevent conception often had to rely on word of mouth or advertising for pills or devices that only hinted at their use.

In the Progressive era, some women began to challenge such restrictive laws. **Margaret Sanger,** a nurse practicing among the poor of New York City, became convinced that too-large families contributed to poverty and damaged the mental and physical health of women. And she saw that women died after botched abortions. By 1914, Sanger also concluded, "Women cannot be on an equal footing with men until they have full and complete control over their reproductive function." In 1916, she went to jail for informing women about *birth control*, a term she originated. The year before Sanger's arrest, in 1915, a group of women (not including Sanger) formed the National Birth Control League to seek the repeal of laws that barred contraceptive information.

Other women also formed organizations to advance specific causes. Some, like the settlement houses, were oriented to service. The National Consumers' League (formed in 1890) and the Women's Trade Union League (1903) tried to improve the lives of working women. Such efforts received a tragic boost in 1911 when fire roared through the Triangle Shirtwaist Company's clothing factory in New York City, killing 146 workers—nearly all women—who were trapped in a building with no outside fire escapes and with exit doors locked to deter workers from taking breaks. The public outcry produced a prominent state investigation and, in 1914, a new state factory safety law.

Some states passed laws specifically to protect working women. In *Muller v. Oregon* (1908), the Supreme Court approved the constitutionality of one such law, limiting women's hours of work. Louis Brandeis, a lawyer working with the Consumers' Union, defended the law on the grounds that women were "in general weaker than men in muscular strength and in nervous energy" and needed special protection because of their social roles as mothers. Such arguments ran contrary to the New Woman's rejection of separate spheres and ultimately raised questions for women's drive for equality. At the time, however, the decision was widely hailed as a vital and necessary protection for women wage earners. By 1917, all but nine states had laws restricting women's working hours.

Although prominent in reform causes, most women could neither vote nor hold office. Support for suffrage grew, however, as more women recognized the need for political action to bring social reforms. By 1896, four western states had extended the vote to women. Then came the doldrums from 1896 to 1910, when no state approved extension of the franchise. Finally, in 1910, Washington approved female suffrage and seven more western states followed over the next five years. In 1916, a western state dissolved another separate sphere when **Jeannette Rankin** of Montana—born on a ranch, educated as a social worker, experienced as a suffrage campaigner—became the first woman elected to the House of Representatives. Suffrage scored few victories outside the West, however.

Convinced that only a federal constitutional amendment would gain the vote for all women, the **National American Woman Suffrage Association, (NAWSA),** led by Carrie Chapman Catt and Anna Howard Shaw, developed a national organization geared to lobbying in Washington. Alice Paul advocated public demonstrations and civil disobedience, tactics she learned from English suffragists while she was a settlement house worker there from 1907 to 1910. In 1913, Paul and her followers formed the Congressional Union, to pursue their more militant strategies. Some white suffragists tried to build an interracial movement for suffrage—NAWSA, for example, condemned lynching in 1917—but most white suffragists feared that attention to other issues would weaken their position.

Despite the predominantly white and middle-class cast of its leaders, the cause of woman suffrage ignited a mass movement during the 1910s, mobilizing young, old, rich, poor, black, and white women of all socioeconomic classes. Opponents of woman suffrage had long argued that voting would bring women into the male sphere, make them subject to the same corrupting influences as men, and thereby render them unsuitable as guardians of the moral order. But some suffrage advocates now turned the domesticity argument to their favor, claiming that, instead of politics corrupting women, women would purify politics, making them more morally righteous and family-oriented. Others, especially feminists, argued that women should vote because they deserved full equality with men. The broadbased suffrage movement could embrace both the former, who argued that women were morally superior to men, and the latter, who argued that women were essentially similar to men. Such unity was unlikely to continue, though, once suffrage was accomplished.

Perhaps the most publicized event in women's lives was national woman suffrage. In June 1919, by a narrow margin, Congress proposed the **Nineteenth Amendment,** to enfranchise women over 21, and sent it to the states for ratification. After a grueling, state-by-state battle, ratification came in August 1920, enabling women to participate in the 1920 election.

As women began to participate in the political mainstream, the unity of the suffrage movement quickly disintegrated in squabbles over the proper political role for women. Both major political parties soon modified the structure of their national committees to provide that each state be represented by a national committeeman and a national committeewoman, and both parties welcomed women as voters. Some suffrage activists, however, joined the League of Women Voters, a nonpartisan group committed to social and political reform. The Congressional Union, led by Alice Paul, converted itself into the National Woman's Party and, after 1923, focused its efforts largely on securing an **Equal Rights Amendment** to the Constitution. The League of Women Voters disagreed, arguing that such an amendment would endanger laws that provided special rights and protections for women. In the end, woman suffrage did not dramatically change either women or politics.

<u>**EXERCISE 18.7**</u>   **"Conversation"**

Use the *introduction*, *subheadings*, *numbers*, and *italics* to guide you in marking the following passage.

Conversation

People use a variety of communication strategies and types at various stages of their relationships. In this section we will consider the kinds of communication that are most <u>prevalent</u> in starting conversations with strangers, keeping conversations going, and sharing ideas and feelings with close friends and intimates.

Starting Conversations   Many people have great difficulty starting conversations with complete strangers. We don't know what kind of potential relationship we might have with a person until we talk with the person. The first step to establishing a relationship, then, is building up the courage to say something.

In male-female encounters, same-sex encounters, and business encounters, what happens in the first few minutes of an initial conversation will have a <u>profound</u> effect on the nature of the relationship that develops. How do you go about striking up a conversation with strangers? For some people, the advice given in this next section will be second nature. For those who find starting conversations difficult, however, the following suggestions for initial interaction with a stranger may be some of the most important information in this chapter.

1. *Formally or informally introduce yourself.* Start a conversation with a person by introducing yourself (or by getting someone else to introduce you). For example, "Hi, my name is Gordon. What's yours?" may sound <u>trite,</u> but it works. Or you might have a friend introduce you by saying, "Doris, I'd like you to meet my friend Bill. Bill, Doris is Susan's sister."

2. *Refer to the physical context.* One of the safest ways of starting a conversation is by referring to some aspect of the physical <u>context.</u> Certainly, one of the oldest and most effective of these is a comment about the weather: "This is awful weather for a game, isn't it?" Other contextual references include such statements as, "They've really decorated this place beautifully," "I wonder how they are able to keep such a beautiful garden in this climate," and "Doesn't it seem stuffy in here?"

3. *Refer to your thoughts or feelings.* A very direct way to make contact is by commenting on what you are thinking or feeling at the moment: "I really like parties, don't you?" or "I live on this floor, too—do these steps bother you as much as they do me?"

4. *Refer to the other person.* "I don't believe I've ever seen you—have you been working here long?" "President and Mrs. Phillips have sure done a lovely job of remodeling this home. Did you ever see it before the renovation?"

None of these statements is particularly threatening, so if the person you want to meet feels the same way about you, chances are he or she will respond pleasantly.

Keeping Conversations Going   Once two people have begun an interaction, they are likely to engage in relatively unthreatening conversations, that is, "small talk." Small talk typifies early stages of relationships and serves to meet many social needs with relatively low amounts of risk and disclosure of self and personal feelings. Moreover, small talk provides a basis on which to decide whether to move a relationship to the next level.

One common type of small talk is to refer to people you both know. Statements such as "Do you know Bill? I hear he has a really great job," "Would you believe that Mary Simmons and Tom Johnson are going together? They never seemed to hit it off too well in the past," and "My sister Eileen is really working hard at losing weight. I saw her the other day and all she talked about was the diet she's on" are all examples of small talk. This kind of small talk, often referred to as *gossip*, occurs during all phases of a relationship but is most common in the early phase because it is considered safe. You can gossip for a long time with another person without really saying anything about yourself or without learning anything about the other person. Gossip can be a pleasant way to pass the time of day with people you know but with whom you have no desire or need for a deeper relationship. It can also provide a safe way to explore the bases for attraction because it allows each person to see whether the other reacts similarly to the views expressed about the object of the gossip. Gossip can, of course, be malicious. More often than not, however, gossip represents a means of interacting amicably with others without becoming personally involved. This is why conversations at parties are composed largely of gossip.

Another kind of small talk is simple idea exchange. In *idea-exchange communication* people share information that contains facts, opinions, and beliefs, and that occasionally reflects values. Idea exchange is a common type of communication between both new acquaintances and old friends. At the office, Dan may talk with Walt about sports, Martha may talk with Louise about new cars, and Pete may talk with Jack about landscaping. Or, on a more serious level, Jan may talk with Gloria about the U.S. role in the Middle East and Dave may talk with Bill about abortion. Although the discussions of foreign policy and abortion are "deeper" than conversations about sports or cars, both sets of conversations represent idea exchanges. This type of communication is important to early stages of relationships because you learn what the other person is thinking, reassess your attraction level, and decide whether you want the relationship to grow.

<u>**EXERCISE 18.8**</u>   **"Education"**

What helps are provided to guide you in marking the following passage?

Education

More than one-half of today's high school graduates go on to some form of higher education, and some 30 percent of those between ages 18 and 24 are currently in college. A recent study by the American Council on Education reveals that 72 percent of freshmen reported that "making more money" was a very important <u>factor</u> in their decision to go to college. Whatever their reasons, the <u>result</u> is a personal investment. Data from the Bureau of the Census show that education pays off in higher incomes. The higher the educational level of the head of a household, the higher are both average annual family income and average lifetime family income. In a recent year, the annual income of households headed by a person with less than a high school education was $12,800. It was $18,900 for those with a high school diploma, $22,600 for those with one to three years of college, $29,700 for those with four years of college, and $35,200 for those with five years or more of college. The Bureau of the Census reports that four years of college adds about $13,000 a year to a worker's paycheck; going to school for an additional four years adds another $10,000.

Completion of a <u>bachelor's degree</u> is a significant educational achievement. The highest <u>educational attainments</u> of persons 25 years and over are as follows: 7 percent have a graduate or professional degree, 13 percent have a bachelor's degree, 6 percent have an <u>associate degree,</u> 19 percent have some college but no degree, 30 percent have a high school diploma, 14 percent completed ninth through 12th grade but have no diploma, and 10 percent have less than a ninth grade education. Such education and training increase people's **human capital**—the abilities, skills, and knowledge that permit them to perform work or services. Employers generally want to hire a person with a college degree because

TABLE 18.1

Income for Careers That Do Not Require a Bachelor's Degree

Occupation	Average Starting Salary	Average Salary of Experienced Individuals
Personnel clerk	$12,900	$22,600
Aircraft mechanic	26,800	43,000
Dental hygienist	18,300	32,700
Drafter	15,900	27,300
Emergency medical technician	22,300	28,200
Flight attendant	13,400	28,400
Photographer	22,900	34,200
Regulatory inspector	20,400	28,300
Respiratory therapist	18,000	26,700
State police officer	23,100	29,700
Surveying technician	12,600	27,700

Source: U.S. Department of Labor, Bureau of Labor Statistics, *Occupational Outlook Handbook* (Washington, DC, May 1993); authors' extrapolations to January 1994.

FIGURE 18.5

How Education
Affects Income

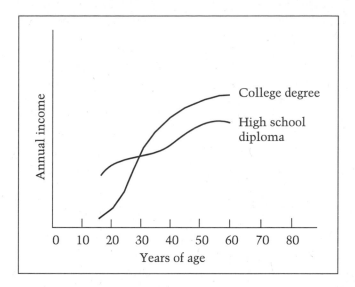

it is evidence of training in selected areas. Table 18.1 shows the starting salaries for various technical career positions that do not require a bachelor's degree. As noted in Figure 18.5, by about age 30 a worker who is a college graduate generally earns more than someone with only a high school diploma, and the college-educated person's income typically continues to rise after age 50. As you can see, education is an excellent predictor of earnings.

Education is also an excellent predictor of net worth. **Net worth** is the amount left when you subtract what you owe from what you own. Recent data from the Bureau of the Census indicate that households headed by a college graduate had a median net worth of $78,542, but net worth was only $4246 for households headed by a high school graduate and $3048 for those headed by someone with less than a high school education. Data from the U.S. Department of Labor show the relationship between education and unemployment. In a recent year, the unemployment rate was 2.5 percent for those with four or more years of college, 5.3 percent for those with one to three years of college, 8.1 percent for those with a high school diploma, and 14.4 percent for those with less than a high school education.

EXERCISE 18.9   **"Developing a Professional Presence"**

This is the second of five exercises for applying study skills to the sample textbook chapter on pages 299–319 of the appendix. The other exercises are for previewing (Exercise 17.2), making notes (Exercise 19.9), reciting and rehearsing (Exercise 20.4), and test taking (Exercise 21.3).

Marking a Chapter

Mark the information in the sample chapter on pages 299–319 of the appendix that answers the following thirteen questions. Each question is followed by a suggestion to help you in underlining or highlighting.

1. What is a professional presence? (Use the term **professional presence** printed in boldface on page 302.)

2. What is the primacy effect? (Use the term **primacy effect** printed in boldface on page 302.)

3. Why are the first few minutes of a meeting extremely important? (Use the heading on page 303.)

4. What are some common assumptions, or stereotypes, that persist because of cultural influence? (Use the term **cultural influences** printed in boldface and the bulleted list on page 306.)

5. What are the elements that comprise one's image? (Use the heading on page 306 and Figure 11.1 on page 307).

6. According to Susan Bixler, what three factors should influence your choice of clothing for work? (Use the numbered list on page 308.)

7. What are some wardrobe suggestions about which most wardrobe engineers and image consultants agree? (Use the heading and sentences printed in boldface on page 311 and the numbered list on pages 311–312.)

8. What is the business casual look? (Use the heading on page 313.)

9. How can facial expression create a positive impression? (Use the subheading on page 313.)

10. How can your carriage create a positive impression? (Use the heading on page 314.)

11. How can your voice create a positive impression? (Use the heading on page 314.)

12. How can your handshake create a positive impression? (Use the heading on page 314 and the numbered list on page 315.)

13. What rules of etiquette are particularly important to working in an organization? (Use the heading on page 315 and the numbered list on pages 315–317.)

Make Notes for Books

The first way to organize information in a textbook is to mark it using methods that are explained in Chapter 18. The second way is to make notes on the information.

Making notes will help you learn in three ways. First, to make notes, you must think about what you read and restate it in your own words. In many instances, you will learn information as you process it in this way. Second, because notes are summaries, you will have much less to learn when you study from notes than when you study directly from textbooks. Third, when you make notes, you don't need to learn information exactly as it is presented in a book—you can rearrange it in formats that make it easier for you to learn.

Read the following summary and examine the examples of notes on pages 219–224 before you continue your study of this chapter.

How to Make Notes for Books

Use the underlining and other marks you made in your textbook to guide you in making notes on a passage.

- Decide what format you will use for notes (see Figure 19.1 and pages 219–224).
- Begin the notes with a title that accurately describes the information you want to learn.
- Make major details stand out in notes.
- Include some minor details.
- Include examples; they help in understanding and learning information.

Notes on Cards

Most students make notes on notebook paper, but some very successful students prefer to study from notes written on index cards. Figure 19.1 below illustrates how to make notes on 3-by-5-inch index cards.

How to Make Notes on Index Cards

■ Write a descriptive title on the blank side of a card.

■ Write details on the back of the card upside down in relation to the title on the front.

When you make notes in this way, the information on the backs of the cards is in the proper position for reading when you turn the cards over.

FIGURE 19.1

Notes on an Index Card

Factors in Mate Selection

1. Age - Husbands tend to be about two years older
2. Social class - Mates tend to be from the same class and to share tastes and interests
3. Religion - Mates tend to share the same faith
4. Education - Mates generally have similar educational levels
5. Racial and ethnic background - People tend to marry within their own groups; interracial marriages are rare
6. Propinquity - People tend to marry those who live near them

There are four advantages to making notes on 3-by-5-inch cards rather than on notebook paper. First, because cards are small, they require you to summarize and condense information. Second, cards make it easy to integrate class notes and textbook notes because you can copy information in your class notes onto related textbook notes so that all the information about a topic is in one place for efficient study. Third, cards make it possible to separate information that you have learned from information that you have not learned. By separating "learned" notes from "unlearned" notes, you can readily direct your attention toward studying information that you have not yet learned. Fourth, cards are convenient to study at times when studying from a notebook is inconvenient. You can study notes on cards while walking from class to class or even while standing on a bus; notes on notebook paper are inconvenient to study at such times.

Major and Minor Details

American Values

<u>Positive values</u>

1. The work ethic — we believe that work is good and necessary and that it will lead to wealth.
2. Pragmatism — we try to find solutions to problems.
3. Thrift and delayed gratification — we believe it is better to save for tomorrow than to spend today.
4. Activism — we work hard to do things better and to make our lives better.

<u>Negative values</u>

1. Wastefulness — we spend money on things we don't need, and we waste our natural resources.
2. Indifference to social needs — we believe the strong are the ones who should survive, and we don't look after the basic needs of all our people.

When you make textbook notes, first consider whether you should prepare them so that major and minor details stand out, as you learned to do when you studied Chapter 9. The notes above have the following charactcristics:

- The title describes the content of the notes, and it is written in the center of the page.
- A line is left blank before each major detail.
- Minor details are indented and listed neatly under major details.

Exercises 19.1 and 19.2 provide practice in making textbook notes that give prominence to major and minor details.

Paragraph Summaries

Reasons for Immigration to America

<u>Economic</u> People in the Old World had difficulty finding employment, and they had little opportunity to acquire land. Many of them didn't have adequate food, clothing, housing, or health care. They believed they would find in America these things that they didn't have in the Old World.

<u>Social Equality</u> Europeans believed they would find greater equality in America. They knew that higher earnings made it possible for poor Americans to dress, eat, and acquire property in ways that were not possible for poor people in the Old World.

<u>American Persuasiveness</u> American businesses used advertising to encourage immigration because they wanted immigrants who would work for low pay. In addition, they wanted to make money by selling passages on ships and by selling land in America.

When you cannot organize information in notes that emphasize major and minor details, it may be appropriate to make notes in paragraph summaries. The paragraph summary notes above have the following characteristics:

- The title describes the content of the notes and it is written in the center of the page.
- A line is left blank before each paragraph.
- Each paragraph is indented.
- Each paragraph begins with an underlined title, which is the topic of the paragraph.

Exercise 19.3 provides practice in making textbook notes in the paragraph summary format.

Definitions of Terminology

Psychology

hormones — Chemicals formed in and given off by organs of the body that affect growth and behavior

rationalization — The giving of reasonable reasons for unreasonable or unacceptable behavior (Ex) A child with a poor report card claims, "The teacher doesn't like me."

hallucination — The seeing or hearing of something that is not there (Ex) A mentally ill person reports things he heard God say to him

pornography — Writings, pictures, and other materials that are intended to be sexually arousing

syndrome — A group of symptoms that occur together and that are typical of a particular disease or reactive pattern

On many college tests, 70 percent or more of questions directly or indirectly test knowledge of terminology; therefore, it is extremely important for you to learn the terminology that is defined in your textbooks. The definitions-of-terminology notes above have the following characteristics:

- Terms are written on the left side of the page.
- Definitions and examples are written on the right side of the page.
- Blank space is left before each new term.

This note-taking format facilitates learning terminology by using the method that is explained on pages 231–232.

Exercise 19.4 provides practice in making textbook notes in the definitions-of-terminology format.

Classification Charts

The Psychosexual Stages, According to Freud

	Age	Characteristics
Oral Stage	Birth to 1 year	Gets pleasure from mouth by sucking, eating, biting, and chewing.
Anal Stage	1 year to 3 years	Gets pleasure from holding and letting go of body waste.
Phallic Stage	3 years to 6 years	The child derives pleasure from his or her own primary sex organs.
Latency Period	6 years to about 11 years	Child denies attraction for parent of opposite sex and identifies with parent of the same sex.
Genital Stage	Adolescence	Awakening of sexuality and desire for heterosexual love

Classification charts are useful for organizing information that explains how two or more persons, places, or things are alike or different in two or more ways. The chart above summarizes Sigmund Freud's theory about the psychosexual stages of human development, which is explained in many psychology textbooks. The information is summarized under headings that explain the two ways in which the stages differ from one another: "Age" and "Characteristics." The notes also emphasize the sequence the stages occur.

When you have difficulty making good notes, ask this question: "Does this information explain how two or more persons, places, or things are alike or different in two or more ways?" If the answer to this question is yes, make notes in a classification chart.

Exercise 19.5 provides practice in making a classification chart.

Time Lines

Major Inventions (1875-1895)

1875
— Telephone
— Phonograph

— Cash register
1880 — Hearing aid

— Electric fan
— Rayon
— Modern bicycle
1885 — Motorcycle

— Contact lens
— Ballpoint pen

1890

— Submarine

— Movie machine
1895 — Safety razor

A time line is useful when you want to learn the chronological sequence of events. To prepare a time line, draw a line, and mark it off in equal time intervals. In the example above, a line is marked off in five-year intervals; however, in other time lines the intervals may represent one week, one month, one year, one hundred years, or any other period. The major advantage of time lines is that they make it easy to visualize the passage of time between events.

After you have marked off the intervals on a time line, write events in the places where they belong. In the example above, "Cash register" is written on the line before 1880 because it was invented in 1879 and "Motorcycle" is written next to 1885 because it was invented in 1885.

Exercise 19.6 provides practice in making textbook notes in a time line.

Maps

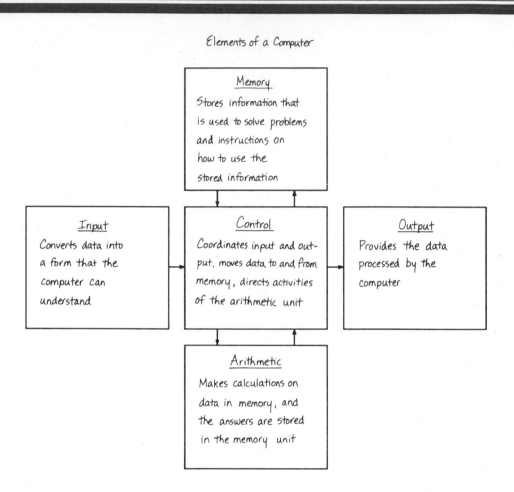

Elements of a Computer

Memory
Stores information that is used to solve problems and instructions on how to use the stored information

Input
Converts data into a form that the computer can understand

Control
Coordinates input and output, moves data to and from memory, directs activities of the arithmetic unit

Output
Provides the data processed by the computer

Arithmetic
Makes calculations on data in memory, and the answers are stored in the memory unit

Maps used in traveling show the relations between places; maps used for notes show the relations between ideas, information, and concepts. In maps, information enclosed within squares, circles, or other forms is connected by lines to information enclosed within other forms to indicate how the information is interrelated.

In the map above, descriptions of the elements of a computer are enclosed within rectangles, which are connected by arrows to show how the elements of a computer are interrelated. For example, one arrow between "Input" and "Control" indicates that data flow from input to control, but not from control to input. The two arrows between "Memory" and "Control" indicate that data flow back and forth between memory and control.

Exercise 19.7 provides practice in making a map.

EXERCISE 19.1   **Index Card**

Use the form for an index card to make notes for "The SQ3R Study Method" on pages 197–198. See pages 191 and 218 for examples of the type of notes you should make.

EXERCISE 19.2   **Major and Minor Details**

Use notebook paper to make major-and-minor-detail notes for "A Healthy Lifestyle" on pages 198–202. See page 219 for an example of the type of notes you should make.

EXERCISE 19.3   **Paragraph Summary**

Use notebook paper to make paragraph summary notes for "Maslow's Hierarchy of Needs" on pages 202–206. See page 220 for an example of the type of notes you should make.

EXERCISE 19.4   Definitions of Terminology

Use notebook paper to make definitions-of-terminology notes for "Defense Mechanisms" on pages 206–207. See page 221 for an example of the type of notes you should make.

EXERCISE 19.5   Classification Chart

Use notebook paper to make classification chart notes for "Learning to Think" on pages 207–209. See page 222 for an example of the type of notes you should make. Use the following headings from left to right across the top of your chart: "Stage," "Age Range," and "Intellectual Processes."

EXERCISE 19.6   Time Line

Use notebook paper to make time-line notes for "Women and Reform" on pages 209–211. See page 223 for an example of the type of notes you should make. Your notes should include events that occurred during the following years: 1890, 1896, 1903, 1908, 1910, 1911, 1913, 1914, 1916, 1917, 1919, and 1920.

EXERCISE 19.7   Map

Use the form on page 227 to make a map of the information in "Conversation" on pages 212–213. Write "Conversation" in the box at the top of the page, "How to Start" in the shaded box on the left, "How to Keep Going" in the shaded box on the right, and list the details in the other boxes.

EXERCISE 19.8   "Education"

Use notebook paper to make notes for "Education" on pages 214–215. Use the format your teacher requests.

EXERCISE 19.9   "Developing a Professional Presence"

This is the third of five exercises for applying study skills to the sample textbook chapter on pages 299–319 of the appendix. The other exercises are for previewing (Exercise 17.2), marking books (Exercise 18.9), reciting and rehearsing (Exercise 20.4), and test taking (Exercise 21.3). Use the suggestions on page 228 to make notes for the chapter in the appendix.

FIGURE 19.2
Form for Exercise 19.7

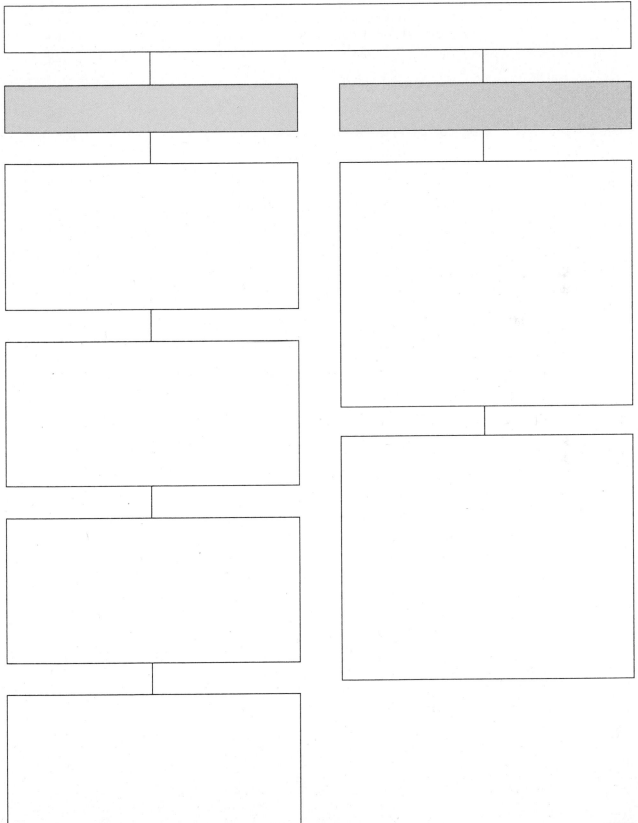

Making Notes for a Chapter

Use the marks you made when you did Exercise 18.9 and the guidelines on page 217 to make notes on the information in the sample textbook chapter on pages 299–319 of the appendix. Use the following titles for your notes—they correspond to the questions in Exercise 18.9.

1. Professional Presence

2. The Primacy Effect

3. The First Few Minutes

4. Assumptions or Stereotypes

5. Elements of One's Image

6. Choosing Work Clothing: Susan Bixler

7. Wardrobe Engineering Suggestions

8. The Business Casual Look

9. Positive Facial Expression

10. Positive Carriage

11. Positive Voice

12. Positive Handshake

13. Important Rules of Etiquette

Remember and Recall Information

If you have ever sat in a test room upset because you could not recall answers that you were certain you knew, you will probably be grateful for this chapter—it explains how to store information so that you can retrieve it when you want it. The suggestions are based on the following concepts about memory, which were introduced in Chapter 5.

Important Memory Concepts

- Most information stays in your memory for less than one minute unless you store it there.
- Prepare information for storage by organizing it in a logical manner.
- Store information with a retrieval cue.
- Use recitation and rehearsal to store information.

In this chapter, the terms storage, recitation, rehearsal, and retrieval have the same meanings as in Chapter 5, and **memory** is used to mean "the total of what one remembers." Following is a summary of the instruction in this chapter.

How to Remember and Recall Information

Organize the information you want to learn into notes that have the characteristics explained in Chapters 15 and 19.

1. Use descriptive titles in your notes as retrieval cues for recalling the information in them.
2. Use good organization of details in your notes to help you store and recall the information in them.
3. Recite the information in your notes.
   - Read the title.

- Try to say the information in your notes silently or aloud to yourself without reading your notes.
- Read the information in your notes to make certain that you recited it correctly; if you did not, reread the information and then immediately try to recite it again.

4. Rehearse the information in your notes.
   - Analyze the information into parts to study and understand how the parts are related.
   - Relate the information to other information in your memory.

5. Review the information frequently to ensure that you can retrieve it quickly when you need it.

6. Use one or more of the following aids to facilitate recitation and rehearsal.
   - Schedule many short study sessions over a long period rather than a few long sessions over a short period.
   - Join a study group.
   - Recite while walking outside rather than while sitting inside.
   - Rehearse by writing on paper rather than by repeating information silently or aloud to yourself.
   - Record hard-to-learn information on audiocassettes and recite it after you have listened to it enough times to learn it.
   - Use mnemonic acronyms, mnemonic sentences, and visualizations as retrieval cues (see pages 235–238).

Retrieval Cues

In preparing information for storage, the first step is to write good retrieval cues, which are words or images that will later help in retrieving, or recalling, information. In Figure 20.1 on page 232, the descriptive title "Types of Advertising" is a retrieval cue for recalling the information written on the back of the card. The student who prepared the card will read "Types of Advertising" and use the words to help her retrieve from her memory what she has stored there about selective advertising, primary demand advertising, and institutional advertising.

There are suggestions for creating retrieval cues on pages 235–238 of this chapter.

Logical Organization

It has been noted several times that information is easier to recite and rehearse if it is logically organized. Figure 20.1 is an example of notes that are logically organized on a 3-by-5-inch card; the major thought, or descriptive title of the notes, is prominently written on the front of the card, and the details are listed neatly on the back. On pages 219–224 there are examples of six other formats for logically organized notes.

Another level of organization is to integrate class notes with textbook notes so that all information about a topic is in one place. If you make textbook notes on 3-by-5-inch cards, prepare class notes for rehearsal by summarizing them on cards. Then, organize the cards by topic so that textbook notes and class notes about a single topic are together. Rehearsal is more efficient when all notes about a topic are together rather than in different places.

Recitation

Recitation is the act of repeating information silently or aloud for the purposes of storing it in memory. Use the procedure below to recite information in notes.

How to Recite

- Read the descriptive title of your notes and use it as a retrieval cue to recollect the information about it in your notes.

- Try to say the information in your notes silently or aloud to yourself without reading your notes.

- Read the information in your notes to make certain that you recited it correctly; if you did not, reread the information and then immediately try to recite it again.

Compare the example of recitation and rehearsal in Figure 20.2 on page 233 to the notes in Figure 20.1 on page 232 to notice the differences in the wordings. When you recite and rehearse, do not engage in rote, word-for-word memorization. Rather, learn the general meaning of information using your own words whenever possible. However, keep in mind that when you change wordings you risk changing meanings, and if you change meanings you will learn incorrect information. When you recite and rehearse, take great care not to change the meaning of things you learn.

Reciting Notes in the Traditional Format   If you recite directly from your class notes in the traditional format shown on page 150, highlight the major headings in your notes and use the highlighted words as retrieval cues. For instance, if "Types of Conflict" is a topic in the notes, highlight these words and use them to recall information about the three types of conflict in the notes: approach-approach, avoidance-avoidance, and approach-avoidance.

Reciting Notes in the Cornell Format   When you take class notes in the Cornell format illustrated on page 151, use your questions in the cue column as retrieval cues to recollect information in your notes. For instance, you could use the question "What are the six ways to transfer information from short-term memory to long-term memory?" as a cue to recall that transfer can be done by associating, organizing, understanding, frameworking, reorganizing, and rehearsing.

Reciting Terminology   On page 221, there is an example of a format for making notes for learning the definitions of terminology. In those notes, terms are written on the left side of the page and definitions are written on

FIGURE 20.1

Notes Used for
Reciting

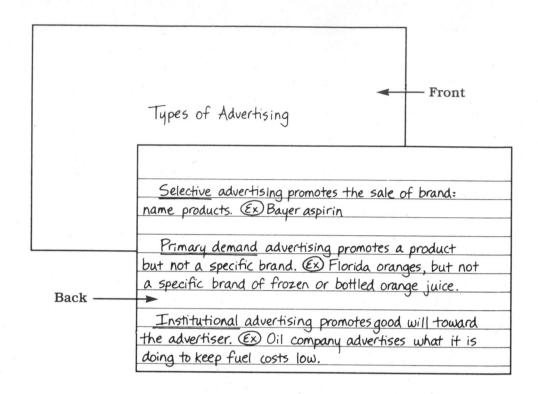

the right side of the page so that the definitions can be covered when the terms
are used as retrieval cues to recollect the definitions. For instance, with the
definitions covered, *syndrome* could be used as a retrieval cue to recollect that
the term refers to "a group of symptoms that occur together and that are
typical of a particular disease or reactive pattern."

Rehearsal

Use recitation in conjunction with rehearsal, or **elaborative rehearsal**, which
is the act of analyzing information and relating it to information that is
already stored in memory. To analyze is to separate something into its parts
for the purpose of studying its parts or understanding how they are related.
Compare the example of rehearsal in Figure 20.2 with the notes in Figure 20.1
to observe how the student analyzed the information in her notes and related
it to other information in her memory.

Examples of Analyzing and Relating

- **Analyzing.** In the student's first response in Figure 20.2, she analyzed that
  the information is divided into three categories—three types of advertising.
  In the other three responses, she further analyzed that each category is
  explained by a definition and an example.

- **Relating.** In the last three responses in Figure 20.2, the student related the
  information in her notes to information in her memory by giving examples
  of products that are different from the examples of products in the notes.

Storage of information is further enhanced by systematic review.

FIGURE 20.2

Recitation of the Information in Figure 20.1

A student read the title on the front of the card in Figure 20.1 and changed it into the following question:

What types of advertising are there?

She then answered her question by reciting the information on the back of the card in the following way:

- Primary demand, selective, and institutional advertising.
- Primary demand advertising sells a product without trying to sell any particular brand-name product . . . for example, sells cotton as a desirable material with many uses, rather than selling specific products, such as Arrow shirts or Cannon towels.
- Selective advertising is used to sell specific brand-name products, such as Comet cleanser and Skippy peanut butter.
- Institutional advertising tries to increase good will toward the advertiser . . . as when Mobil Oil sponsors a movie on public television.

Review

Review is an essential but often overlooked step in the study process. To **review** is to repeatedly recite and rehearse information to ensure that it can be retrieved quickly when it is needed.

When you study, you will often find that you are unable to remember information that you knew the day before. This loss of information is due to the normal process of forgetting—we tend to forget 30 to 40 percent of what we learn within twenty-four hours after we learn it! For example, after reciting and rehearsing for an hour, a student had learned the information on twenty of eighty cards she had prepared to study for a physics test. However, when she reviewed the twenty "learned" cards the next day, she discovered that she had forgotten information on six of them. What happened to her is what happens to all of us; we tend to forget a substantial portion of what we learn within twenty-four hours after we learn it. This is the reason that review is an essential part of the study process.

How to Review Notes on Cards

Maintain a deck of "learned" cards and a deck of "unlearned" cards. Then each time you recite,

- Begin by reviewing the deck of "learned" cards. If you have forgotten information on a card, put it back in the "unlearned" deck.
- Recite and rehearse the "unlearned" cards, attempting to move as many as you can into the "learned" deck.

Continue in this way until you can accurately recall all the information twenty-four hours after you have moved all cards to the "learned" deck.

How to Review Notes on Notebook Paper

Place checks in pencil next to information as you learn it. Then, each time you recite,

- Begin by reviewing checked information and erase checks next to information you have forgotten.
- Recite and rehearse the information that is not checked, attempting to place checks next to as much of it as you can.

Continue in this way until you can accurately recall the information twenty-four hours after you have placed pencil checks next to all of it.

Aids to Recitation and Rehearsal

One or more of the following strategies may help you learn more quickly when you recite and rehearse information.

Schedule Study Time Properly   Learning can be improved by scheduling study time in a way that fosters the effective storage of information. The most common error students make in scheduling study time is to plan insufficient time for reciting and rehearsal. As a result, they experience the stress of having to learn too much in too little time and the stress interferes with their ability to concentrate on studying. You cannot learn efficiently when you are worrying that you have too little time to learn everything you need to learn.

A less obvious error is to schedule sufficient time for rehearsal but to schedule it in too few study sessions over too few days. Learning is more effective when material is learned during short study sessions over as many days as possible. You know, for example, that you are likely to be a better typist if you practice typing one hour a day for thirty days in a row than if you practice six hours a day for five days in a row. The same principle that applies to learning how to type applies to learning information and skills for your college courses.

In scheduling study time, it is also essential to keep in mind that there is not a one-to-one relationship between the amount of information to store and the amount of time needed to store it. For instance, if you study the meanings of sixty terms for a psychology test, you may learn thirty of them in an hour and, as a result, schedule one hour to learn the other thirty terms. However, it might take you two or three hours to learn the remaining thirty terms because some of them may have meanings that are especially difficult for you to understand or remember.

Study with Others   Some students learn better when they study with a group of other students (see page 35).

Walk While Reciting   When I was a college student, I told a friend that I was having extreme difficulty learning information for a test. She suggested that I might benefit from the advice her drama coach gave her, that she could learn parts in plays more quickly if she studied them while walking rather than while sitting. I did what she recommended and found that I learned information more quickly when I recited it while walking outside rather than while sitting at a desk. When you have difficulty learning material, experiment to find out whether you learn more efficiently while walking than while sitting.

Rehearse by Writing   Writing is used to learn many of the skills that are taught in colleges, such as the skills that you need to solve mathematical problems and to translate a foreign language into English. You can also use writing to learn information of the kind that is usually recited silently or aloud. If you have difficulty learning material by reciting and rehearsing it, try writing it on paper. Some students report that writing provides them with the additional reinforcement they need when they recite.

Use Audiocassettes   Some students find that the most efficient way for them to recite is by listening to notes recorded on audiocassettes. One of my students, for example, had a job that required him to spend much time driving. To take advantage of his time in his car, he recorded his class notes and listened to them as he drove from place to place. He checked his learning by turning off his cassette player, reciting what he heard, and replaying the material to make certain he had recited it correctly.

If you are an auditory learner, audiocassettes can be useful learning tools for you, whether you listen to them in a car, at home, or over headphones as you walk from place to place.

Mnemonic Devices as Retrieval Cues

You may recall from Chapter 5 that two prominent theories about forgetting agree that once information is stored in memory, it stays there. As a result, these theories propose that forgetting is not a matter of losing information from memory but of being unable to retrieve it. When logical organization and descriptive titles are insufficient for retrieving information from memory, you may need to use a mnemonic device as a retrieval cue.

Mnemonic (ni-mon'ik) means "to help the memory." There are many different kinds of **mnemonic devices**. For example, the rhyming jingle "*i* before *e*, except after *c*" is a mnemonic for remembering a spelling principle. The following sentence is a mnemonic for remembering the reciprocal of pi = .318310:

$$\frac{\text{Can}}{3} \frac{\text{I}}{1} \frac{\text{remember}}{8} \frac{\text{the}}{3} \frac{\text{reciprocal?}}{10}$$

By counting the number of letters in each word of this sentence, one can recall that the reciprocal of pi is .318310.

The following discussions explain three types of mnemonic devices that are widely used as retrieval cues: mnemonic acronyms, mnemonic sentences, and visualizations.

Mnemonic Acronyms   A **mnemonic acronym** is a word made from the first letters of words you want to recall. One of the best-known mnemonic acronyms is HOMES, which is used to recall the names of the Great Lakes: Huron, Ontario, Michigan, Erie, Superior. H recalls Huron, O recalls Ontario, and so on.

In Figure 20.3 below the acronym SIP is written in the lower right-hand corner of the index card as a reminder of the letters with which the three types of advertising begin: Selective, Institutional, Primary demand.

FIGURE 20.3

A Mnemonic Device on an Index Card

Types of Advertising

SIP ← — Mnemonic Acronyms

Acronyms are widely used by students who have a great deal to learn, such as students studying for medical professions. Mnemonics such as the following are passed on among students in much the same way nursery rhymes are passed on among children:

- SKILL is used to recall the excretory organs of the body: Skin, Kidneys, Intestines, Liver, Lungs.
- A PAIL is used for remembering the five types of wounds: Abrasion, Puncture, Avulsion, Incision, Laceration.

Acronyms may also be used to recall phrases. The American Cancer Society recommends using the acronym CAUTION to remember the common warning signs of cancer:

- Change in bowel or bladder habits
- A sore that does not heal
- Unusual bleeding or discharge
- Thickening or lump in the breasts or elsewhere
- Indigestion or difficulty in swallowing
- Obvious change in a wart or mole
- Nagging cough or hoarseness

Though these are not certain signs of cancer, the American Cancer Society advises that they indicate the advisability of visiting a physician for an examination and consultation.

When you have difficulty recalling information, try using acronyms as retrieval cues. Your acronyms do not need to be real words—any combination of letters that you recall easily can serve as a mnemonic acronym for you.

Mnemonic Sentences   A **mnemonic sentence** is a sentence made of words that begin with the same letters as the first letters of words you want to recall. They are particularly useful for learning information in a specific sequence. For instance, the acronym <u>HOMES</u> may be used to recall the names of the Great Lakes, but the following sentence may be used to remember the names of the Great Lakes in correct sequence going from West to East.

<u>S</u>he <u>M</u>ust <u>H</u>ave <u>E</u>aten <u>O</u>nions.

The first letters of the words in this sentence are the same as the first letters of the names of the Great Lakes in correct sequence from West to East: <u>S</u>uperior, <u>M</u>ichigan, <u>H</u>uron, <u>E</u>rie, <u>O</u>ntario.

Some mnemonic sentences are passed on from student to student in the same way as acronyms. Here are some well-known ones.

<u>M</u>y <u>V</u>ery <u>E</u>arthy <u>M</u>other <u>J</u>ust <u>S</u>erved <u>U</u>s <u>N</u>ine <u>P</u>izzas.

In this sentence, the underscored letters are the same as the first letters in the names of the planets, starting with the one nearest the sun and proceeding to the one farthest from the sun: <u>M</u>ercury, <u>V</u>enus, <u>E</u>arth, <u>M</u>ars, <u>J</u>upiter, <u>S</u>aturn, <u>U</u>ranus, <u>N</u>eptune, <u>P</u>luto.

The first letters of the words in the following sentence are used to recall the order of operations in algebra:

<u>P</u>lease <u>E</u>xcuse <u>M</u>y <u>D</u>ear <u>A</u>unt <u>S</u>ally.

The order of operations is <u>P</u>arentheses, <u>E</u>xponents, <u>M</u>ultiplication, <u>D</u>ivision, <u>A</u>ddition, <u>S</u>ubtraction.

In the following example, the underscored letters are used by biology students to recall the categories into which living things are divided:

<u>K</u>ing <u>P</u>hilip <u>C</u>ame <u>O</u>ver <u>F</u>rom <u>G</u>reece <u>S</u>inging.

The categories for living things are <u>K</u>ingdom, <u>P</u>hylum, <u>C</u>lass, <u>O</u>rder, <u>F</u>amily, <u>G</u>enus, <u>S</u>pecies.

Mnemonic sentences are also useful when the first letters of words to be recalled do not spell a word. The following sentence is used to remember the four sections of a symphony orchestra:

<u>S</u>inners <u>W</u>ill <u>B</u>e <u>P</u>unished.

Because it is not possible to make an acronym from the letters *SWBP*, this sentence helps in recalling the orchestra sections: <u>S</u>tring, <u>W</u>oodwind, <u>B</u>rass, <u>P</u>ercussion.

Consider using mnemonic sentences as retrieval cues whenever you want to learn information in a specific sequence or when the first letters of words you want to remember do not spell a word.

Visualizations A **visualization** is anything that can be visualized, or pictured in the mind, to aid the retrieval of information. Visualizations are usually examples, and this is one reason I suggested in Chapter 18 that you mark examples in your textbooks and in Chapter 19 that you include examples in your textbook notes.

In rehearsing the notes in Figure 20.1 on page 232, the student used visualizations—products she could picture in her mind, such as Comet cleanser and Skippy peanut butter. Another student devised the following visualizations to help himself understand and retrieve the definitions of three types of social mobility for his sociology course:

Types of Social Mobility	Visualizations
Horizontal (from one status to a similar status)	I changed jobs from pumping gas to parking cars.
Vertical (from one status to a higher or lower status)	I changed jobs from parking cars to being a management trainee for an insurance company.
Intergenerational (when the status of family members changes from one generation to another)	My grandfather was a laborer, but my father supervises skilled factory workers.

The student used the images of himself, his father, and his grandfather to help himself understand, remember, and recall the three types of social mobility.

EXERCISE 20.1   ## Mnemonic Acronyms

This exercise provides practice in writing mnemonic acronyms.

1. There are four major types of wounds:
   - A *laceration* is a tear.
   - An *incision* is a cut.
   - A *crush* is an injury caused by pressure.
   - A *puncture* is a wound caused by piercing.

   Use the first letters of the italicized words to write an acronym for remembering the four types of wounds.

2. Some health care providers believe that there are five emotional stages through which people pass when they learn they are about to die:
   - Denial
   - Anger
   - Bargaining
   - Depression
   - Acceptance

   Use the first letters of these words to write a nonsense word that can be used to remember the names of the stages in the correct sequence.

3. A microbiology textbook explains three measures that can be taken to reduce the incidence of rabies:

   ■ *Immunize* more dogs and cats.

   ■ Enforce *leash* laws.

   ■ *Educate* the public about the dangers of rabies.

   Use the first letters of the italicized words to write a word for remembering the three measures for reducing rabies.

EXERCISE 20.2   ## Mnemonic Sentences

This exercise provides practice in writing mnemonic sentences.

1. There are four major categories of drugs:

   ■ *Depressants* slow body functions.

   ■ *Stimulants* speed up body functions.

   ■ *Hallucinogens* cause people to see or hear things that are not actually present.

   ■ *Marijuana* produces various effects.

   Write a mnemonic sentence in which the first letters of the words are the same as the first letters of the names of the four major types of drugs.

2. On pages 202–206 there is an explanation of Abraham Maslow's "hierarchy of needs"—a theory that there are five basic human needs, which people tend to satisfy in the following order:

   ■ Physiological needs

   ■ Safety needs

   ■ Social needs

   ■ Esteem needs

   ■ Self-actualization needs

   Write a mnemonic sentence in which the first letters of the words are the same as the first letters of the names of the human needs, arranged in the correct sequence.

3. Following are the six principal components of soil:

   ■ Air

   ■ Humus

   ■ Mineral salts

   ■ Water

   ■ Bacteria

   ■ Rock particles

   Write a mnemonic sentence in which the first letters of the words are the same as the first letters of these ingredients.

EXERCISE 20.3   Visualizations

This exercise provides practice in writing visualizations.

1. On page 194, there is a passage that describes four zones of private space. Read the passage and then devise visualizations for remembering the differences between the four zones: intimate distance; personal distance; social distance; and public distance.

2. On page 84, there is a passage that explains three types of advertising. Read the passage and then devise visualizations for remembering the differences between the three advertising categories: selective advertising; primary demand advertising; and institutional advertising.

3. On page 121, there is a passage that explains three kinds of conflict. Read the passage and then devise visualizations for remembering the three kinds: approach-approach, avoidance-avoidance, approach-avoidance.

EXERCISE 20.4   "Developing a Professional Presence"

This is the fourth of five exercises for applying study skills to the sample textbook chapter on pages 299–319 of the appendix. The other exercises are for previewing (Exercise 17.2), marking books (Exercise 18.9), making notes (Exercise 19.9), and test taking (Exercise 21.3).

Reciting and Rehearsing

Use the suggestions in this chapter to recite and rehearse the notes you took for Exercise 19.9. Use the following questions as retrieval cues:

1. What is a professional presence?
2. What is the primacy effect?
3. Why are the first few minutes of a meeting extremely important?
4. What are some common assumptions, or stereotypes, that persist because of cultural influence?
5. What are the elements that comprise one's image?
6. According to Susan Bixler, what three factors should influence your choice of clothing for work?
7. What are some wardrobe suggestions about which many wardrobe engineers and image consultants agree?
8. What is the business casual look?
9. How can facial expression create a positive impression?
10. How can your carriage create a positive impression?
11. How can your voice create a positive impression?
12. How can your handshake create a positive impression?
13. What rules of etiquette are particularly important to working in an organization?

PART

IV

Do Well on Tests

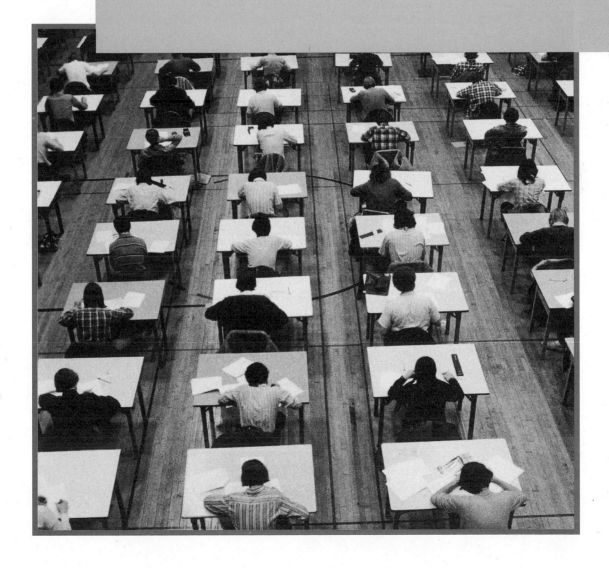

Preview of PART IV

Considering the importance test scores have in determining course grades, it is surprising that schools give little attention to teaching students how to do their best when they take tests. But test taking is a skill that can be learned in the same way the skills of reading and writing are learned. The following chapters explain strategies you may use when you take any test and specific techniques to use when you answer the following kinds of questions:

- True-false questions
- Multiple-choice questions
- Matching questions
- Fill-in questions
- Essay questions

Prepare for tests using the strategies that are explained in Chapters 13 through 20. Then, try using the suggestions in the following chapters to do your best when you take tests.

Strategies for Any Test

Virtually all teachers give a midterm and a final exam, and many teachers give two, three, or more additional tests or quizzes during a term. Following are some of the reasons you will take many tests during your college career.

Reasons for Tests

- Test scores are used to help decide students' course grades.
- Tests motivate students to study and learn course content.
- Students' test scores provide teachers with feedback about the effectiveness of their teaching.
- Tests provide students with feedback about how well they are doing in their courses.

Chapters 13 through 20 explain what to do before you take tests; this chapter suggests what you should do while you take them. Specific strategies for answering true-false, multiple-choice, matching, fill-in, and essay questions are explained in Chapters 22 through 27; following is a summary of strategies that apply to all tests.

How to Take a Test

- Reduce anxiety by reminding yourself that you studied thoroughly before the test and you know how to use good test-taking strategies.
- Preview the test to learn what types of questions you must answer, whether questions are printed on both sides of each page, and where you must write your answers.
- Read the directions carefully and follow them exactly.
- Listen attentively to everything the teacher says before and during the test.
- Plan your test-taking time so you will answer all the questions you know in case time runs out.

- Answer the easiest questions first.
- Answer all the questions unless you are instructed not to.
- Check your answers, but be careful not to change correct answers to incorrect answers.
- Don't let other students see your answers. (You may be accused of cheating.)
- When a test is returned, study your incorrect answers to learn how you might do better on the next test the teacher gives.

Reduce Your Test Anxiety

Test anxiety is the uneasiness or apprehension students experience because they must take a test. Check the statements in the following checklist that describe you.

Test Anxiety Checklist

- ❑ I worry about failing tests.
- ❑ I do not sleep well the night before a test.
- ❑ I sometimes try to figure out how I can avoid taking a test.
- ❑ Before or during a test I often perspire excessively, have an upset stomach, feel my heart beating rapidly, or experience shortness of breath.
- ❑ I have difficulty concentrating when I take tests.
- ❑ While taking tests, I am often unable to recall information that I learned.
- ❑ I make foolish mistakes when I answer test questions.
- ❑ I become upset when I don't know the answer to a test question.
- ❑ I become very nervous if time runs out before I am able to answer all the questions on a test.
- ❑ While taking tests, I worry that other students will finish before me or do better than me.

All students experience some test anxiety; however, if you checked five or more items in this list, you suffer from a greater amount of test anxiety than most students do.

Because anxiety results from fear, you can usually avoid test anxiety by preparing thoroughly for tests, using the methods that are explained in Chapters 13 through 20. If you are well prepared for a test, you will not have much to fear. Be certain you attend all test reviews and that you learn the answers to all the questions in the checklist on page 123 before each test.

It is also important to arrive at tests well rested and without rushing. You will not do your best on a test if you are tired or if you have created unnecessary anxiety for yourself by rushing into the test room at the last minute. Also, ignore students who are nervously quizzing each other or cramming; the negative energy they generate could cause you to become upset and lose your concentration.

In addition, knowing and using good test-taking procedures will help you to reduce test anxiety. Anxiety directs thoughts inward, to think about discomfort; but good test-taking methods direct thoughts outward, to think about answering test questions correctly. If you use the methods that are explained in this chapter and in Chapters 22 through 27 when you take tests, you will be so busy in the worthwhile pursuit of answering questions correctly that your mind will probably not turn to futile thoughts of fear of taking tests.

If you become excited during a test, keep in mind that it is normal to be excited and that excitement can help you do your best, in the same way it helps athletes do their best during athletic competition. You may also find that the following exercise helps you to relax when you are anxious.

Relaxation Exercise

- Without actually smiling, relax your face and feel yourself smiling on the inside.
- Take a very deep breath—a breath so deep that you imagine it reaches to the soles of your feet.
- Then, still smiling inside, let your breath out very slowly.

If you cannot conquer test anxiety by using these methods, seek professional help. Many colleges have counselors who provide assistance to students who experience acute and disabling test anxiety.

Preview Tests

Before you answer any questions on a test, survey it to learn what types of questions you must answer, whether questions are printed on one or both sides of each page, and where you must write your answers.

Then read the test directions; they may be different from what you expect. For example, students usually expect that they are to answer all questions on tests; however, the directions for the essay test in Figure 21.1 instruct students to answer only two of the four questions. Students who answer all four questions make a serious mistake because they will not receive credit for their answers to the third and fourth questions (and their answer to the third or fourth question might be better than their answer to the first or second question).

FIGURE 21.1
An Essay Test

Test: Mass Communication

Answer any two of the following four questions. Each answer has a value of 50 points. You have 50 minutes to write your answers.

1. What part should the media play in changing the public's attitudes and opinions?
2. Compare the importance of movies as a mass medium in the 1940s to their importance today.
3. What issues and problems would each of the following disciplines emphasize in studying mass communication: psychology, sociology, and linguistics?
4. What questions and issues are of concern when studying broadcasting from a content point of view?

Listen to Everything Teachers Say

It is absolutely essential to listen attentively to everything that teachers say on test days. Before tests they often explain directions that give students difficulty, and during tests they sometimes warn students about typographical errors on tests.

Also, when there are only a few students left in a test room, instructors sometimes answer questions or make comments that help the remaining students give a correct answer to a difficult question. If you leave a test room before the end of a test period, you may miss information other students received and used to answer a question correctly.

Plan Test-taking Time

Because there is often too little time to answer all test questions, you must plan how to use the available time. Allocate your test-taking time by finding the answers to the following questions.

Questions to Ask for Planning Test-taking Time

- How many questions must I answer?
- How many points is each question worth?
- How much time do I have to answer the questions?

For example, a student took a psychology test with the following directions: "You have fifty minutes to answer twenty-five multiple-choice questions (2 points each) and five short-answer questions (10 points each)." He computed that the multiple-choice questions had a value of 50 points ($2 \times 25 = 50$) and the short-answer questions had a value of 50 points ($10 \times 5 = 50$). Therefore, he allotted twenty-five minutes for answering the multiple-choice questions and twenty-five minutes for answering the short-answer questions (about one minute for each multiple-choice question and about five minutes for each short-answer question).

Answer the Easiest Questions First

After you have planned how to use your test-taking time, determine which questions are easiest to answer and answer these questions first. There are at least three benefits to answering the easiest questions before answering the more difficult ones.

Reasons You Should Answer the Easiest Questions First

- **You will answer all the questions you can answer correctly**, in case time runs out before you answer all the questions. When test-taking time is limited, do not waste it trying to answer questions that you will almost certainly answer incorrectly.
- **You might think of answers to some of the difficult questions**. While you are answering other questions, you will often remember answers to questions that you could not answer the first time you read them.

■ **You might find answers to some of the difficult questions.** True-false and multiple-choice questions are sometimes interrelated, so that one question suggests the correct answer to another question. As you take tests, look for information in questions that can help you select correct answers to other questions that you could not answer the first time you read them.

When you answer true-false or multiple-choice questions, read each question twice and answer it or move on to the next question. When you have read each question twice and answered as many as you can, reread the first unanswered question twice again and answer it or move on to the next unanswered question. Work through the test in this way as many times as necessary to select an answer to each question.

Check the time every ten minutes to make certain that you are answering questions at the rate that will help you get the highest possible score. During the last minute or two of the test period, mark some answer for each question. For instance, you might mark all unanswered true-false questions *true*, and you might mark *c* for all unanswered multiple-choice questions.

Write Clearly

When you take tests, remember that your teachers have to read your answers. Be considerate of them—write using the best handwriting you possibly can while working under the pressure of time limitations. Also, write clearly when you answer true-false and multiple-choice questions. Do not write a *T* that could be mistaken for an *F*, an *a* that looks like a *d*, or a *c* that resembles an *e*. All teachers are familiar with these ploys, and they are annoyed by students who use them.

Usually Answer All Questions

Give an answer to every question on a test unless you are specifically told not to answer all questions, as on an essay test (see Figure 21.1 on page 245). When you do not know an answer to a true-false or a multiple-choice question, guess the answer—you might guess correctly.

When you guess the answer to a true-false question, you have a 50 percent chance of guessing the correct answer. There is a 50 percent chance the answer is true and a 50 percent chance the answer is false. When you guess the answer to a multiple-choice question with four answers (*a*, *b*, *c*, and *d*), you have a 25 percent chance of guessing the correct answer. There is a 25 percent chance the answer is *a*, a 25 percent chance the answer is *b*, and so on.

Check Your Answers

Always carefully check your answers before you give a test to a teacher. If, after careful consideration, you are certain you answered questions incorrectly, write the correct answers, but cross out the original answers in a way that leaves them visible. After the teacher has graded your test, analyze whether you tend to change incorrect answers to correct answers or change correct answers to incorrect answers. If you find that you have a tendency to change correct answers to incorrect ones, you will want to use extreme care in changing test answers in the future.

Ignore Other Test Takers

Do you ever worry that students who finish a test before you may receive higher grades than you? If so, there is no need to have this concern. Some of the people who finish tests quickly do receive high test grades, but others complete tests quickly because they do not know the answers to many questions. Some students who finish tests last receive the highest test grades because they use every minute of test-taking time to make certain that their answers are correct. Therefore, when you take a test, ignore other students and concentrate on answering questions correctly.

Also, if a classmate should ever ask you to share answers to test questions, don't do so. If another student is poorly prepared for a test, do not let this be your problem. If you let another student read your test answers, you may be accused of cheating; those who allow others to read their answers are as guilty of cheating as those who read them! Cheating in college is a serious offense that could result in disciplinary action or dismissal. Therefore, during tests, sit so other students cannot see your answers (and so you cannot see their answers).

Learn from Incorrect Responses

Test taking is a skill, and skills are improved by making mistakes and learning not to make them. For instance, if you are a good automobile driver, you have learned not to make mistakes you made while you were learning to drive. Similarly, you may become an expert test taker by learning not to make mistakes that you now make when you take tests.

When tests are returned to you, analyze them to understand why you answered questions incorrectly. You may decide that you did not plan test-taking time carefully enough or that you did not review class notes as much as you should have. You may also find it helpful to discuss your incorrect test answers with classmates and teachers. Use what you learn from your analyses and discussions to do better when you take future tests.

EXERCISE 21.1 ## Planning Test-taking Time

Practice planning test-taking time by answering the following questions.

1. You have fifty minutes to solve ten mathematical problems, which have a value of 10 points each. How many minutes should you spend solving each problem?

   _____

2. You have one hour and forty minutes to answer four essay questions. One answer has a value of 40 points and three answers have a value of 20 points

each. How many minutes should you plan to spend answering the 40-point question?

_____

How many minutes should you plan to spend answering each of the 20-point questions?

_____

3. You have sixty minutes to answer twenty-five multiple-choice questions and ten short-answer questions. The multiple-choice questions have a value of 2 points each, and the short-answer questions have a value of 5 points each. How many minutes should you plan to spend answering the twenty-five multiple-choice questions?

_____

How many minutes should you plan to spend answering each short-answer question?

_____

EXERCISE 21.2   **Test-taking Methods Checklist**

Use the following checklist to evaluate your test-taking strategies. Write checks in pencil so you can erase them and reuse the checklist after each test you take.

- ❑ I prepared for the test using the methods that are explained in Chapters 13 through 20 of *College Study Skills*.
- ❑ Before I answered any questions, I surveyed the test to learn what types of questions I would answer, whether questions were printed on both sides of pages, and where to write answers.
- ❑ I read the test directions and followed them exactly.
- ❑ I listened attentively to everything the teacher said before and during the test.
- ❑ I planned my test-taking time carefully so I was able to answer all the questions for which I knew answers.
- ❑ I checked the time every ten minutes to make certain that I would answer questions at the rate that would help me get the highest possible score.
- ❑ I answered the easiest questions first.
- ❑ I picked up extra points by correctly guessing the answers to some questions.
- ❑ I double-checked my answers after I wrote them.
- ❑ I was careful not to let any classmate see my answers during the test.
- ❑ When the test was returned, I studied my incorrect answers to learn how I might do better on the next test.

If there is a statement you did not check, use it as a hint to how you might do better the next time you take a test for the course.

<u>**EXERCISE 21.3**</u>   **"Developing a Professional Presence"**

This is the fifth of five exercises for applying study skills to the sample textbook chapter on pages 299–319 of the appendix. The other exercises are for previewing (Exercise 17.2), marking books (Exercise 18.9), making notes (Exercise 19.9), and reciting and rehearsing (Exercise 20.4).

Test Taking

You may take a true-false, multiple-choice, or short-answer test your instructor distributes, or you may answer some of the following questions.

15-Point Questions

Check the boxes in front of the four questions in the following list that your instructor requests you to answer. Each correct answer has a maximum value of 15 points.

❑   1. What is a professional presence?

❑   2. What is the primacy effect?

❑   3. Why are the first few minutes of a meeting extremely important?

❑   4. Give examples of stereotypes that are sometimes used to form impressions of others during a first meeting.

❑   5. According to Susan Bixler, what three factors should influence your choice of clothing for work?

❑   6. What is the business casual look?

❑   7. How can your handshake create a positive impression?

40-Point Question

Check the box in front of the question in the following list that your instructor requests you to answer. A correct answer has a maximum value of 40 points.

❑   8. Discuss the basic points regarding business dress about which most wardrobe engineering experts agree.

❑   9. Explain the rules of etiquette that are particularly important to working in an organization.

True-False Questions

True-false questions are statements that test takers must decide are either true or false. They are well suited for testing whether students have learned facts such as the following:

❑ T ❑ F   The United States entered World War II in 1941.

The United States either entered World War II in 1941 or it did not. It did; the statement is true.

   True-false questions are easy for teachers to write and grade, and students can answer them in a very short time. As a result, true-false questions appear frequently in tests for psychology, history, business, and other college courses for which instructors want to determine whether students have learned factual information.

   Following is a summary of the methods for answering true-false questions that are explained in this chapter.

How to Answer True-False Questions

Answer all questions that you know are true or false. When you are uncertain whether a question is true or false, use the following hints to help in locating statements that are likely to be false:

■ Questions that contain extreme modifiers such as *always, all, only,* and *never* tend to be false.

■ Questions that state a reason tend to be false (and they often contain the words *reason, because,* or *therefore*).

When you are uncertain whether a statement is true or false, guess that it is true.

Assume Statements Are True

When you answer true-false questions on college tests, mark *true* those statements that you know are true and mark *false* those that you know are false. When you are uncertain whether a statement is true or false, assume it is true. The reason for assuming that statements are true is that there is a definite *tendency* for true-false tests to include more true statements than false ones. As a result, when you guess the answer to a true-false question, you are more likely to guess the correct answer if you guess it is true.

However, keep in mind that a true-false statement is false if any part of it is false. For example,

❑ T   ❑ F   George Washington, Benjamin Franklin, and Abraham Lincoln were presidents of the United States.

This statement is false because Benjamin Franklin was not a president of the United States.

Extreme Modifiers

A **modifier** is a word that limits meaning, such as *old* in the phrase "old man." **Extreme modifiers** are words such as *all, always, only,* and *never,* which do not allow for exceptions—they tend to appear in false statements. However, statements that include modifiers such as *some, frequently, many,* and *sometimes,* which do allow for exceptions, tend to appear in true statements. Compare the following statements.

❑ T   ❑ F   **All** businesses adopt and use new technology.
❑ T   ❑ F   **Many** businesses adopt and use new technology.

The first statement is false, but the second statement is true. All businesses do not adopt and use new technology, but many of them do. Compare the following false and true statements, paying attention to the words printed in boldface.

False Statements	True Statements
1. Parents **always** love their children.	1. Parents **usually** love their children.
2. **All** children love chocolate.	2. **Many** children love chocolate.
3. The **only** reason people work is to earn money.	3. A **major** reason people work is to earn money.
4. Men are **never** secretaries.	4. Men are **seldom** secretaries.
5. **Nobody** reads dictionaries for pleasure.	5. **Few** people read dictionaries for pleasure.

The false statements in the left column contain extreme modifiers, such as *always* and *all,* which do not allow for exceptions. Following are more examples of extreme modifiers.

Extreme Modifiers Often in False Statements

all	none	best	absolutely
always	never	worst	absolutely not
only	nobody	everybody	certainly
invariably	no one	everyone	certainly not

The true statements in the right column on page 252 contain modifiers such as *usually* and *many*, which allow for exceptions. Following are more examples of these kinds of modifiers.

Modifiers Often in True Statements

usually	frequently	often	sometimes
some	seldom	many	much
probably	a majority	apt to	most
might	a few	may	unlikely

Some students have difficulty deciding which words are extreme modifiers. If you have this problem, keep in mind that an extreme modifier is simply a modifier that identifies the greatest degree and does not allow for exceptions, such as *always*. In contrast, *usually*, *frequently*, and *often* are not extreme modifiers—they are modifiers that allow for exceptions.

Though true-false statements that contain extreme modifiers tend to be false, they can, of course, be true. For instance,

❑ T   ❑ F   Identical twins are **always** the same sex.

This statement is true; if twins are not the same sex, they are not identical.

Reasons

True-false questions that state reasons tend to be false, either because they state an incorrect reason or because they do not state all the reasons. For instance,

❑ T   ❑ F   The **reason** the government protects consumers is that consumer lobbyists fought for this protection.

This statement is false because it states an incomplete reason. The government protects consumers as a result of the actions of *many* groups and individuals who were not or are not necessarily lobbyists. Though we tend to think of the consumer movement as a new force in our society, it has been very strong since the 1880s and it was not started by lobbyists.

The following true-false questions illustrate that the statement of a reason does not have to contain the word *reason*.

❑ T   ❑ F   The government protects consumers **because** lobbyists fought for this protection.

❑ T   ❑ F   Consumer lobbyists fought to protect consumers; **therefore** the government now protects them.

The words *because* and *therefore* indicate that these true-false questions state reasons.

True-false questions that state reasons can, of course, be true. For instance,

❑ T   ❑ F   Stores make much use of newspaper advertising **because** it is low in cost and has a high impact on consumers.

This statement is true—it gives two of the reasons stores use newspaper advertising.

Exercises 22.1 through 22.5 provide practice in learning how to select correct answers to true-false questions; the answers to the questions in the exercises are correct according to the sources on which they are based. Use what you learn by doing the exercises to answer more true-false questions correctly on college tests.

Negatives and Double Negatives

When you answer test questions, be alert for **negative** words, such as *not*, and negative prefixes, such as *un-*. Compare the following questions, paying special attention to the word *not*, which is printed in boldface in the second version of the question.

❑ T   ❑ F   Alcohol is a depressant.
❑ T   ❑ F   Alcohol is **not** a depressant.

The first statement is true, but the word *not* in the second statement makes it false.

Also, compare the following questions, paying special attention to the negative prefix *un-*, which is printed in boldface in the first version of the question.

❑ T   ❑ F   Most **un**saturated fats are of vegetable origin.
❑ T   ❑ F   Most saturated fats are of vegetable origin.

The prefix *un-* in the first statement makes it true, but the second statement is false.

Negatives   *Not* and *cannot* are the most common negative words. Following are the most common negative prefixes. Learn any that are new to you.

Prefix	Example
un-	**Un**truthful means **not** truthful.
non-	**Non**alcoholic means **not** alcoholic.
in-	**In**direct means **not** direct.
im-	**Im**perfect means **not** perfect.
il-	**Il**legal means **not** legal.
ir-	**Ir**responsible means **not** responsible.
dis-	**Dis**agreeable means **not** agreeable.

Double Negatives   Test writers also sometimes include double negatives in questions. **Double negatives** are statements that include two negatives, usually *not* and a negative prefix. A double negative is printed in boldface in the following sentence.

She is **not un**intelligent.

To interpret a statement of this type, cross out both negatives.

She is ~~not un~~intelligent.

Then read the statement as though it contains no negatives.

She is intelligent.

"She is not unintelligent" means "she is intelligent."

The most common double negatives are printed in boldface in the following list on the left.

Double Negative	Interpretation
not untruthful	truthful
not nonalcoholic	alcoholic
not indirect	direct
not imperfect	perfect
not illegal	legal
not irresponsible	responsible
not disagreeable	agreeable

Exercises 22.6 and 22.7 provide practice in interpreting statements that include negatives and double negatives.

EXERCISE 22.1   True-False Questions

The following statements are true, except for those that have an extreme modifier or that state a reason. Check **T** for true statements and **F** for false statements. When you check **F**, underline the word in the statement that indicates it is false.

1. ❑ T   ❑ F   Young people tend to consider as necessities many products that adults categorize as luxuries.

2. ❑ T   ❑ F   Criminologists are concerned only with the reasons people commit crimes and not with what happens to people after they are imprisoned.

3. ❑ T   ❑ F   We do not know for certain what causes lightning.

4. ❑ T   ❑ F   Men seem to fall in love more quickly and easily than women.

5. ❑ T   ❑ F   Laws do nothing to diminish discrimination because it is not possible to legislate morality.

6 ❑ T   ❑ F   All people are psychologically mature at age eighteen.

7. ❑ T   ❑ F   The right hemisphere of the brain is believed to be the center for nonverbal reasoning.

8. ❑ T   ❑ F   The reason for underlining textbooks is that, if they are underlined, students do not need to make notes on the information in them.

9. ❑ T   ❑ F   The halo effect refers to the tendency always to rate individuals positively.

10. ❑ T   ❑ F   Joggers can maintain the same physical fitness as runners by jogging the same distances that runners run.

11. ❑ T   ❑ F   Markup pricing complicates the process of deciding what prices to charge for products; therefore, retailers do not use it often.

12. ❑ T   ❑ F   In the past, population growth was sometimes controlled by killing newborn babies.

EXERCISE 22.2 True-False Questions

The following statements are true, except for those that have an extreme modifier or that state a reason. Check **T** for true statements and **F** for false statements. When you check **F**, underline the word in the statement that indicates it is false.

1. ❑ T ❑ F International trade is not vital to our economy because we are the world's leading economic and military power.

2. ❑ T ❑ F In American society, people tend to marry others who are much like themselves with regard to age, social class, education, and so on.

3. ❑ T ❑ F Prejudice is based only on fear, ignorance, and cultural conditioning.

4. ❑ T ❑ F During the Civil War, more Northern soldiers died from diseases or accidents than from combat.

5. ❑ T ❑ F Psychologists have shown that all six-year-olds can perform the thinking skills needed to learn to read.

6. ❑ T ❑ F College graduates usually earn more money than high school graduates.

7. ❑ T ❑ F People who divorce and remarry are more likely to divorce than people who marry for the first time.

8. ❑ T ❑ F The reason tropical Africa has a very good agricultural economy is that it has a very long growing season.

9. ❑ T ❑ F The decision to commit suicide is never made suddenly or impulsively.

10. ❑ T ❑ F Gambling is usually more profitable to organized crime than either prostitution or drugs.

11. ❑ T ❑ F The Old Testament does not report an incident in which a woman was put to death for sleeping with a man other than her husband.

12. ❑ T ❑ F It makes sense to choose a college major in the same field as one's intended career because most graduates are employed in the general field of their college major.

EXERCISE 22.3   True-False Questions

The following statements are true, except for those that have an extreme modifier or that state a reason. Check **T** for true statements and **F** for false statements. When you check **F**, underline the word in the statement that indicates it is false.

1. ❑ T ❑ F   The United States has one of the most severe systems for punishing criminals in the civilized world.

2. ❑ T ❑ F   Highly talented people always have highly positive self-concepts.

3. ❑ T ❑ F   Of the slaves who were taken from Africa, approximately 6 percent were brought to the United States.

4. ❑ T ❑ F   The population is increasing rapidly in less developed countries of the world because of the high birthrates in those regions.

5. ❑ T ❑ F   People are more likely to be murdered in their homes by somebody they know than on the streets by a stranger.

6. ❑ T ❑ F   Women seem to fall out of love more quickly and with less difficulty than men.

7. ❑ T ❑ F   Colorblindness is a vision problem of men, but never of women.

8. ❑ T ❑ F   Average weekly movie attendance in the United States dropped from 90,000,000 in the 1940s to 22,5000,000 in the 1980s.

9. ❑ T ❑ F   There are almost as many independent nations in Africa as there are states in the United States.

10. ❑ T ❑ F   Churchmen formed the only substantial block of white Southerners who criticized slavery during the years before the Civil War.

11. ❑ T ❑ F   Women have less education than men; therefore, they earn less money than men.

12. ❑ T ❑ F   Sleep was not scientifically investigated until recently because there was no interest in this subject until after World War II.

EXERCISE 22.4 **True-False Questions**

The following statements are true, except for those that have an extreme modifier or that state a reason. Check **T** for true statements and **F** for false statements. When you check **F**, underline the word in the statement that indicates it is false.

1. ❑ T ❑ F   The reason Napoleon sold Louisiana to the United States was that he feared we would take it by force.

2. ❑ T ❑ F   It is healthy for us to express our anger.

3. ❑ T ❑ F   Most human behavior is learned.

4. ❑ T ❑ F   Stock certificates must be issued by all corporations.

5. ❑ T ❑ F   People judge others on traits they are born with, such as height, skin color, hairiness, and nose shape.

6. ❑ T ❑ F   Psychologists agree that our value systems are always formed by the time we are six years old.

7. ❑ T ❑ F   Drug pushers usually become members of criminal organizations because they themselves are addicted and need a source of drugs.

8. ❑ T ❑ F   Today, retail stores are staffed largely by part-time sales workers.

9. ❑ T ❑ F   The lack of black police officers is due to the fact that there is discrimination against well-qualified black applicants for positions in the police force.

10. ❑ T ❑ F   Most jobs contain some dreary activities.

11. ❑ T ❑ F   Employers provide orientation for new employees only.

12. ❑ T ❑ F   There are at least 7,000 people in the United States over one hundred years old.

EXERCISE 22.5   True-False Questions

The following statements are true, except for those that have an extreme modifier or that state a reason. Check **T** for true statements and **F** for false statements. When you check **F**, underline the word in the statement that indicates it is false.

1. ❑ T ❑ F   People of similar intellectual levels tend to marry one another.

2. ❑ T ❑ F   Despite great temptation, President Lincoln never used political deception or trickery.

3. ❑ T ❑ F   When "senseless" violence occurs, it is always illegal and usually brought about by the victim.

4. ❑ T ❑ F   A powerful narcotic was at one time an ingredient in Coca-Cola.

5. ❑ T ❑ F   American women were not guaranteed the right to vote until 1920.

6. ❑ T ❑ F   Convertible bonds are considered to be more conservative investments than nonconvertible bonds because they may be exchanged for common stock.

7. ❑ T ❑ F   Many couples maintain an active sexual relationship into their sixties and seventies.

8. ❑ T ❑ F   States with the death penalty actually have higher rates of murder than states without it.

9. ❑ T ❑ F   The tone of your voice often creates a strong positive or negative impression.

10. ❑ T ❑ F   When employees are fired it is usually because they lack the technical skills to do their jobs.

11. ❑ T ❑ F   Children with hearing and vision difficulties should be taught only by specially trained teachers.

12. ❑ T ❑ F   All property will increase in value; therefore, the purchase of real estate is a good hedge against inflation.

EXERCISE 22.6 **Negatives**

In the following pairs of questions, one statement contains a negative word or prefix and the other one does not. Underline the negatives, and check **T** for true statements and **F** for false statements.

1. ❑ T ❑ F   Most people really do not want to work.
   ❑ T ❑ F   Most people really do want to work.

2. ❑ T ❑ F   Job security is unimportant to most workers.
   ❑ T ❑ F   Job security is important to most workers.

3. ❑ T ❑ F   Psychologists agree on the definition of intelligence.
   ❑ T ❑ F   Psychologists disagree on the definition of intelligence.

4. ❑ T ❑ F   Lack of ability to do work is the reason given most often for firing workers.
   ❑ T ❑ F   Lack of ability to do work is not the reason given most often for firing workers.

5. ❑ T ❑ F   Lateness or absence from work is a frequent reason given for firing workers.
   ❑ T ❑ F   Lateness or absence from work is an infrequent reason given for firing workers.

6. ❑ T ❑ F   When you want to help friends who have a problem, it is well to be impatient with them.
   ❑ T ❑ F   When you want to help friends who have a problem, it is well to be patient with them.

7. ❑ T ❑ F   When you want to learn about an occupation by reading published materials, it is relevant when the material was published.
   ❑ T ❑ F   When you want to learn about an occupation by reading published materials, it is irrelevant when the material was published.

8. ❑ T ❑ F   American society has no social classes.
   ❑ T ❑ F   American society has social classes.

EXERCISE 22.7 Double Negatives

Cross out the double negatives in the following statements, and check **T** for true statements and **F** for false statements.

Part 1

1. ❑ T ❑ F Fine crystal drinking glasses are not unbreakable.

2. ❑ T ❑ F A lie is not an untrue statement.

3. ❑ T ❑ F People can write if they are not illiterate.

4. ❑ T ❑ F The totally blind are not unable to see.

5. ❑ T ❑ F Milk is not a nonalcoholic beverage.

6. ❑ T ❑ F A straight line is not an indirect path between two points.

7. ❑ T ❑ F We trust those whom we know we cannot distrust.

8. ❑ T ❑ F If a painting by a dead artist is destroyed by fire, it is not irreplaceable.

Part 2

1. ❑ T ❑ F A surprise is something that is not unexpected.

2. ❑ T ❑ F One million dollars is not an insubstantial sum of money.

3. ❑ T ❑ F Under federal law, it is not illegal to pay women less than men for doing the same or similar work.

4. ❑ T ❑ F Friends should not be inconsiderate of our feelings.

5. ❑ T ❑ F It is not dishonest to tell the truth.

6. ❑ T ❑ F Unfinished work is work that is not uncompleted.

7. ❑ T ❑ F Identical objects are not dissimilar.

8. ❑ T ❑ F It is not unwise to be alert for double negatives in test questions.

Multiple-Choice Questions

Multiple-choice questions are incomplete statements followed by possible ways to complete them or they are questions followed by possible answers. The incomplete statement or question that begins a multiple-choice question is called the **stem,** and the choices for answers are written so that one is the correct answer and the others are **distracters.**

1. United States senators serve
   - ❑ a. two-year terms.
   - ❑ b. four-year terms.
   - ❑ c. six-year terms.
   - ❑ d. eight-year terms.

In this example, the stem is "United States senators serve." The question is written with the intention that students who know the correct answer will select *c* (six-year terms), whereas other students will be distracted and select one of the distracters—*a*, *b*, or *d*.

Following is a summary of the methods for answering multiple-choice questions that arc explained in this chapter.

How to Answer Multiple-Choice Questions

1. Anticipate the answer to a question and look for it among the choices by eliminating the distracters.
2. Answer all questions for which you know the correct answer.
3. When you are uncertain of a correct answer, look for clues to correct answers:
   - "All of the above"
   - one of two similar-looking answers
   - the most inclusive answer

4. When you cannot find a clue to a correct answer, look for clues to incorrect answers:
   - an extreme modifier (such as *always*)
   - an unfamiliar term
   - a joke or insult
   - the highest and lowest number in a set

Popularity of Multiple-Choice Questions

There are at least three reasons multiple-choice questions are popular among college teachers.

Reasons for Popularity of Multiple-Choice Questions

- They can be used to test all aspects of students' knowledge and their ability to reason using information they have learned.
- When answers are recorded on answer sheets, multiple-choice answers are easy to grade.
- Students with poor writing ability are not penalized when they answer multiple-choice questions (as they may be when they are required to give written answers to questions).

For these reasons, you will probably take many multiple-choice tests during your college career.

Anticipate Answers and Eliminate Distracters

Multiple-choice questions are prepared by first writing a stem and the correct answer. For instance,

2. A speech that has as its purpose to inform how to plan a successful party must use
   - ❑ a. exposition.
   - ❑ b.
   - ❑ c.
   - ❑ d.

After putting this much on paper, the question writer then fills in the distracters and decides where to locate the correct answer. As a result, the test taker's job is to locate the correct answer that was "hidden" by the question writer. This is done by anticipating the answer to a question and by looking for it among the choices by eliminating the distracters.

One way to eliminate distracters is to analyze a multiple-choice question as though it is a series of true-false questions. For instance,

❑ T ❑ F   a. United States senators serve two-year terms.
❑ T ❑ F   b. United States senators serve four-year terms.
❑ T ❑ F   c. United States senators serve six-year terms.
❑ T ❑ F   d. United States senators serve eight-year terms.

Most multiple-choice questions are actually a series of true-false statements, only one of which is true. When you answer a multiple-choice question, analyze it to eliminate distracters and to select as the correct answer the choice that makes the stem a true statement.

Clues to Correct Answers

When you have difficulty eliminating the distracters in a multiple-choice question, analyze it for the following clues to correct answers.

"All of the Above"   When "all of the above" is a choice in a multiple-choice question, it tends to be the correct answer. Check the correct answer to the following question.

3. Teenage love involves
    ❑ a. sexual attraction.
    ❑ b. crushes.
    ❑ c. a search for identity.
    ❑ d. all of the above

You should have checked *d*; it is the correct answer.
   The question could, of course, have been written so that "all of the above" is not the correct answer. Check the correct answer to the following question.

4. Teenage love involves
    ❑ a. crushes.
    ❑ b. expensive dates.
    ❑ c. guilt and shame.
    ❑ d. all of the above

According to the source on which this question is based, the correct answer is *a*; however, keep in mind that in college tests "all of the above" is the correct answer much more frequently than it should be.
   Also, when you know that two answers are correct and another choice is "all of the above," you must select "all of the above" as the correct answer. For instance,

5. Silver is used to make
    ❑ a. knives and forks.
    ❑ b. jewelry.
    ❑ c. film for photography.
    ❑ d. all of the above

If you know that silver is used to make knives, forks, and jewelry, you must select "all of the above" as the correct answer even if you do not know that it is also used to make film for photography. If you select *a*, you do not include jewelry; if you select *b*, you do not include knives and forks. You must select *d* to include knives, forks, and jewelry in your answer.

Two Similar-looking Answers   When two answers are similar looking, the correct answer is often one of the two similar-looking answers. Check the correct answer to the following question.

6. In the brain, language functions are associated mainly with the
   - ☐ a. left hemisphere.
   - ☐ b. right hemisphere.
   - ☐ c. cerebellum.
   - ☐ d. corpus callosum.

You should have eliminated answers *c* and *d* and made your choice between the two similar-looking answers *a* and *b*. The correct answer is *a*.

Question writers sometimes write multiple-choice questions to eliminate the clue to two similar-looking answers. For instance,

7. Loss of all sensation in your hand would most likely result from damage to
   - ☐ a. afferent spinal nerves.
   - ☐ b. efferent spinal nerves.
   - ☐ c. afferent cranial nerves.
   - ☐ d. efferent cranial nerves.

When questions are written in this way, you cannot use two similar-looking answers as a clue to the correct answer, which in this case is *a*.

Most Inclusive Answer   When one answer to a multiple-choice question is more inclusive than other answers, it is likely to be the correct answer. Check the most inclusive answer to the following question.

8. Output devices on computers produce
   - ☐ a. a permanent copy.
   - ☐ b. a soft copy.
   - ☐ c. both *a* and *b*
   - ☐ d. none of the above

You should have checked *c*, which includes the possibilities stated in answers *a* and *b*; answer *c* is the most inclusive answer, and it is also the correct answer.

It can be a challenge to identify the most inclusive answer. Check the most inclusive answer to the following question.

9. Weight is likely to vary most among a group of
   - ☐ a. men who are football linebackers.
   - ☐ b. women who are ballet dancers.
   - ☐ c. people who are jockeys.
   - ☐ d. people who are college students.

Football linebackers tend to include only heavy people; women ballet dancers and jockeys tend to include only light people. College students, though, include people who are heavy, light, and medium in weight. Answer *d* is the most inclusive, and it is the correct answer.

Clues to Incorrect Answers

When you find no clue to a correct answer in a multiple-choice question, analyze it to see if you can find one of the following clues to incorrect answers.

Extreme Modifiers   In Chapter 22, you learned that extreme modifiers tend to be included in true-false questions that are false; in multiple-choice questions, extreme modifiers tend to appear in distracters. Underline the extreme modifiers in the following question and check the correct answer.

10. Mentally healthy people
     ❑ a. never change their goals.
     ❑ b. are always happy when alone.
     ❑ c. are sometimes anxious or afraid.
     ❑ d. never examine their mistakes.

You should have underlined *always* and *never*, and you should have checked *c*.

Unfamiliar Terms   Unfamiliar terms or phrases are often included in distracters. Underline the unfamiliar terms in the following question and check the correct answer.

11. Mass hysteria results when large numbers of people
     ❑ a. believe something that is not true.
     ❑ b. fear an invasion of iconoclasts.
     ❑ c. have concomitant exigencies.
     ❑ d. share incontrovertible perceptions.

You should have underlined *iconoclasts, concomitant exigencies*, and *incontrovertible perceptions*; and you should have checked *a*. The only time it is wise to pick answers with unfamiliar terms is when you are certain that all the other answers are incorrect. For instance,

12. Jeans are always
     ❑ a. dark blue.
     ❑ b. well worn.
     ❑ c. too tight.
     ❑ d. bifurcated.

You know that jeans are not always dark blue, well worn, or too tight; therefore, you are forced to conclude that they are *bifurcated*, even though you probably don't know the meaning of the word. To bifurcate is to divide into two parts or branches; the legs of jeans are in two parts, one for each leg. Skirts, in contrast, are not bifurcated.

Jokes or Insults   Answers that are jokes or insults are usually distracters. Check the answer in the following question that is not ridiculous or insulting.

13. A common reason students give for leaving college is that they
    ❑ a. aren't smart enough to do college work.
    ❑ b. find that they dislike other college students.
    ❑ c. are treated badly by their instructors.
    ❑ d. decide that something else interests them more.

Answers *a*, *b*, and *c* are either ridiculous or insulting; you should have eliminated them as distracters and checked *d*, which is the correct answer.

Extreme Numbers   When answers are a series of numbers that go from high to low, the extreme numbers (the highest and lowest ones) tend to be incorrect. Answer the following question by eliminating the extreme numbers as distracters.

14. According to the U.S. Department of Agriculture, how many servings of vegetables should we eat each day?
    ❑ a. one to three
    ❑ b. two to four
    ❑ c. three to five
    ❑ d. four to six

You should have eliminated the extreme numbers in answers *a* and *d* and made your choice between *b* and *c*. The correct answer is *c*. According to the U.S. Department of Agriculture, we should eat three to five servings of vegetables and two to four servings of fruit each day.

EXERCISE 23.1 **Multiple-Choice Questions**

Use the clues to correct and incorrect answers summarized on pages 263–264 to select the correct answers to the following questions.

1. Learning how to play the piano while singing occurs in the
   - ❑ a. motor domain.
   - ❑ b. cognitive domain.
   - ❑ c. affective domain.
   - ❑ d. motor and cognitive domain.

2. After the Civil War, Reconstruction legislatures in the South were successful in
   - ❑ a. making prison reforms.
   - ❑ b. integrating public schools.
   - ❑ c. improving facilities for the handicapped.
   - ❑ d. achieving all of the foregoing.

3. On June 21, the sun is found directly over the
   - ❑ a. tropic of Cancer.
   - ❑ b. tropic of Capricorn.
   - ❑ c. equator.
   - ❑ d. North Pole.

4. The normal adult temperature of 98.6°F is equivalent to
   - ❑ a. 18°C.
   - ❑ b. 27°C.
   - ❑ c. 37°C.
   - ❑ d. 42°C.

5. Those who believe in the work ethic believe that
   - ❑ a. all people will do good work.
   - ❑ b. hard work is always rewarded.
   - ❑ c. work is good and important.
   - ❑ d. only workers should receive money.

6. The biosphere consists of
   - ❑ a. air above the earth.
   - ❑ b. the earth's surface.
   - ❑ c. bodies of water on earth.
   - ❑ d. air, earth surface, and water bodies.

7. The median is a measure that is similar to
   - ❑ a. the average.
   - ❑ b. a histogram.
   - ❑ c. the skewness.
   - ❑ d. a coefficient.

8. Educators refer to individuals of very low intelligence as
   - ❑ a. idiots.
   - ❑ b. morons.
   - ❑ c. imbeciles.
   - ❑ d. totally dependent.

9. Studies of workers' attitudes have found that
   - ❑ a. most workers feel they should have better jobs.
   - ❑ b. many workers would rather have better jobs than more pay.
   - ❑ c. workers are motivated by conflicting drives.
   - ❑ d. all of the above.

10. Children begin to understand some of the concepts associated with religious beliefs when they are
    - ❑ a. toddlers.
    - ❑ b. preschoolers.
    - ❑ c. school aged.
    - ❑ d. teenagers.

EXERCISE 23.2   Multiple-Choice Questions

Use the clues to correct and incorrect answers summarized on pages 263–264 to select the correct answers to the following questions.

1. Most Jewish immigrants to the United States came from
   - ❑ a. Eastern Europe.
   - ❑ b. Western Europe.
   - ❑ c. Israel.
   - ❑ d. Africa and Asia.

2. Partners in a marriage are likely to be similar in
   - ❑ a. height and weight.
   - ❑ b. hair and skin color.
   - ❑ c. general health.
   - ❑ d. size, coloring, and health.

3. People work because they
   - ❑ a. need to feel productive.
   - ❑ b. must pay for necessities.
   - ❑ c. want to achieve dignity.
   - ❑ d. all of the above.

4. Brazil was colonized by
   - ❑ a. Indians.
   - ❑ b. North Americans.
   - ❑ c. a heterogeneous group of Europeans.
   - ❑ d. a homogeneous group of Europeans.

5. A zero-growth family is one that has
   - ❑ a. no children.
   - ❑ b. one child.
   - ❑ c. two children.
   - ❑ d. three children.

6. Members of one's family of orientation are
   - ❑ a. blood relatives.
   - ❑ b. affinal relatives.
   - ❑ c. tertiary relatives.
   - ❑ d. misogynistic relatives.

7. The difficulty of reading material can be estimated by studying the lengths of
   - ❑ a. words.
   - ❑ b. sentences.
   - ❑ c. both *a* and *b*.
   - ❑ d. none of the above.

8. Which of the following statements about ability is true?
   - ❑ a. People differ in their abilities.
   - ❑ b. All people are equal in abilities.
   - ❑ c. There is only one basic type of ability.
   - ❑ d. Ability never changes over one's lifetime.

9. More doctors are males than females, probably because
   - ❑ a. women don't want prestigious jobs.
   - ❑ b. of established occupational expectations.
   - ❑ c. males make better doctors.
   - ❑ d. most women crack under pressure.

10. A common physical symptom of depression is
   - ❑ a. constipation.
   - ❑ b. decreased pulse.
   - ❑ c. decreased blood pressure.
   - ❑ d. all of the above.

EXERCISE 23.3 Multiple-Choice Questions

Use the clues to correct and incorrect answers summarized on pages 263–264 to select the correct answers to the following questions.

1. About how much time should one spend doing aerobic activity to attain top conditioning?
   ❑ a. 1 hour 6–7 days a week
   ❑ b. ½ hour 3–5 days a week
   ❑ c. ¼ hour 3–5 days a week
   ❑ d. ½ hour 6–7 days a week

2. Harmony between one's beliefs and behavior is called
   ❑ a. cognitive consonance.
   ❑ b. cognitive dissonance.
   ❑ c. personality agreement.
   ❑ d. belief-system integration.

3. Our sexual attitudes develop
   ❑ a. solely from what we learn from our parents.
   ❑ b. from positive and negative sexual experiences.
   ❑ c. from satisfying sexual experiences.
   ❑ d. from unfortunate sexual experiences.

4. The burning of fossil fuel is causing a build-up of carbon dioxide that may eventually
   ❑ a. affect the global radiation balance.
   ❑ b. create a warming trend on earth.
   ❑ c. irreversibly alter world ecosystems.
   ❑ d. all of the above.

5. In the 1840s, the great potato famine in Ireland resulted from
   ❑ a. wet weather.
   ❑ b. dry weather.
   ❑ c. population growth.
   ❑ d. potato disease.

6. Which of the following age groups most commonly experiences frightening dreams?
   ❑ a. two-year-olds
   ❑ b. three-year-olds
   ❑ c. six-year-olds
   ❑ d. adolescents

7. The abbreviation SEM refers to a type of
   ❑ a. serological technique.
   ❑ b. anaerobic bacteria.
   ❑ c. microscope.
   ❑ d. avian embryo.

8. In New England prior to 1780, there were
   ❑ a. no banks.
   ❑ b. no schools.
   ❑ c. no hospitals.
   ❑ d. Both *a* and *c*.

9. If a five-year-old says, "I flied to New York," this indicates that the child
   ❑ a. has ignorant parents.
   ❑ b. has inferior intelligence.
   ❑ c. knows language rules but not their exceptions.
   ❑ d. prefers using incorrect grammatical forms.

10. Cancers cells
    ❑ a. lack contact inhibition.
    ❑ b. are "immortal."
    ❑ c. will not readily rejoin cells of the organ from which they originate.
    ❑ d. all of the above.

EXERCISE 23.4 **Multiple-Choice Questions**

Use the clues to correct and incorrect answers summarized on pages 263–264 to select the correct answers to the following questions.

1. If worry over a pet's safety prevents a person from leaving
home more than twice a week,
he or she is
   - ❑ a. obsessive-compulsive.
   - ❑ b. a dipsomaniac.
   - ❑ c. somewhat abnormal.
   - ❑ d. a fruitcake.

2. The first book published in the
New World was printed in
   - ❑ a. Peru in 1473.
   - ❑ b. New York in 1486.
   - ❑ c. Mexico in 1539.
   - ❑ d. Massachusetts in 1626.

3. The return to a less mature
behavior pattern is called
   - ❑ a. repression.
   - ❑ b. regression.
   - ❑ c. reaction formation.
   - ❑ d. none of the above.

4. A nurse's first concern upon
discovering a fire is to
   - ❑ a. close doors and windows.
   - ❑ b. put out the fire.
   - ❑ c. safeguard patients.
   - ❑ d. set off the fire alarm.

5. Engaging in aerobic exercise at
least three times a week may
produce
   - ❑ a. positive body perception.
   - ❑ b. more endorphins in the
     brain.
   - ❑ c. cardiovascular
     conditioning.
   - ❑ d. all of the above.

6. Mary jogs every day because it
makes her feel good about
herself. She is motivated by
   - ❑ a. an intrinsic reward.
   - ❑ b. an extrinsic reward.
   - ❑ c. a psychological need.
   - ❑ d. peer-group pressure.

7. Children begin to understnad
that death is final when they
are about
   - ❑ a. 5–6 years old.
   - ❑ b. 8–9 years old.
   - ❑ c. 11–13 years old.
   - ❑ d. 15–16 years old.

8. The central processing unit of a
computer
   - ❑ a. controls computer
     operations.
   - ❑ b. performs arithmetic
     operations.
   - ❑ c. contains memory for the
     program and data.
   - ❑ d. all of the above.

9. The major problem with selling
beverages in throwaway cans is
that these containers
   - ❑ a. create costly garbage-
     disposal problems.
   - ❑ b. are expensive to make
     and dispose of.
   - ❑ c. use a great deal of
     expensive metal.
   - ❑ d. require much expensive
     energy to produce.

10. Most psychologists agree that
   - ❑ a. institutionalized children
     never succeed in life.
   - ❑ b. fatherless boys always
     become homosexuals.
   - ❑ c. unloved infants often have
     personality problems.
   - ❑ d. abused children always
     abuse their own children.

Examples in Questions

Questions on college tests may often be stated in ways that are impossible for you to anticipate. The surprise of reading questions worded in ways that you do not expect may unnerve you and cause you to select incorrect answers to questions that you would otherwise answer correctly.

Examples in Stems

If you learn in a psychology course that *frustration* is that which prevents a person from reaching a goal, you could probably correctly answer questions about the definition of *frustration*. However, you may have difficulty correctly answering questions that require you to analyze an *example* of frustration, such as the one in the stem of the following question.

1. John earns a good salary at a job he doesn't like. He has a chance to get a job doing something he would like to do, but the pay is so low that it won't give him the money he needs for his family. So he's still working at his old job. John's frustration is
   ❑ a. his feelings of unhappiness and discontent.
   ❑ b. the present job that he doesn't like.
   ❑ c. the job that he would like to have.
   ❑ d. the low pay for the job he'd like to have.

To answer this question, you must compare the example in the stem to the definition of *frustration* (that which prevents a person from reaching a goal). You must ask yourself, "What is John's goal?" and "What is preventing him from reaching it?" John's goal is to have a job he would like, but he is prevented from reaching his goal because the job he would like pays too little money. The correct answer to the question is *d*.

Examples in Answers

A multiple-choice question may have examples in answers rather than in the stem, as in the following question:

2. Which of the following statements does *not* contain a frustration?
   ❑ a. Al wants to be a doctor, but he can't get into medical school.
   ❑ b. Ann wants to go to work, but she has children to care for.
   ❑ c. Bob wants to be a firefighter, but he isn't tall enough.
   ❑ d. Mary wants to be a dancer, but she also wants to be a singer.

To answer this question, you must compare examples in the answers to the definition of *frustration* (that which prevents a person from reaching a goal). You must ask questions such as the following to eliminate the distracters.

- For *a*, ask "Does this state what is preventing Al from reaching his goal of being a doctor?" Yes, he cannot get into medical school.

- For *b*, ask, "Does this state what is preventing Ann from reaching her goal of going to work?" Yes, she has children to care for.

- For *c*, ask, "Does this state what is preventing Bob from reaching his goal of being a firefighter?" Yes, he is not tall enough.

- For *d*, ask, "Does this state what is preventing Mary from reaching her goal of being a singer or dancer?" No, singers may be dancers and dancers may be singers.

The correct answer is *d*; it does *not* state a frustration.

The following exercises provide practice in answering multiple-choice questions that have examples in stems or answers. By doing the exercises, you should become more confident that you will select correct answers to these types of questions when they appear on tests you take for your college courses.

EXERCISE 24.1   **Examples in Questions**

Answer the questions about the passages by eliminating distracters and checking the boxes in front of correct answers.

A **euphemism** is an acceptable or inoffensive word or phrase used to describe something that is distasteful, unpleasant, or intimate. "I'm going to wash my hands" is sometimes a euphemism for "I'm going to use the toilet." "Not too good-looking" is a euphemism when it's used to describe an extremely ugly object or person.

1. Which of the following is *not* a euphemism for describing an elderly person?
   - ❑ a. She's a senior citizen.
   - ❑ b. She's in her golden years.
   - ❑ c. She has the benefit of experience.
   - ❑ d. She's older than God.

2. Which of the following is *not* a euphemism for describing a person who has died?
   - ❑ a. He kicked the bucket.
   - ❑ b. He passed away.
   - ❑ c. He went to his reward.
   - ❑ d. He is enjoying eternal rest.

The **one-plus-one rule** is a useful but seldom-taught spelling rule. It applies when (1) joining two words, (2) joining a prefix and a base word, and (3) joining a base word and a suffix. The basic idea is that when elements begin and end with the same consonant at the place where they are joined, both consonants are kept. Thus, *jack* plus *knife* is *jac**kk**nife*; *mis-* plus *spell* is *mi**ss**pell*; and *brown* plus *-ness* is *brow**nn**ess*.

3. Which of the following correctly spelled words does *not* follow the one-plus-one rule?
   - ❑ a. glowworm
   - ❑ b. soulless
   - ❑ c. eighteen
   - ❑ d. dissimilar

4. According to the one-plus-one rule, which of the following words is spelled correctly?
   - ❑ a. unecessary
   - ❑ b. newstand
   - ❑ c. transshipment
   - ❑ d. bathouse

EXERCISE 24.2   Examples in Questions

Answer the questions about the passages by eliminating distracters and checking the boxes in front of correct answers.

Palindromes are words, phrases, or sentences that spell the same backward and forward: for instance, *radar, civic,* and *nun.* The most famous palindromic sentence is probably "A man, a plan, a canal—Panama," which is spelled *amanaplanacanalpanama* forward and backward.

1. Which of the following is *not* a palindrome?
   - ❑ a. noon
   - ❑ b. repaper
   - ❑ c. pump
   - ❑ d. level

2. Which of the following is *not* a palindrome?
   - ❑ a. a Toyota
   - ❑ b. Don't give in.
   - ❑ c. Dennis sinned.
   - ❑ d. Madam, I'm Adam.

The **average** is found by adding numbers together and dividing the sum by the total number of numbers. To find the average of 5, 7, and 9, add the numbers (21) and divide by the number of numbers (3); the average is 7. The **median** is the middle number in a set—it has the same number of numbers above and below it. The median for the following numbers is 7: 2, 2, 7, 8, 9.

3. What is the median for the following set of numbers: 2, 4, 6, 5, 8, 2, 1?
   - ❑ a. 2
   - ❑ b. 4
   - ❑ c. 5
   - ❑ d. 6

4. What are the average and median for the following set of numbers: 4, 6, 8, 8, 9?
   - ❑ a. 6
   - ❑ b. 9
   - ❑ c. 7 and 8, respectively
   - ❑ d. 6 and 8, respectively

EXERCISE 24.3   **Examples in Questions**

Answer the questions about the passages by eliminating distracters and checking the boxes in front of correct answers.

Phonemes are the sounds that are heard when words are spoken. For example, the word *can* has three phonemes (*k, a,* and *n*). Many words have more letters then phonemes. For instance, *wreck* has five letters but only three phonemes (*r, e,* and *k*).

1. Which of the following is *not* a phoneme?
   - ❑ a. n
   - ❑ b. r
   - ❑ c. c
   - ❑ d. k

2. How many phonemes are there in the word *laugh?*
   - ❑ a. two
   - ❑ b. three
   - ❑ c. four
   - ❑ d. five

In a court action, the **plaintiff** is the one who claims a wrong has been done, and the **defendant** is the one who is accused of having done the wrong. For instance, if your landlord takes you to court because you do not pay rent, you are the defendant and your landlord is the plaintiff.

3. When Harry's luggage was lost, he took an airline company to court, but the company said Harry lost the luggage. The airline company was the
   - ❑ a. aggressor.
   - ❑ b. prosecutor.
   - ❑ c. defendant.
   - ❑ d. plaintiff.

4. Ted and Alice are married, but Ted runs around with Freda, and Alice goes out with Tony. Alice is taking Ted to court to divorce him. Who is the plaintiff?
   - ❑ a. Freda
   - ❑ b. Tony
   - ❑ c. Ted
   - ❑ d. Alice

EXERCISE 24.4   **Examples in Questions**

Answer the questions about the passages by eliminating distracters and checking the boxes in front of correct answers.

Open questions are ones that call for rather long answers. For instance, "What are some of your favorite ways to spend leisure time?" is an open question. **Closed questions** are ones that can be answered in a word or two. For instance, "How old are you?" is a closed question.

1. Which of the following is an open question?
   - ❑ a. Do you have a job?
   - ❑ b. How can you become a better conversationalist?
   - ❑ c. Where did you eat lunch on Friday?
   - ❑ d. What grade did you get for your chemistry course?

2. Which of the following is a closed question?
   - ❑ a. What can you do to earn higher grades?
   - ❑ b. What can your teachers do to help you learn?
   - ❑ c. How can you answer more test questions correctly?
   - ❑ d. Do you think it's worthwhile to study test-taking skills?

Parents engage in **sex-typing** when they encourage their children to behave in ways that have been traditionally considered appropriate for males and females. For instance, when parents encourage a son to wrestle but discourage a daughter from wrestling, they are sex-typing.

3. Parents are sex-typing when they encourage a
   - ❑ a. girl to ride a bike.
   - ❑ b. boy to care for a cat.
   - ❑ c. girl to clean house.
   - ❑ d. boy to learn to cook.

4. Which of the following is *not* an example of sex-typing?
   - ❑ a. Telling a boy not to cry
   - ❑ b. Teaching a boy to fight back
   - ❑ c. Telling a girl to be sweet
   - ❑ d. Teaching a girl to fight back

Matching Questions

Matching questions present two lists of items and require test takers to associate items in one list with items in the other list. In properly written questions, all items in each list are similar. For example, the following matching question for a music appreciation course requires students to match operas with their composers.

Music Appreciation

_____	1. *Dido and Aeneas*	a. Puccini
_____	2. *Don Giovanni*	b. Mozart
_____	3. *Tosca*	c. Monteverdi
_____	4. *Tristan and Isolde*	d. Purcell
_____	5. *Orfeo*	e. Wagner
_____	6. *Rigoletto*	f. Donizetti
_____	7. *Carmen*	g. Verdi
_____	8. *Lucrezia Borgia*	h. Bizet

It is extremely difficult to guess correct answers to properly written matching questions, such as this one. If you guess at the composers of the operas, you are not likely to guess more than one correct answer.

Answering Matching Questions

When you answer a matching question, scan both lists to understand the types of items you are to match, and then use one list as the starting place for making all the matches. Take care to match only those items that you are absolutely certain are matches because each time you make a mistake, you will be led to

279

make another error. For instance, if you match *3* with *b* when you should match *3* with *f*, you will make the mistake of matching *3* with an incorrect letter and you will make another mistake when you match *f* with an incorrect number.

Following is a summary of the methods for answering matching questions that are explained in this chapter.

How to Answer Matching Questions

- Examine both lists to understand the types of items you are to match.
- Use one list as the starting place for making all the matches.
- If one list has longer statements, use it as the starting place for making matches.
- Cross out items as you match them.

Match first only those items that you are certain are matches. If possible, use logical clues to match items about which you are uncertain.

Lists with Longer Statements

If one list in a matching question has longer statements, use the list of longer statements as the starting place for making matches. For example,

Introduction to Business

_____	1. advertising media	a. telling customers that an advertised special is sold out but offering them a more expensive substitute
_____	2. sales promotion	b. nonpaid information about the company or its products in the mass media
_____	3. bait-and-switch	c. the element of promotional strategy other than personal selling, advertising, and publicity
_____	4. promotional mix	d. radio, TV, newspapers, magazines, and direct mail
_____	5. publicity	e. combination of advertising, personal selling, sales promotion, and publicity
_____	6. frequency	f. average number of times an advertising message reaches a person or household

There are only eleven words in the first column of this matching question, but there are sixty-eight words in the second column. Therefore, if you use the column with the longer statements as the starting place for making matches, you will not have to read through all of the long items each time you attempt to make a match.

Logical Clues

When matching questions are improperly prepared, you may be able to use logical clues to figure out answers to them, as in the following improperly prepared matching question for a psychology course.

Psychology

_____ 1. located in the ear   a. James B. Watson

_____ 2. behaviorist   b. ideographic study

_____ 3. childhood crisis   c. frequency distribution

_____ 4. tally of scores   d. to trust others

_____ 5. study of an individual   e. organ of Corti

Because this question is improperly written, you should be able to use logical clues to guess some correct answers to it. For example, you will not match *1* with *a* because you know that James B. Watson is not located in the ear. Guess the answers.

EXERCISE 25.1   Starting with Longer Answers

Use the list with the longer statements as the starting place to make matches. Match first only those items that you are certain are matches and cross out items as you match them.

_____   1. lecture

_____   2. syllabus

_____   3. curriculum

_____   4. mnemonic

_____   5. acronym

_____   6. dean

_____   7. bibliography

_____   8. registrar

_____   9. tutor

_____ 10. bursar

_____ 11. appendix

_____ 12. transcript

a. a word made from the initial letters of other words

b. the part of a book that contains any supplementary materials or information

c. a list of the books, articles, or other sources of information that are referred to by a writer

d. the title of a person at a college who is responsible for money transactions

e. a member of the administration of a college who is in charge of specified aspects of the school's functioning

f. a talk during which an instructor communicates information to students

g. a device used to aid memory

h. the title of a person at a college who is responsible for registering students in courses and for maintaining their academic records or transcripts

i. a summary or outline distributed by an instructor that states the main topics to be discussed in a course

j. the official record of courses taken, grades received, and grade point averages

k. a person who gives individual instruction to students

l. the courses required to earn a particular degree

EXERCISE 25.2   **Using Logical Clues**

Use logical clues to locate the correct answers to the following poorly written matching questions. Match first only those items that you are certain are matches and cross out items as you match them.

_____ 1. indentured servant

_____ 2. largest city on the eve of the American Revolution

_____ 3. He established the American factory system.

_____ 4. She advocated better care for the insane.

_____ 5. state where Prohibition was strongest

_____ 6. number of Southern slaves in 1860

_____ 7. painters of American life

_____ 8. the Fourteenth Amendment

_____ 9. contribution of black musicians

_____ 10. needed for frontier farming

_____ 11. describes U.S. policy toward Indians

_____ 12. average yearly income in 1890

_____ 13. percent of population living in cities in 1910

_____ 14. popular nineteenth-century entertainment

_____ 15. year the Great Depression started

a. Maine

b. made blacks citizens

c. thirty-eight

d. barbed wire

e. temporary laborer

f. Currier and Ives

g. 1929

h. $486

i. Samuel Slater

j. 4,000,000

k. Dorothea Dix

l. two-faced

m. melodrama

n. jazz

o. Philadelphia

EXERCISE 25.3   Guessing Answers

In order to understand how difficult it is to guess the answers to well-written questions, try to match the items in the right column to the names in the left column. If you are unfamiliar with the facts being tested, you should make no more than one correct match by guessing at the answers. Use all but one of the items in the right column, and use an item one time only.

_____   1. Democritus   a. Law of Triads

_____   2. Van Helmont   b. naming of cathode rays

_____   3. Proust   c. conceived of the atom

_____   4. Berzelius   d. discovered sulfanilamide

_____   5. Döbereiner   e. discovered DDT

_____   6. Zeidler   f. Law of Definite Composition

_____   7. Gelmo   g. discovered element 106

_____   8. Urey   h. first atomic pile

_____   9. Goldstein   i. modern symbols for elements

_____ 10. Fermi   j. discovered deuterium

                                    k. foundations of chemical physiology

Fill-in Questions

Fill-in questions are statements with deleted portions that test takers must supply. For instance,

> Approximately _____ percent of American land is devoted to the raising of crops.

It is usually impossible to guess the correct answers to fill-in questions that appear on college tests. If you do not know how much American land is devoted to raising crops, you are not likely to guess the correct answer (17 percent).

Following is a summary of the methods for answering fill-in questions that are explained in this chapter.

How to Answer Fill-in Questions

- Decide what type of answer is required.
- When a question contains two blanks with a space between them, give a two-word answer.
- When a blank is preceded by the word *an*, give an answer that begins with a vowel (*a, e, i, o,* or *u*).

Decide the Type of Answer

The basic strategy for answering a fill-in question is to decide what type of answer is required. What type is needed for this question?

> After reading _____, President Theodore Roosevelt ordered an investigation of the meat-packing industry.

You should have decided that the answer for this question is the name of a book, magazine, newspaper, or other written material. However, it is probably impossible that you would have guessed the answer is a book titled *The Jungle*.

When it is unclear what type of answer is required, ask the instructor for clarification. For instance,

Alexander Hamilton was born in _____.

Because it is unclear what type of answer is needed for this question, you might ask a teacher, "Do you want me to give the place where he was born or the year in which he was born?" Prepare your question carefully. Don't, for example, point to a question and ask a teacher, "What do you mean?" Request clarification by asking questions that help your teacher understand why you are confused. (Alexander Hamilton was born on the island of St. Kitts in the West Indies; the year was 1755.)

Two Blanks

When a fill-in question contains two blanks with a space between them, a two-word answer is required. For instance,

Always and *never* are examples of _____ _____.

If you studied Chapters 22 and 23, you should know that the correct answer to this question is *extreme modifiers*.

The "An" Clue

The word *an* before a blank is a clue that the answer is a word that begins with a vowel sound, such as those represented by the letters *a, e, i, o,* and *u.* For instance,

Compliments satisfy an _____ need.

Those who have studied the basic human needs know that they are of five basic types: physiological, safety, social, esteem, and self-realization. The word *an* before the blank suggests that the correct answer is the human need that begins with a vowel; the correct answer is *esteem*. However, most instructors eliminate this clue by writing *a(an)*, *a(n)*, or *a/an* instead of *an* before blanks.

EXERCISE 26.1 Fill-in Questions

Guess the answers to the following questions to understand that it is practically impossible to guess the correct answers to fill-in questions.

1. The sixth letter of the Greek alphabet is _____.

2. Mukilteo is located in the state of _____.

3. Tirana is the capital of _____.

4. There are _____ inches in a rod.

5. The two parts of a ratchet are a wheel and a(n) _____.

The basic strategy for answering a fill-in question is to decide what type of answer is required and to give that type of answer. Use the words in the following list to write the type of answers required by the following nine fill-in questions: Walt Whitman; morpheme; fifteen; 1962; 4,160; first; cyclone; sadist; Hinduism.

6. The Nile River is approximately _____ miles long.

7. Until as recently as _____, slavery existed somewhere in the world.

8. It was _____ _____ who said, "In the faces of men and women I see God."

9. A(n) _____ killed 300,000 people in Bangladesh on November 13, 1970.

10. A person who derives pleasure from causing others to suffer physical or mental pain is a(n) _____.

11. A(n) _____ is the smallest unit of language that has meaning.

12. One belief of _____ is that life in all forms is an aspect of the divine.

13. If a federal court gives a criminal a life sentence, the earliest possible parole date is after _____ years of the sentence have been served.

14. United States presidents enjoy the highest public support during the _____ year of their terms.

EXERCISE 26.2   **Fill-in Questions**

The following fill-in questions are based on information in Chapters 21 through 25 of *College Study Skills.*

1. Test anxiety is uneasiness or _____ students experience because they need to take a test.

2. When you guess the answer to a multiple-choice question with four answers (*a, b, c,* and *d*), you have a _____ change of guessing the correct answer.

3. Cheating in college is a serious offense that could result in disciplinary action or _____.

4. When you are uncertain whether a true-false question is true or false, assume it is _____.

5. A true-false question that contains a(n) _____ _____ such as *always* or *never* tends to be false.

6. True-false questions that state reasons often contain the word *reason, because,* or _____.

7. True-false questions tend to be _____ when they state a reason.

8. Double negatives are statements that include two negatives, usually *not* and a(n) _____ _____.

9. The incomplete statement or question that begins a multiple-choice question is called the _____.

10. Jokes and insults tend to be _____ answers in multiple-choice questions.

11. High and low numbers tend to be _____ answers in multiple-choice questions.

12. If one list in a matching question has short statements and the other list has long statements, use the list of _____ statements as the starting place for making matches.

Essay Questions

Essay questions require written responses that are usually a paragraph or more in length.

Students are often instructed not to answer all questions on essay tests. For example, the directions for the essay test in Figure 27.1 on page 290 state that students are to answer only three of the five questions. They will be penalized if they answer more than three questions, because only one of the 50-point answers and two of the 25-point answers will be graded. A good answer to the fifth question on the test is illustrated in Figure 27.2 on page 291.

Following is a summary of the instructions in this chapter.

How to Answer Essay Questions

Use these six procedures when you answer essay questions.

1. Give the type of answer the direction words call for.
2. Answer all parts of questions.
3. Write well-organized answers.
   - Plan the major points.
   - Write an introduction that summarizes the answer.
   - Make the major points stand out.
   - Write a conclusion that reveals your mastery of subject matter or that makes an interesting suggestion.
4. Write complete answers.
   - Include all the information that is relevant to the answer.
   - Write as though you are explaining the subject to a person who is uninformed about it (such as a friend or relative) rather than to a teacher.

5. Write answers that are easy for you to proofread and easy for your teachers to read.
   - Write or print neatly.
   - Use an erasable ballpoint pen, so you can correct errors.
   - Write only on right-hand pages of bluebooks, so you can write additions and changes on left-hand pages.
   - Indent each paragraph.
   - Leave one-inch margins on all four sides of answers.
6. Proofread your answers before you give them to your instructor.

FIGURE 27.1

An Essay Test

Sociology Test

Write your answers to the following questions in the booklet that you have been given. Answer any one of the 50-point questions and any two of the 25-point questions. You have 60 minutes to write your answers.

Answer One (50 points)
1. Describe the five principal types of societies.
2. Compare the functionalist and ecological approaches to understanding cultural variation.

Answer Two (25 points each)
3. Discuss the effects of isolation during childhood on human development.
4. Contrast Freud's, Cooley's, and Mead's theories of how the self emerges.
5. Explain what norms are.

Students often write answers to essay questions in **bluebooks**, which are small booklets that contain lined paper. At one time, the covers of these booklets were always blue, but today covers of bluebooks may be blue, yellow, pink, or some other color.

Variations of the essay test include take-home and open-book tests. A **take-home test** can be test questions that students actually answer at home or test questions that they study at home but answer in class. The questions on take-home tests are usually more difficult than the questions on tests students see for the first time in class. Also, teachers tend to grade answers to take-home tests very strictly.

An **open-book test** is a test during which students may refer to textbooks, and sometimes to notes, as they answer questions. The term open-book is misleading because it suggests that students can copy answers to questions from books; however, open-book tests seldom include questions for which answers can be copied. Whatever benefit students gain by referring to books is directly related to how thoroughly they have studied. Prepare for an open-book test just as you would for any other type of test.

FIGURE 27.2

An Answer to the Fifth Question in Figure 27.1

Norms are guidelines for how people should behave in particular situations; they include folkways, mores, and taboos.

Folkways are norms that pertain to things people do in everyday life. Placing refrigerators in kitchens, watching TV now and then, and eating hot dogs at ball games are some of our folkways. These behaviors are expected but not demanded.

Mores are norms that prohibit such behaviors as theft, murder, and rape. Society severely punishes those who violate mores.

Taboos are norms for behaviors that are unthinkably repulsive. In our society the taboo against eating human flesh is so strong that many states have no law against it. Also, sexual relationships between parents and children are taboos in most societies.

Some norms apply to all members of a society, and others do not. For instance, in the United States nobody may be married to more than one person. However, although we have a norm against killing others, it does not apply to soldiers and police officers in certain situations.

Understand Direction Words

The first step in answering an essay question is to interpret correctly the meanings of direction words. **Direction words** are italicized in the following questions.

Describe the five principal types of societies.
Explain the benefits of aerobic exercise.

Before you take an essay test, learn the meanings of the following direction words. Pay special attention to the often misinterpreted meanings of *compare, criticize, analyze,* and *justify.*

Direction Words

- **Discuss.** Write as much as you can. "Discuss test-taking skills."
- **Describe.** Write about the subject so it can be visualized. "Describe a nutritious diet."

- **Diagram.** Draw a picture and label its parts. "Diagram the parts of the human ear."
- **Illustrate.** Give a long written example. "Illustrate the use of the SQ3R study formula."
- **Enumerate** or **list.** Make a numbered list. "Enumerate (or list) good and bad listening habits."
- **Outline.** Make a numbered or well-organized list. "Outline basic test-taking strategies."
- **Summarize.** Briefly state. "Summarize the accomplishments of President Truman."
- **Define.** Give the meaning. "Define *psychopath*."
- **Relate.** Discuss the connection between topics. "Relate television viewing to reading habits."
- **Trace.** Discuss in a logical or chronological sequence. "Trace the path by which blood flows through the human body."
- **Explain.** Discuss reasons. "Explain why the United States entered World War II."
- **Compare.** Discuss similarities and differences. "Compare democracy and socialism."
- **Contrast.** Discuss differences. "Contrast Catholicism with Protestantism."
- **Criticize** or **evaluate.** Discuss good and bad points of the subject and conclude whether it is primarily good or bad. "Criticize (or evaluate) the death sentence."
- **Argue.** Give reasons for or against a statement. "Argue whether it is morally right or wrong to condemn criminals to death."
- **Analyze.** Discuss the parts of something and show how the parts are related. "Analyze the marketing strategies of Coca-Cola® and Pepsi-Cola®."
- **Justify** or **defend.** Discuss good and bad points and conclude that it is good. "Justify (or defend) U.S. expenditures on military defense."

Answer All Parts of Questions

Failure to answer all the parts of essay questions is a major reason students sometimes get lower grades on essay tests than they should. Compare the following questions.

Relate cigarette smoking to heart disease.
Relate cigarette smoking to heart disease and cancer.

The first question has one part, but the second question has two parts. Answers to the second question must explain how cigarette smoking is related to (1) heart disease and (2) cancer. Answers that respond to only one part of the question will not receive full credit.

Sometimes essay questions are not clearly written. When you cannot understand an essay question, ask the teacher who wrote it for clarification. It is appropriate for you to assume that your teachers want you to understand their test questions.

Write Well-organized Answers

After you have interpreted the direction words and identified all parts of an essay question, write a well-organized answer by planning the major points, by writing a good introduction, and by making major points stand out clearly.

Plan the Major Points   Sometimes the major points you should include in your answers are directly stated in essay questions. For instance,

> Define the following terms: folkways, mores, and taboos.

The three major points to include in the answer are stated in the question; they are definitions of the three terms listed at the end of the question. However, the question is worded in the following way in the essay test illustrated in Figure 27.1 on page 290.

> Explain what norms are.

To answer this question, students must recall that folkways, mores, and taboos are three types of norms.

Write an Introduction   A good introduction to an essay question is a clear summary of the answer. If an answer has several parts, the introduction should state the parts in the way illustrated in the first paragraph of the essay answer in Figure 27.2 on page 291.

When a question requires an answer with one major point, summarize the major point of your answer clearly in the introduction. For example,

Question	Introduction to Answer
Explain whether you believe that advertising benefits consumers.	In my opinion, advertising does not benefit consumers.

Other students may have written, "I believe that advertising benefits consumers." Whichever point of view is taken, it should be clearly stated in the introduction.

Make Major Points Stand Out   Notice in Figure 27.2 on page 291 that major points stand out because they appear in first sentences of paragraphs and because key terms are underlined for additional emphasis. If major points in your essay stand out clearly, it will be easier for your teachers to grade your answers. If you write answers that are easy to read, teachers may show their appreciation by giving your answers higher grades than they give for answers that are difficult for them to figure out.

Write a Conclusion   Write a conclusion that reveals your mastery of subject matter or that makes an interesting suggestion. The conclusion of the essay in Figure 27.2 on page 291 demonstrates that the writer knows more about norms than is needed to give a complete answer to the question. If you write an answer in which you explain why you believe advertising does not benefit consumers, you might conclude it with suggestions about ways in which advertising could better serve the public.

FIGURE 27.3

Comparison of a Short and a Long Answer to a Question

Use point value as a guide in deciding the length and completeness of answers. Compare these examples of a 10-point and a 50-point answer to a question.

Question

What are the four speech-making strategies and how do they differ?

10-point response

There are four basic speech-making strategies. Impromptu speeches are presented on the "spur of the moment"; the speaker has no time to organize or rehearse. Extemporaneous speeches are organized in outline form but are not written word for word. Manuscript speeches are written in advance and then read from a written or typed copy. Memorized speeches are written in advance and then learned word for word, to be presented without a written copy. These four strategies allow speakers to suit their presentations to their speaking situations.

50-point response

Situations for speech making vary and speakers, as a result, choose among four different speech-making strategies to present their ideas most effectively.

Impromptu speeches are given on the "spur of the moment"; the speaker has no chance to organize or rehearse. These highly informal speeches are often unfocused (because they are unplanned) and ineffective (because they were not rehearsed), but they are the usual kinds of speeches given at organization meetings and in class discussions.

Extemporaneous speeches are given from prepared outlines, but they are not completely written. Rather, speakers decide what to discuss and what details or examples to use, and then they choose words as they speak. Extemporaneous speeches have the advantage of being organized, but at the same time they are flexible, allowing speakers to modify what they say to suit the needs of their audiences. For this reason, they are often the most effective speeches at informal meetings.

Manuscript speeches are written in complete form and then read, much like a newscast. Because they are prepared in advance, manuscript speeches are well organized and carefully worded. If they are also well rehearsed, manuscript speeches are effective in formal speaking situations because they present an exact, well-worded version of the speaker's ideas.

Memorized speeches are written in complete form and then committed to memory. Because they are carefully prepared, they often present solid content, but few speakers can memorize a lengthy speech and deliver it well. In addition, memorized speeches are not flexible and only work in highly formal circumstances, like awards ceremonies and formal banquets.

Because of the differences among these four speech-making strategies—in organization, presentation, and flexibility—they provide speakers with a number of ways to share ideas with audiences.

Write Complete Answers

As a general rule, teachers give the highest grades to those answers that include the most relevant information. It is almost always better to include too many facts and details than to include too few. Whenever you are uncertain whether to include a relevant piece of information or example, include it.

You must, of course, use the point value for an answer as a guide in deciding the length and completeness of your answer. Figure 27.3 above contains a 10-point and a 50-point answer to an essay question on a fifty-minute essay test. Compare the one-paragraph 10-point answer to the six-paragraph 50-point answer.

If you tend to write answers to essay questions that are too short, write them thinking that they will be read by a friend or relative rather than by a teacher. The thought that your answers will be read by a person who is uninformed about the subject might help you to write more complete answers and to explain your thoughts more clearly.

An essay test may be printed on sheets of paper with spaces on the paper for writing answers. When a space is not large enough for a complete answer, continue the answer on the back of the page. For instance, if there is not enough space to write a complete answer to a third question, write as much as you can in the space provided and then write *over* in parentheses. On the other side of the page, write 3 and complete the answer.

Write Easy-to-Read Answers

Some teachers give lower grades to sloppy papers written in hard-to-read handwriting. Therefore, write neatly so that your answers are easy for your teachers to read and grade.

- Use an erasable ballpoint pen so you can erase mistakes and correct them.
- Write answers only on right-hand pages of bluebooks so that when you proofread you can write additions and changes on the blank left-hand pages.
- Indent each new paragraph, and leave margins that are at least one inch wide at the top, bottom, left, and right of your answers.

Writing neatly will also help you in proofreading your answers.

Proofread Your Answers

You cannot do your best writing when you answer essay questions under the pressure of time limitations; therefore, plan for time to proofread answers after you write them.

When you proofread, correct errors in spelling, punctuation, and grammar, and add additional relevant information if you can. Any improvements you make when you proofread will benefit you when your answers are graded.

What to Do If Time Runs Out

It is essential to plan test-taking time carefully when answering essay questions (see page 246). However, no matter how carefully you plan, you will not always have enough time to write complete answers to all questions on an essay test. If you do not write an answer, a teacher will assume that you do not know the answer; and if you write a very short answer, a teacher will assume it is the best answer you can write.

One solution to this problem is to write an outline for the answer you would write if you had sufficient time, show it to the teacher, and request additional time to write the complete answer. Another solution is to simply tell a teacher that you did not have enough time to write an answer. A reasonable teacher will offer a solution to this problem.

EXERCISE 27.1   Direction Words

Learn the meanings of the direction words on pages 291–292 and write them on the lines beneath the following questions. Do **not** answer the questions.

1. **Compare** your college teachers to your high school teachers.

_____

2. **Criticize**, or **evaluate**, this statement: "All college teachers should correct spelling and grammatical errors in papers they receive from students."

_____

_____

_____

3. **Justify**, or **defend**, guessing at correct answers to true-false and multiple-choice questions.

_____

_____

4. **Argue** whether or not the United States should adopt a health plan similar to the one in Canada.

_____

_____

5. **Illustrate** how you have used study suggestions explained in *College Study Skills*.

_____

6. **Enumerate** the guidelines for underlining textbooks.

_____

7. **Relate** the use of effective study skills to good grades on college tests.

_____

_____

8. **Trace** the path of the last trip you took.

_____

_____

9. **Analyze** the appeal of last year's three highest-grossing movies.

_____

_____

Direction Words

Learn the meanings of the direction words on pages 291–292 and write them on the lines beneath the following questions. Do **not** answer the questions.

1. **Contrast** your college teachers with your high school teachers.

_____

2. **Diagram** the room in which you are sitting.

_____

3. **Discuss** three types of social mobility.

_____

4. **Describe** clothing you enjoy wearing because it is good looking and comfortable.

_____

5. **Explain** why you have chosen the curriculum in which you are enrolled.

_____

6. **Outline** the characteristics of multiple-choice questions that are sometimes hints to incorrect and correct answers.

_____

7. **Summarize** the basic strategies for answering true-false, multiple-choice, and fill-in questions.

_____

8. **Define** the following: appendix, glossary, references.

_____

EXERCISE 27.3   **Answering All Parts of Questions**

To receive full credit, an answer to an essay question must respond to all parts of the question. Number the parts of the following questions in the way that is illustrated in the first question.

1. Compare narration and exposition and give examples of them.

2. Discuss three methods for making ethical decisions, enumerate the problems associated with each method, and evaluate which method is the most difficult to use.

3. Discuss the differences between modern and traditional dating, identify differences you consider to be most important, and hypothesize how dating might be different twenty years from now.

4. How did the following men challenge the accepted religious views during the Age of Enlightenment: Toland, Bayle, Hume, and Voltaire?

5. Is the women's liberation movement a continuation of the women's rights movement, or are they two different movements? Defend your answer.

EXERCISE 27.4   **Answering an Essay Question**

Write a well-organized and complete answer to the following question, as your instructor requests. Remember to write neatly and to proofread your answer.

Summarize the steps in the study process.

EXERCISE 27.5   **Answering an Essay Question**

Write a well-organized and complete answer to the following question, as your instructor requests. Remember to write neatly and to proofread your answer.

Summarize the basic strategies for taking any test and the specific strategies for answering true-false, multiple-choice, matching, and fill-in questions.

EXERCISE 27.6   **Answering an Essay Question**

Write a well-organized and complete answer to the following question, as your instructor requests. Remember to write neatly and to proofread your answer.

Discuss the methods that may be used to write well-organized and complete answers to essay questions.

Appendix:
Textbook Chapter
for Practice

This appendix contains a textbook chapter titled "Developing a Professional Presence." The underlying assumption of the chapter is that people we come into contact with while we are working form opinions about us using such superficial cues as the way we dress and the way we shake hands; the chapter offers suggestions about what we can do to create a favorable impression of ourselves with people who do not know us.

Use the chapter to practice surveying, underlining or highlighting, making notes, reciting and rehearsing, and test taking.

- Exercise 17.2 on pages 186–188 provides practice in previewing the chapter.
- Exercise 18.9 on pages 215–216 provides practice in marking the chapter.
- Exercise 19.9 on pages 226 and 228 provides practice in making notes from the chapter.
- Exercise 20.4 on page 240 provides practice in reciting and rehearsing information in your notes.

If your instructor assigns these exercises, he or she will probably request you to answer test questions about the chapter, such as those in Exercise 21.3 on page 250.

As you study the following chapter, evaluate whether it contains any suggestions that you want to try out the next time you meet a new person on the job or elsewhere.

Source of textbook material: Reece, Barry L. and Rhonda Brandt, Effective Human Relations in Organizations, Sixth Edition. Copyright © 1996 by Houghton Mifflin Company. Used with permission.

Chapter 11

Developing a Professional Presence

Chapter Preview

After studying this chapter, you will be able to

1. Explain the importance of professional presence.

2. Discuss the factors that contribute to a favorable first impression.

3. Distinguish between assumptions and facts.

4. Define *image* and describe the factors that form the image you project to others.

5. List and discuss factors that influence your choice of clothing for work.

6. Understand how manners contribute to improved interpersonal relations in the workplace.

T HE HERTZ CORPORATION, the U.S. Air Force, Hyatt Hotels Corporation, the City of Dallas, and the Neiman-Marcus Group, Inc. have one thing in common — all have purchased the services of Feedback Plus. Feedback Plus is an agency that dispatches professional shoppers who pose as consumers. These "mystery" shoppers visit the client's business, purchase products or services, and report back to the client on the quality of service they receive. The City of Dallas hired Feedback Plus to see how car-pound employees treat citizens picking up their cars. The Air Force is using professional shoppers to assess customer service at their on-base supply stores. Banks, hospitals, and public utilities are also hiring mystery shoppers. Vickie Henry, chief executive of Feedback Plus, notes that many similar firms compete for clients' business, and service really differentiates one firm from another. Although Henry has a database of 8,800 people who serve as professional shoppers, she sometimes assumes the role of mystery shopper herself. During a recent visit to an upscale women's apparel store, she observed the type of customer service most companies attempt to avoid. None of the many salespeople on the sales floor said hello when she entered the store. When she removed a skirt from a clothing rack, none of the salespeople approached her. Finally, several minutes after entering the store, Henry approached a salesperson and asked to use the dressing room. Needless to say, service at this firm did not receive high marks from Feedback Plus.[1] ■

As organizations experience increased competition for clients, patients, and customers, awareness of the importance of public contact increases.[2] They are giving new attention to the old adage "First impressions are lasting impressions." Research indicates that initial impressions do indeed tend to linger. Therefore, a positive first impression can set the stage for a long-term relationship.

Of course, it is not just those *first* contacts with clients, patients, customers, and others that are important. Positive impressions should be the objective of *every* contact. A major goal of this chapter is to discuss the important factors that help us make positive impressions. Another important goal is to examine the factors that shape the image we project to others.

MAKING A GOOD IMPRESSION

There are many personal and professional benefits to be gained from a study of the concepts in this chapter. You will acquire new insights regarding ways to communicate positive impressions during job interviews, business contacts, and social contacts made away from work. You will also learn how to shape an image that will help you achieve your fullest potential in the career of your choice. Most important, the material in this chapter will very likely increase your self-awareness. As we noted in Chapter 1, self-awareness is an important first step toward building more effective relationships with others.

Chapter 11 Developing a Professional Presence

This is not a chapter about ways to make positive impressions with superficial contacts and quick-fix techniques. We do not discuss the "power look" or the "power lunch." The material in this chapter will not help you become a more entertaining conversationalist or win new customers by pretending to be interested in their hobbies or families. Stephen Covey, author of *The 7 Habits of Highly Effective People,* says that the ability to build effective, long-term relationships is based on character strength, not quick-fix techniques. He notes that outward attitude and behavior changes do very little good in the long run unless they are based on solid principles governing human effectiveness. These principles include service (making a contribution), integrity and honesty (which serve as a foundation of trust), human dignity (every person has worth), and fairness.[3]

Few people can fake a sincere greeting or a caring attitude. If you really do not care about the customer's problem, the customer will probably sense your indifference. Your true feelings will be difficult to hide. Ralph Waldo Emerson was right on target when he said, "What you are shouts so loudly in my ears I cannot hear what you say."

Professional Presence

We are indebted to Susan Bixler, president of Professional Image, Inc., and author of *Professional Presence,* for giving us a better understanding of what it means to possess professional presence. **Professional presence** is a dynamic blend of poise, self-confidence, control, and style that empowers us to be able to command respect in any situation.[4] Once acquired, it permits us to be perceived as self-assured and thoroughly competent. We project a confidence that others can quickly perceive the first time they meet us.

Bixler points out that, in most cases, the credentials we present during a job interview or when we are being considered for a promotion are not very different from those of other persons being considered. It is our professional presence that permits us to rise above the crowd. Debra Benton, a career consultant, says, "Any boss with a choice of two people with equal qualifications will choose the one with style as well as substance."[5] Learning to create a professional presence is one of the most valuable skills we can acquire.

The Primacy Effect

The development of professional presence begins with a full appreciation of the power of first impressions. The tendency to form impressions quickly at the time of an initial meeting illustrates what social psychologists call a **primacy effect** in the way people perceive one another. The general principle is that first impressions establish the mental framework within which a person is viewed, and later evidence is either ignored or reinterpreted to coincide with this framework.[6]

Part III: Personal Strategies for Improving Human Relations

Martha Kelly met a middle-aged man at an outdoor cookout. He was wearing cutoff blue jeans and an old pair of worn-out sneakers. He had had several drinks and tended to interrupt people and monopolize any conversation. Throughout the afternoon, people avoided him whenever possible. About two weeks later, Martha stopped at a drugstore to get a prescription filled. To her surprise, the pharmacist was the same man she had met at the cookout, only now he was dressed in a neatly tailored white jacket, blue shirt, and pin-striped tie. Although he projected a very professional image in dealing with his customers, Martha left the store and went to another pharmacy to get her prescription filled. The positive impression communicated in the store was not strong enough to overcome her first, negative impression.

The First Few Minutes

When two people meet, their potential for building a relationship can be affected by many factors. Within a few moments, one person or the other may feel threatened, offended, or bored. Leonard Zunin and Natalie Zunin, coauthors of *Contact—The First Four Minutes,* describe what they call the **four-minute barrier**.[7] In this short period of time, human relationships are established, reconfirmed (in the case of two former acquaintances meeting), or

A political candidate must be able to build rapport with a variety of people. A good handshake, eye contact and a pleasant smile can help you make a good first impression. (Dan Lamont/Matrix International)

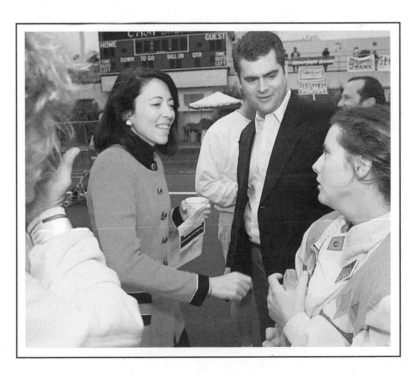

Chapter 11 Developing a Professional Presence

denied. It is during the first few minutes of interaction with others that people's attention spans are at their greatest and powers of retention at their highest.

Why four minutes? According to the Zunins, this is the average time, determined by careful observation, during which two people in a social situation make up their minds to continue the encounter or to separate. During the first few minutes you can benefit from what sociologists call the "halo effect." This means that if you are viewed positively within the first four minutes, the person you made contact with is more likely to assume that everything you say or do is positive.[8]

Thinking / Learning Starters

To test the practical application of the Zunins' theory in a real-life setting, examine it in the context of your past experiences. Review the following questions and then answer each with yes or no.

1. Have you ever gone for a job interview and known instinctively within minutes that you would or would not be hired?

2. Have you ever met a new supervisor who immediately communicated to you the impression that he or she could be trusted and was interested in your welfare?

3. Have you ever entered a restaurant, hotel, or office and experienced an immediate feeling of being welcome after the employee spoke only a few words?

First Impressions in a Work Setting In a work setting, the four-minute period in which a relationship is established or denied is often reduced to seconds. The U.S. Postal Service is concerned about perceptions created during this brief period of time. In selected regions of the nation, postal workers have completed the Dale Carnegie human relations course.[9] The following examples illustrate the effect that immediate first impressions can have in a variety of work situations:

Item: Paula rushed into a restaurant for a quick lunch—she had to get back to her office for a 1:30 P.M. appointment. The restaurant was not crowded, so she knew she would not have to wait for a table. At the entrance of the main dining area was a sign reading, "Please Wait to Be Seated." A few feet away, the hostess was discussing a popular movie with one of the waitresses. The hostess made eye contact with Paula but continued to visit with the waitress. About twenty more seconds passed, and Paula began to feel anxiety build in-

Part III: Personal Strategies for Improving Human Relations

Total Person Insight

"If people aren't quickly attracted to you or don't like what they see and hear in those first two to four minutes, chances are they won't pay attention to all those words you believe are demonstrating your knowledge and authority. They will find your client guilty, seek another doctor, buy another product, vote for your opponent or hire someone else."

JANET G. ELSEA

President, Communication Skills, Inc.

---

side her. She tried to get the hostess's attention, but the hostess did not respond. After another ten seconds had passed, Paula walked out of the restaurant.

Item: Sandy and Mike entered the showroom of a Mercedes-Benz dealer. They noticed two salespeople seated at desks near the entrance. One salesperson was wearing a well-tailored blue blazer, gray slacks, and a white shirt with a blue tie highlighted by subtle stripes. The other salesperson was wearing sport slacks (khaki color), a blue knit pullover shirt (short sleeve), and casual shoes. The salesperson wearing the casual clothing walked over to Sandy and Mike and asked, "May I be of assistance?" Mike said, "We're just looking today." The salesperson returned to his desk. As they left the showroom Sandy said, "I can't believe someone selling a $40,000 automobile would wear such casual clothing." "I agree," Mike said.

In each of these examples, the negative first impression was created in less than sixty seconds. The anxiety level of the restaurant customer increased because she was forced to wait while two employees talked about a personal matter. And the potential customers were making judgments about the car salesperson based solely on his appearance. Unfortunately, these employees were probably not fully aware of the impression they communicated to customers.

Assumptions Versus Facts The impression you form of another person during the initial contact is made up of both assumptions and facts. Most people tend to rely more heavily on **assumptions** during an initial meeting. As the Zunins state, people live in an assumptive world:

> When you meet a stranger, and sometimes with friends, much of the information you get is based on assumption. You form positive or negative feelings or impressions but you must realize that only superficial facts can be gathered in four minutes.

Chapter 11 Developing a Professional Presence

Depending on assumptions is a one-way ticket to big surprises and perhaps disappointments.[10]

Cultural influences, especially during the early years of your life, lead you to form impressions of some people even before you meet them. People often stereotype entire groups. Here are a few of the common stereotypes that still persist in our society:

- "Older workers are set in their ways."
- Men have a "competition mentality."
- "Executive women are aggressive."

These are just a few of the assumptions that some people perceive as facts. With the passing of time some assumptions tend to lose support as factual information surfaces. The idea that all married couples should have children receives less support today than it did a generation ago. Women are now less likely to be viewed as unacceptable candidates for executive positions. Nevertheless, people rarely reach the point in life where they are completely free of assumptions. In fact, the briefer the encounter with a new acquaintance, the greater is the chance that misinformation will enter into your perception of the other person.

THE IMAGE YOU PROJECT

Image is a term used to describe how other people feel about you. In every business or social setting, your behaviors communicate a mental picture that others observe and remember. This picture determines how they react to you. Your image depends on more than exterior qualities such as dress and grooming. In the words of James Gray, author of *The Winning Image,* "Image is more than just a veneer."[11] He observes,

> Image is a tool for communicating and for revealing your inherent qualities, your competence, abilities and leadership. It is a reflection of qualities that others associate with you, a reflection that bears long-lasting influence in your bid for success. Image is not a tool for manipulation. Nor is it a false front. It cannot substitute for substance.[12]

In many respects, the image you project at work is very much like a picture puzzle, as illustrated in Figure 11.1. It is formed by a variety of factors, including manners, self-confidence, voice quality, versatility (see Chapter 5), integrity (see Chapter 7), entrance and carriage, facial expression, surface language, competence, positive attitude, and handshake. Each of these image-shaping components is under your control.

A growing number of organizations have discovered a direct link between profitability and the image projected by employees. Financial institutions, public utilities, airlines, retail stores, restaurants, hospitals, and manufacturers face

Part III: Personal Strategies for Improving Human Relations

FIGURE 11.1

Major Factors That
Form Your Image

the problem of not only gaining but also retaining the patronage of clients and customers. When the Oldsmobile division of General Motors Corp. decided to reshape the image projected by dealers, it developed a $25 million training program. Dealers and employees learned how to improve service to customers and to sell the Aurora, a more luxurious car than Olds dealers have sold in the past.[13]

Surface Language

As noted earlier, we form opinions about other people based on both facts and assumptions. Unfortunately, assumptions often carry a great deal of weight. Many of the assumptions you develop regarding other people are based upon what the Zunins describe as "surface language." **Surface language** is defined as a pattern of immediate impressions conveyed by appearance. The clothing you wear, your hair style, the fragrances you use, and the jewelry you display all combine to make a statement about you to others.

According to many writers familiar with image formation, clothing is particularly important. John Molloy, author of *Dress for Success* and *The Woman's*

Chapter 11 Developing a Professional Presence

Dress for Success Book, was one of the first to acknowledge publicly the link between image and wardrobe. According to his research, what you wear influences your credibility and likability.[14] The view that clothing is a very important component of image formation is supported by many other image consultants, including Susan Bixler, William Thourlby, Emily Cho, and Jacqueline Thompson.

Although a more relaxed dress code has evolved in recent years, people judge your appearance long before they judge your talents. It would be a mistake not to take your career wardrobe seriously. Bixler suggests that those making career wardrobe decisions should keep in mind that three things haven't changed:[15]

1. *If you want the job, you have to look the part.* Establish personal dress and grooming standards appropriate for the organization where you wish to work. Before you apply for a job, try to find out what the workers there are wearing. If in doubt, dress conservatively. Some of America's most successful companies still maintain a formal dress code. Roger Penske, best known for his successes in IndyCar racing, owns six auto dealerships in southern California. Men who sell cars at Penske dealerships must follow a strict dress code: No beards, no sunglasses, and wear proper business attire, with neckties pulled tight.[16]

2. *If you want the promotion, you have to look promotable.* Employees can communicate with their clothing that they are satisfied with their position. A good rule to follow is to dress for the job you want, not the job you have. If you are currently an office clerk and want to become an office manager, identify the successful office managers and emulate their manner of dress. Emily Cho, author of *Looking Terrific,* says that the right wardrobe can transform a person from being part of the corporate scenery to being in the forefront.

3. *If you want respect, you have to dress as well as or better than your industry standards.* One would expect to find conservative dress standards in the fields of banking, insurance, accounting, and law, and more casual dress standards in the fields of advertising, sports entertainment, and agriculture. Spend time researching the dress and grooming standards in the industry where you hope to find a job.

Thinking / Learning Starter

Do you recall a teacher, coworker, or supervisor whose surface language impressed you—either positively or negatively? What specific elements (dress, hairstyle, etc.) were evident in this person's surface language? What type of image do you think he or she was trying to project?

Selecting Your Career Apparel

Over 23 million American workers wear a uniform especially designed for a particular job. The judges on the U.S. Supreme Court and the technicians at the local Midas Muffler and Brake shop have one thing in common — both wear a special uniform to work. Today more and more people are donning uniforms to go to work. Companies that have initiated extensive career apparel programs rely on uniforms to project an image of consistent quality, good service, and uniqueness. Uniforms enhance company credibility, which in turn increases customer confidence in the firm.[17] Wearing a uniform can also have a positive effect on employees. Wearing the same uniform seems to create a sort of bond among coworkers. Thus, a uniform can make at least a small contribution to building company spirit at your local McDonald's restaurant or Holiday Inn hotel.

Dress was the focus of a management decision at the GenCorp Automotive plant at Shelbyville, Indiana. The work force there is divided into twenty-five teams of twelve to fifteen production workers. To build company spirit, a decision was made to adopt the same "uniform" for all employees. Everyone, including managers, wears navy blue skirts or trousers and light blue shirts.[18]

Many workers wear special-dress uniforms. Unitog, based in Kansas City, rents and sells uniforms to companies such as Exxon and Anheuser-Busch. A uniform worn by employees will often contribute to a spirit of teamwork. (Eli Reichman)

Chapter 11   Developing a Professional Presence

The uniforms worn by United Postal Service employees, airline reservation clerks, and the employees at your local restaurant might be classified as special-design **career apparel**. Some work uniforms are designed by top talents in the fashion industry. In addition to special-design uniforms, there is another type of career apparel, somewhat less predictable, worn by large numbers of people in our labor force. Here are some examples:

- A female lawyer representing a prestigious firm would be appropriately dressed in a gray or blue skirted suit. A dress with a suit jacket would also be acceptable. She should avoid clothing in brash colors or casual styles that might reduce her credibility.
- A male bank loan officer would be appropriately dressed in a tailored gray or blue suit, white shirt, and tie. This same person dressed in a colorful blazer, sport shirt, and plaid slacks would be seen as too casual in most bank settings.
- A female receptionist at a prominent accounting firm would be appropriately dressed in a skirt and blouse. This same person would be inappropriately dressed if she showed up for work wearing designer jeans, a sweater, and sneakers.
- A mechanic employed by an auto dealership that sells new cars would be appropriately dressed in matching gray, tan, or light blue shirt and pants. The mechanic would be inappropriately dressed in jeans and a T-shirt.

Many organizations seek advice about career apparel from image consultants. One source of image consultants is the Association of Image Consultants International.

FOR BETTER OR WORSE © 1994 Lynn Johnston Prod., Inc. Reprinted with permission of UNIVERSAL PRESS SYNDICATE. All rights reserved.

Part III: Personal Strategies for Improving Human Relations

Wardrobe Engineering

The term **wardrobe engineering** was first used by John Molloy to describe how clothing and accessories can be used to create a certain image. This concept was later refined by several other noted image consultants in hundreds of books and articles on dress and grooming. Although these authors are not in complete agreement on every aspect of dress, they do agree on a few basic points regarding wardrobe.

The quality of your wardrobe will influence the image you project. A wardrobe should be regarded as an investment, with each item carefully selected to look and fit well. Purchase a few basic items each year and you will soon have everything you need.

The newest dress fad is often inappropriate in a business or professional setting. In most cases, the world of work is more conservative than college, the arts, or the world of sports. If you are a fashion setter, you might be viewed as unstable or insincere. To be taken seriously, avoid clothing that is faddish or too flashy.

Women generally have more latitude than men in selecting appropriate attire, but they should still exercise some caution in choosing their wardrobe. In some cases, women are entering positions formerly dominated by men. They need to be taken seriously, and the wardrobe they select can contribute to this end.

Your wardrobe should be appropriate for your field and for you. Although you should consider the dress and grooming standards of others in your field, don't give in to blind conformity or duplication. As one image consultant noted, "Effective packaging is an individual matter based on the person's circumstances, age, weight, height, coloring, and objectives."[19] In addition to these personal factors, you need to consider what's appropriate for your career. In general, four factors influence your choice of clothing for work:

1. *Products and services offered.* In some cases the organization's products and services more or less dictate a certain type of dress. For example, a receptionist employed by a well-established law firm would likely wear clothing that is conservative, modest, and in good taste. These same dress standards would apply to a pharmaceutical sales representative who calls on medical doctors.
2. *Type of person served.* Research indicates that first impressions created by dress and grooming are greatly influenced by unconscious expectations. Throughout life we become acquainted with bank loan officers, nurses, police officers, and others employed in a wide range of occupations. We form mental images of the apparel common to each of these occupations. When

Chapter 11 Developing a Professional Presence

In an effort to improve quality, Kim Woo-Chong, chairman of the Daewoo Group, frequently puts on a uniform and inspects operations on the floor of the Daewoo Motor plant. By wearing the same attire, he can better relate to his plant employees. (Ki Ho Park/Kistone Photography)

we encounter someone whose appearance does not conform to our past experiences, we feel uncomfortable.

3. *Desired image projected by the organization.* Some companies establish dress codes that help shape the image they project to the public. Walt Disney Company, for example, maintains a strict dress and grooming code for all its theme-park employees. They are considered "cast members" and must adhere to dress and grooming standards that complement the image projected by Disney theme parks.

4. *Geographic region.* Dress in the South and Southwest tends to be more casual than in the Northeast. Climate is another factor that influences the clothing people wear at work. In Texas, for example, the warm climate calls for short sleeves and open collars in some work settings.

Thinking / Learning Starter

Assume you are planning to purchase (1) a life insurance policy, (2) a Rolex wristwatch, and (3) eyeglasses. What types of career apparel would you expect persons selling these products to wear? What grooming standards would you recommend?

Part III: Personal Strategies for Improving Human Relations

The Business Casual Look

The terms *business casual* or *corporate casual* have recently been used to describe the movement toward dress standards that emphasize greater comfort and individuality. **Business casual** usually means slacks and sports coats for men, and slacks, casual dresses, or skirts for women.[20] Business casual bridges the gap between the suits, white shirts, and silk blouses traditionally worn in business, and more casual dress, such as jeans, shorts, and T-shirts. Some companies have established "casual Fridays" or "dress-down weeks," while others have shifted from a strict dress code to a relaxed dress code. The casual look in corporate America was triggered, in part, by efforts to improve teamwork and empower employees. Bottom-up initiatives often emphasize getting rid of symbols of top-down authority.[21] The casual trend has also been fueled by the influx of Generation Xers who are entering the work force. These new workers are more relaxed and are looking for ways to express their individuality.

Now that the casual look is gaining acceptance, many companies are struggling to develop casual dress guidelines for their employees. Levi Strauss & Co., maker of jeans, Dockers and other nonjean clothes, is offering companies an informational kit containing suggestions on how to develop a casual dress code.[22] Image consultants are also offering advice. Most agree that business casual still means dressing for success.

Your Facial Expression

After your overall appearance, your face is the most visible part of you. Facial expressions are the cue most people rely on in initial interactions. They are the "teleprompter" by which others read your mood and personality.[23]

Studies conducted in nonverbal communication show that facial expressions strongly influence people's reactions to each other. The expression on your face can quickly trigger a positive or negative reaction from those you meet. How you rate in the "good-looks" department may not be nearly as important as your ability to communicate positive impressions with a pleasant smile.

If you want to identify the inner feelings of another person, watch the individual's facial expressions closely. A frown may tell you "something is wrong." A smile generally communicates "things are OK." Everyone has encountered a "look of surprise" or a "look that could kill." These facial expressions usually reflect inner emotions more accurately than words.

In many work settings, a cheerful smile is an important key to creating a positive first impression. A deadpan stare (or frown) can communicate a negative first impression to others. If you find it hard to smile, take time to consider the reasons. Are you constantly thinking negative thoughts and simply find nothing to smile about? Are you afraid others may misinterpret your intentions?

Your Entrance and Carriage

The way you enter someone's office or a business meeting can influence the image you project, says Susan Bixler. She notes that "your entrance and the way you carry yourself will set the stage for everything that comes afterward."[24] A nervous or apologetic entrance may ruin your chances of getting a job, closing a sale, or getting the raise you have earned. If you feel apprehensive, try not to let it show in your body language. Hold your head up, avoid slumping forward, and try to project self-assurance. To get off to the right start and make a favorable impression, follow these words of advice from Bixler: "The person who has confidence in himself or herself indicates this by a strong stride, a friendly smile, good posture, and a genuine sense of energy. This is a very effective way to set the stage for a productive meeting. When you ask for respect visually, you get it."[25] Bixler says the key to making a successful entrance is simply believing—and projecting—that you have a reason to be there and have something important to present or discuss.

Your Voice

Several years ago, a Cleveland-based company, North American Systems, Inc., developed and marketed Mr. Coffee, which makes coffee quickly and conveniently. Some credited the quick acceptance of this product to an effective advertising campaign featuring baseball Hall of Famer Joe Di Maggio. He came across to the consumer as an honest, sincere person. When Joe Di Maggio said Mr. Coffee worked and made good coffee, people believed him.

The tone of your voice, the rate of speed at which you speak (tempo), and the volume of your speech contribute greatly to the meaning attached to your verbal messages. In the case of telephone calls, voice quality is critical because the other person cannot see your facial expressions, hand gestures, and other body movements. You cannot trade in your current voice for a new one, but you can make your voice more pleasing to other people and project a positive tone.

Although there is no ideal voice for all business contacts, your voice should reflect at least these four qualities: confidence, enthusiasm, optimism, and sincerity. Above all, try to avoid a speech pattern that is dull and colorless. Joanne Lamm, founder of Professional Speech Associates, says the worst kind of voice has no projection, no color, and no feeling.[26]

Your Handshake

When two people first meet, a handshake is usually the only physical contact between them. The handshake can communicate warmth, genuine concern for the other person, and strength. It can also communicate aloofness, indiffer-

Part III: Personal Strategies for Improving Human Relations

ence, and weakness. The message you send the other party via your handshake depends on a combination of the following factors.

1. *Degree of firmness.* Generally speaking, a firm handshake communicates a caring attitude, whereas a weak grip communicates indifference.
2. *Degree of dryness of hands.* A moist palm is unpleasant to feel and can communicate the impression that you are nervous. A clammy hand is likely to repel most people.
3. *Duration of grip.* There are no specific guidelines for the ideal duration of a grip. Nevertheless, by extending the handshake, you can often communicate a greater degree of interest in and concern for the other person.
4. *Depth of interlock.* A full, deep grip is more apt to convey friendship and strength to the other person.
5. *Eye contact during handshake.* Visual communication can increase the positive impact of your handshake. Maintaining eye contact throughout the handshaking process is important when two people greet each other.[27]

Most individuals have shaken hands with hundreds of people but have little idea whether they are creating positive or negative impressions. It is a good idea to obtain this information from those coworkers or friends who are willing to provide you with candid feedback. Like all other human relations skills, the handshake can be improved with practice.

Your Manners

The study of manners (sometimes called etiquette) reveals a number of ways to enhance our professional presence. A knowledge of good manners permits us to perform our daily work with poise and confidence. Letitia Baldrige, author of *Letitia Baldrige's New Complete Guide to Executive Manners,* provides us with a basic definition of good *manners:* "It's consideration and kindness and thinking about somebody other than oneself."[28] Another writer says, "Manners are the grace woven into the knotty fabric of our lives. Without them, it's all knots and thorns."[29] Good manners represent an important key to improved interpersonal relations.

Good manners is a universal passport to positive relationships and respect. One of the best ways to develop rapport with another person is to avoid behavior that might be offensive to that individual. Although it is not possible to do a complete review of this topic, some of the rules of etiquette that are particularly important in an organizational setting are covered here.

1. *When you establish new relationships, avoid calling people by their first names too soon.* Jacqueline Thompson, author of *Image Impact,* says assuming that all work-related associates prefer to be addressed informally by their first names is a serious breach of etiquette.[30] Use titles of respect—Ms., Miss, Mrs., Mr., or Dr.—until the relationship is well established. Too much familiarity can breed

Chapter 11 Developing a Professional Presence

Total Person Insight

"In a society as ridden as ours with expensive status symbols, where every purchase is considered a social statement, there is no easier or cheaper way to distinguish oneself than by the practice of gentle manners."

JUDITH MARTIN

Author, *Miss Manners' Guide for the Turn-of-the-Millennium,* in "Low Income Is Not Low-Class"

---

irritation. When the other party says, "Call me Susan," or "Call me Roy," it is all right to begin using the person's first name. Informality should develop by invitation, not by presumption.

2. *Avoid obscenities and offensive comments or stories.* In recent years, standards for acceptable and unacceptable language have changed considerably. Obscenity is more permissible in everyday conversation than it was in the past. But it is still considered inappropriate to use foul language in front of a customer, a client, or, in many cases, a coworker. According to Bob Greene, syndicated columnist, an obscenity communicates a negative message to most people.

> What it probably all comes down to is an implied lack of respect for the people who hear you talk. If you use profanity among friends, that is a choice you make. But if you broadcast it to people in general, you're telling them that you don't care what their feelings might be.[31]

Never assume that another person's value system is the same as your own. Foul language and off-color stories can do irreparable damage to interpersonal relations.

3. *Watch your table manners.* Business is frequently conducted at breakfast, lunch, or dinner these days, so be aware of your table manners. When you invite a customer to lunch, do not discuss business before the meal is ordered unless the client initiates the subject. Begin eating only when most of the people around you have their plates. If you have not been served, however, encourage others to go ahead. Assume responsibility for making sure the conversation moves from topic to topic and person to person. No one likes to be left out. Ann Humphries, president of Eticon, Etiquette Consultants for Business, says that knowledge of table manners gives employees the confidence they need to do their jobs well.[32]

4. *Express appreciation at appropriate times.* A simple thank-you can mean a lot. Failure to express appreciation can be a serious human relations blunder. The office worker who works hard to complete a rush job for the boss is likely to feel frustrated and angry if this extra effort is ignored. The customer who makes a purchase deserves a sincere thank-you. You want your customers to know that their business is appreciated.

5. *Be familiar with meeting etiquette.* Business meetings should start and end on time. When you attend a meeting, arrive on time and don't feel obligated to comment on each item on the agenda. Yes, sometimes silence is golden. In most cases, you should not bring up a topic unless it is related to an agenda item. If you are in charge of the meeting, end it by summarizing key points, reviewing the decisions made, and recapping the responsibilities assigned to individuals during the meeting. Always start and end the meeting on a positive note.[33]

6. *Be aware of personal habits that may offend others.* Sometimes an annoying habit can be a barrier to establishing a positive relationship with someone else. Chewing gum is a habit that bothers many people, particularly if you chew gum vigorously or "crack" it. Biting fingernails, cracking knuckles, scratching your head, and combing your hair in public are additional habits to be avoided. If you wear a fragrance (cologne or after-shave lotion), apply it in moderation when going to work. Do not risk causing a client or coworker discomfort with your fragrance.[34]

Letitia Baldrige says that in the field of manners, "Rules are based on kindness and efficiency." She also believes that good manners are those personal qualities that make life at work more livable.[35] In a civilized community, there have to be some restraints.

Assessing Your Professional Presence

To assess your professional presence and determine if small changes are needed, plan to spend ten to fifteen minutes making an informal presentation to someone in front of a video camera. The video footage will let you see what you really look like and how you sound to others. Play the tape several times and pay special attention to your posture, gestures, eye movement, tone of voice, and body movement. After you determine how you come across to others, plan to change the things you don't like. For example, if you notice that you frequently speak in a monotone, make a mental note to work on this problem.[36]

Summary

Professional presence permits us to be perceived as self-assured and competent. These qualities are quickly perceived the first time someone meets us. People tend to form impressions of others quickly at the time they first meet them, and these first impressions tend to be preserved. The four-minute barrier is a term used to describe the average time people spend together before a relationship is either established or denied. In an organizational setting, the time interval is often reduced to seconds. Positive impressions are important because they contribute to repeat business and customer referrals.

The impression you form of another person during the initial contact is made up of assumptions and facts. When meeting someone for the first time, people tend to rely heavily on assumptions. Many of your assumptions can be traced to early cultural influences. Assumptions are also based on perceptions of surface language. Surface language is a pattern of immediate impressions conveyed by appearance. The clothing and jewelry you wear, your hairstyle, and the fragrances you use all combine to make a statement about yourself to others.

Image consultants contend that discrimination on the basis of appearance is still a fact of life. Clothing is an important part of the image you communicate to others. Four factors tend to influence your choice of clothing for work: (1) the products or services offered by the organization, (2) the type of person served, (3) the desired image projected by the organization, and (4) the region where you work.

In addition to clothing, research indicates that facial expressions strongly influence people's reactions to each other. The expression on your face can quickly trigger a positive or negative reaction. Similarly, your entrance and carriage, voice, handshake, and manners also contribute to the image you project when meeting others.

Career Corner

Q. In the near future I will begin my job search, and I want to work for a company that will respect my individuality. Some companies are enforcing strict dress codes and other policies that, in my opinion, infringe on the rights of their employees. How far can an employer go in dictating my lifestyle?

A. This is a good question, but one for which there is no easy answer. For example, most people feel they have a right to wear the fragrance of their choice, but many fragrances contain allergy-producing ingredients. In some parts of California, you will find "non-fragrance" zones. Second-hand smoke is another major issue in the workplace because some research indicates that it can be harmful to the health of workers. Rules regarding weight, hair length, and the type of clothing and jewelry that can be worn to work have also caused controversy. There is no doubt that many companies are trying to find a balance between their interests and the rights of workers. Blockbuster Entertainment Corporation has placed restrictions on the length of an employee's hair and the amount of jewelry that can be worn during work hours. The company believes employee appearance is crucial to the success of the company. The best advice I can give you is to become familiar with the employer's expectations before you accept a job. The company has a responsibility to explain its personnel policies to prospective employees, but sometimes this information is not covered until after a person is hired.

Part III: Personal Strategies for Improving Human Relations

Key Terms

professional presence
primacy effect
four-minute barrier
assumptions
cultural influences

image
surface language
career apparel
wardrobe engineering
business casual

Review Questions

1. Image has been described as "more than exterior qualities such as dress and grooming." What other factors shape the image we project?
2. Define the term *primacy effect*. How would knowledge of the primacy effect help someone who works in patient care or customer service?
3. Why do people tend to rely more heavily on assumptions than on facts during the initial meeting?
4. Why should career-minded people be concerned about the image they project? What factors contribute to the formation of a person's image?
5. What are some of the major decisions people make about others based on career apparel?
6. Susan Bixler suggests that when making wardrobe decisions, you should keep in mind that three things have not changed. List and discuss these three factors.
7. What is meant by the term *unconscious expectations*?
8. Describe the type of speaking voice that increases a person's effectiveness in dealing with others.
9. Provide a basic definition of good manners. Why is the study of manners important?
10. Stephen Covey says that changing outward attitudes and behaviors does very little good in the long run unless we base such changes on solid principles that govern human effectiveness. Do you agree or disagree with his views? Explain your answer.

Vocabulary List

The vocabulary list in this section contains information about the meanings and pronunciations of the words that are underscored in blue in Chapter 18, "Mark Your Books." Your instructor may request you to learn the meanings of the words in this vocabulary list.

Information in Entries

The following entry for the word *pit* illustrates the five types of information that are provided for words listed in this section.

> **pit** (pit) *v.* To set in competition; to set against, match [to *pit* the two best teams in a championship play-off]

1. The *spelling* is printed in boldface: **pit.**

2. The *pronunciation* is enclosed in parentheses: (pit).

3. The *part of speech* is printed in italics: *v.*

4. The *definition* begins with a capital letter: To set in competition; to set against, match.

5. An *example* of the way the word is used is enclosed in brackets following the definition: [to *pit* the two best teams in a championship play-off]

The meaning of each word in the vocabulary list corresponds to the ways the word is used in this book. For instance, the word *pit* has many meanings, including "the hard stone in a fruit [a cherry *pit*]" and "an area where animals are kept [a bear *pit*]." However, the entry above indicates that in this book, *pit* is used as a verb that means "to set in competition."

Parts of Speech

The following abbreviations are used for the traditional parts of speech:

noun (*n.*)
noun plural (*n.pl.*)
verb (*v.*)
adjective (*adj.*)
adverb (*adv.*)

The words in the vocabulary list do not include a conjunction (*conj.*), interjection (*interj.*), or preposition (*prep.*).

Pronunciation Spelling

Interpret pronunciation spellings using the pronunciation key at the bottom of some of the pages in this section. For instance, by using the key you can determine that *chaos* (kā´os´) is pronounced using the following sounds:

k
ā as in **pay**
o as in p**o**t
s

Vowels   Vowel sounds present the major problem in interpreting pronunciation spellings because the five vowels, *a, e, i, o,* and *u,* are used to represent a variety of sounds.

pat (pat)	**pet** (pet)	**pit** (pit)	**pot** (pot)	**cut** (cut)
pay (pā)	**be** (bē)	**pie** (pī)	**toe** (tō)	**cute** (kyo͞ot)
care (câr)		**pier** (pîr)	**paw** (pô)	
arm (ärm)		**firm** (fûrm)	**took** (to͝ok)	
			boot (bo͞ot)	

In addition, pronunciation spellings include the two-vowel combinations found in the term *boy scout* (boi skout) and the de-emphasized sound in words such as ***ago, agent, sanity, comply,*** and *focus,* which is represented by a symbol called the schwa: **ago** (ə´gō). The schwa, which looks like the letter *e* printed upside down (ə), has the vowel sound heard in *of* when the phrase "bag *of* candy" is said quickly (bag əv kan´dē).

Consonants   Consonant letters are used to represent consonant sounds in pronunciation spellings. For example:

half (haf)	phone (fōn)
ghost (gōst)	wrap (rap)
gem (jem)	his (hiz)
knit (nit)	rhyme (rīm)
debt (det)	sign (sīn)

The letters *c, q,* and *x* are not used in pronunciation spellings. The letter *c* is usually pronounced *k* as in *can* (kan) or *s* as in *cent* (sent); the letter *q* is usually pronounced *kw,* as in *quit* (kwit); and the letter *x* is usually pronounced *ks,* as in *tax* (taks).

ə ago/a pat/ā pay/â care/ä arm/e pet/ē be/i pit/ī pie/î pier/o pot/ō toe/ô paw/o͞o took/o͞o boot/
oi boy/ou scout/u cut/yo͞o cute/û firm

Accent Marks   Pronunciation spellings usually include accent marks to indicate the relative force with which syllables are spoken. Compare the placement of the primary accents marks (´) in the pronunciations for the verb and noun forms of the word *extract*:

> **extract** (ek-strakt´) *v.* To pull out [to *extract* a tooth]
> **extract** (ek´-strakt) *n.* A passage selected from a book [to read a short *extract* from a long book]

The second syllable of *extract* is stressed when the word is used as a verb [*ex-tract´* a tooth], whereas the first part of the word is stressed when the word is used as a noun [to read a short *ex´-tract* from a long book].

The secondary accent mark (´) is used to indicate stress that is weaker than primary stress but stronger than the stress of unaccented syllables. Primary and secondary accent marks in the following words indicate which syllables receive primary and secondary stress.

rec´ og nize´
in´ dis pen´ sa ble

Say *recognize* and *indispensable* aloud, giving primary and secondary stress to the syllables with the primary and secondary accent marks.

Words Underscored in Blue

The following words are underscored in blue in Chapter 18, "Mark Your Books."

☐ **absorption** (ab-sôrp´shən) *n.* The state of being very interested in or completely occupied by someone or something [total *absorption* in one's work]

☐ **abstract** (ab-strakt´) *adj.* Existing as an idea in the mind rather than in physical form [the *abstract* ideas of beauty, love, perfection, and freedom]

☐ **adhere** (ad-hîr´) *v.* To follow closely; to keep to, stand by [to *adhere* to the rules of a game]

☐ **adolescence** (ad´l-es´əns) *n.* The time in a person's life that begins with the development of secondary sex characteristics and ends with maturity [to be in high school during *adolescence*]

☐ **aerobic** (â-rō´bik) *adj.* Improving physical conditioning of the circulatory and respiratory systems [jogging, swimming, and other *aerobic* activity]

☐ **alternative** (ôl-tûr´nə-tiv) *n.* A choice among or between things [the *alternative* of attending college or going to work]

☐ **amicably** (am´i-kə-blē) *adv.* Showing good will; friendly [respected for dealing *amicably* with others]

☐ **antipathy** (an-tip´ə-thē) *n.* A deep-seated dislike; distaste [an *antipathy* for people who eat with food falling out of their mouths]

☐ **appraisal** (ə-prā´zəl) *n.* The act of evaluating; estimate, assessment [an *appraisal* of the value of one's possessions]

☐ **associate degree** (ə-sō´shē-it di-grē´) *n.* An academic degree offered by two-year colleges, usually the Associate of Arts, Associate of Science, or Associate of Applied Science [to earn an *associate degree* in computer technology]

☐ **assumption** (ə-sump´shən) *n.* Something accepted as true without proof; belief, supposition, theory, hypothesis [the *assumption* that evil deeds will be punished]

□ **attainment** (ə-tan′mənt) *n.* The act of arriving at a goal; acquisition, realization [the *attainment* of success in business]

□ **attribute** (ə-trib′yōōt) *v.* To regard as belonging to someone or something [to *attribute* success to hard work]

□ **autonomy** (ô-ton′ə-mē) *n.* Independence or self-government; the state of functioning independently [unmarried people who value their *autonomy*]

□ **bachelor's degree** (bach′ə-lərz di-grē′) *n.* An academic degree offered by four-year colleges and universities, usually the Bachelor of Arts or Bachelor of Science [to be awarded a *bachelor's degree*]

□ **botch** (boch) *v.* To ruin by poor performance or lack of skill; bungle, spoil [to *botch* a chance for a good grade by not studying]

□ **brainstorm** (brān′stôrm′) *v.* To work on the solution to a problem with a group of people who all contribute their ideas [to *brainstorm* with one's study group about what questions might appear on a test]

□ **causality** (kô-zal′i-tē) *n.* The interrelation of cause and effect [searching for *causality* in a scientific experiment]

□ **chair** (châr) *v.* To act as chairperson [to *chair* a meeting]

□ **circuit** (sûr′kit) *n.* A route that is traveled regularly [to be on the lecture *circuit*]

□ **cognitive** (kog′ni-tiv) *adj.* Involving mental processes such as memory, reasoning, and judgment [the *cognitive* act of remembering]

□ **colleague** (kol′ēg′) *n.* A fellow worker in a profession; associate, coworker [to have dinner with one's *colleagues* after work hours]

□ **colon** (kō′lən) *n.* A section of the large intestine

□ **concept** (kon′sept′) *n.* An idea, thought, notion [the *concepts* of right and wrong]

□ **conception** (kən-sep′shən) *n.* Something developed in the mind; idea, concept, notion [the *conception* of a perfect society]. The beginning of a pregnancy [a birth following nine months after *conception*]

□ **concrete** (kon-krēt′) *adj.* Specific, particular, factual, definite [*concrete* evidence that the murder was committed with a butcher knife]

□ **constructive** (kən-struk′tiv) *adj.* Leading to improvements or advancements; helpful, useful [*constructive* suggestions for vocabulary development]—**constructively,** *adv.*

□ **consumption** (kən-sump′shən) *n.* The act of using something up; depletion, exhaustion [the *consumption* of champagne at a wedding]

□ **context** (kon′tekst) *n.* The entire background or environment of a particular event; framework, surroundings [the inappropriateness of hysterical laughter in the *context* of a funeral]

□ **contraception** (kon′trə-sep′shən) *n.* The intentional prevention of a pregnancy through the use of devices, drugs, surgery, or other means [taking medication for the purpose of *contraception*]

□ **crucial** (krōō′shəl) *adj.* Of great importance; critical, decisive, essential, urgent [the *crucial* decision to wage a war]

□ **cult** (kult) *n.* Devotion to a person or principle; followers, disciples [the *cult* of youth and beauty]

□ **derive** (di-rīv′) *v.* To get from a source [to *derive* maple syrup from a tree]

□ **deter** (di-tûr′) *v.* To discourage, hinder, prevent [Cold, wet, and windy weather may *deter* outside activities.]

□ **differentiate** (dif′ə-ren′shē-āt′) *v.* To observe the difference between; distinguish [to *differentiate* identical twins]

□ **disclosure** (dis-klō′zhər) *n.* The act of revealing or disclosing; revelation, communication, making known [the *disclosure* of one's affection for another]

ə ago/a pat/ā pay/â care/ä arm/e pet/ē be/i pit/ī pie/î pier/o pot/ō toe/ô paw/ōō took/ōō boot/oi boy/ou scout/u cut yōō cute/û firm

☐ **divert** (dĭ-vûrt´) *v.* To turn aside from a course or direction; sidetrack [for police to *divert* traffic around the scene of an accident]

☐ **doldrums** (dōl´drəmz´) *n.pl.* Low spirits; gloom, sluggishness, depression, blues [in the *doldrums* over the end of a love affair]

☐ **domesticity** (dō´me-stĭs´ĭ-tē) *n.* Devotion to home life and family [involved in the *domesticity* of family life]

☐ **ego** (ē´gō) *n.* The part of the personality that is conscious, most in touch with external reality, and that controls behavior [to have an *ego* that accepts all challenges]

☐ **elicit** (ĭ-lĭs´ĭt) *v.* To draw out or bring forth [to *elicit* an answer to a question]

☐ **enfranchise** (en-fran´chīz´) *v.* To give the right to vote [to be *enfranchised* by citizenship]

☐ **esteem** (ĭ-stēm´) *n.* Favorable opinion or regard; respect [to be a professor held in high *esteem* by students]

☐ **ethics** (eth´ĭks) *n.pl.* A code of morals and standards of conduct [the *ethics* of the medical profession]

☐ **explicit** (ek-splĭs´ĭt) *adj.* Clearly stated; definite, precise [*explicit* directions that a child can understand]—**explicitly,** *adv.*

☐ **facilitate** (fə-sĭl´ə-tāt´) *v.* To make easy or less difficult; to ease, help [a well-written textbook that *facilitates* learning]

☐ **factor** (fak´tər) *n.* A circumstance or condition that brings about a result; reason, influence [a *factor* to consider when selecting a mate]

☐ **franchise** (fran´chīz´) *n.* The constitutional right to vote [to exercise one's *franchise* on election day]

☐ **gender** (jen´dər) *n.* A person's sexual identity [the male and female *gender*]

☐ **gratification** (grat´ə-fĭ-kā´shən) *n.* The condition of being pleased or satisfied; satisfaction, delight [the *gratification* of knowing you have done your best]

☐ **grueling** (grōō´lĭng) *adj.* Extremely physically or mentally demanding; exhausting [a *grueling* week of working, studying, and taking tests]

☐ **hail** (hāl) *v.* To greet or welcome enthusiastically; acclaim, cheer [to *hail* the discovery of a cure for a previously incurable disease]

☐ **hierarchy** (hī´ə-rär´kē) *n.* A group of people or things arranged in order, such as order of rank or class [a *hierarchy* of animal life with apes near the top and sponges near the bottom]

☐ **hypothesis** (hī-poth´ĭ-sĭs) *n.* A tentative explanation that can be tested by further investigation or experimentation; an unproved theory [a *hypothesis* about the causes of a new disease]

☐ **hypothetical** (hī´pə-thet´ĭ-kəl) *adj.* Supposed, assumed, possible [a *hypothetical* problem on an examination for nurses]

☐ **id** (id) *n.* According to Freud, the primitive part of the personality that demands immediate satisfaction of needs, drives, and desires [a rapist driven by his *id*]

☐ **inanimate** (in-an´ə-mit) *adj.* Not possessing animal life; spiritless, dead [*inanimate* rocks, sand, and sea]

☐ **incentive** (in-sen´tiv) *n.* Something that stimulates one to take action; encouragement, motivation [a test as an *incentive* to study]

☐ **incompetent** (in-kom´pə-tənt) *adj.* Lacking the ability or knowledge necessary for a task; unskillful, incapable, unqualified [an open-and-shut case that was lost by an *incompetent* lawyer]

☐ **inconsistency** (in´kən-sis´tən-sē) *n.* The state of not being consistent, regular, or predictable [The *inconsistency* of his employment made it impossible for him to support his family.]

☐ **initiative** (ĭ-nĭsh´ə-tĭv) *n.* The capacity to begin or complete a task; enterprise [taking the *initiative* in keeping friendships alive]

☐ **intimate** (in´tə-mit) *adj.* To be close, familiar, personal [an *intimate* relationship between husband and wife]

☐ **invariably** (in-vâr´ē-ə-blē) *adv.* Unchangingly, constantly, unvaryingly [to be *invariably* kind to others]

☐ **limbo** (lim´bō) *n.* A place or condition of neglect or confinement [to be in *limbo* during a ten-hour airplane flight]

☐ **lust** (lust) *n.* Powerful desire; sexual craving [to *lust* for wealth and power]

☐ **malicious** (mə-lish´əs) *adj.* Deliberately harmful; hateful, spiteful [a *malicious* attack with a hammer]

☐ **militant** (mil´i-tənt) *adj.* Aggressive in support or promotion of a cause; combative, assertive [a *militant* opponent of abortion rights]

☐ **modest** (mod´ist) *adj.* Not showy; simple, plain, quiet, humble [a *modest* little house]

☐ **morals** (mor´əlz) *n.pl.* Rules of conduct; standards of right and wrong; principles, standards [to have *morals* that forbid cheating]

☐ **motivate** (mō´tə-vāt´) *v.* To provide a reason to be moved to action; to stimulate, activate, arouse [to *motivate* a student to learn]

☐ **negotiate** (ni-gō´shē-āt´) *v.* To settle by mutual agreement; bargain for; come to terms [to *negotiate* an end to the employees' strike]

☐ **norm** (nôrm) *n.* A standard for behavior that is considered to be appropriate; yardstick, criterion [*norms* that govern the courteous treatment of others]

☐ **nuclear family** (nōō´klē-ər fam´ə-1ē) *n.* Parents and children living in one household

☐ **nutrient** (nōō´trē-ənt) *n.* A nourishing substance in food [the *nutrients* in a bowl of chicken and vegetable soup]

☐ **obsessive** (əb-ses´iv) *adj.* To be preoccupied with a thought; fixated [to be *obsessive* about cleanliness]

☐ **orient** (ôr´ē-ənt) *v.* To adjust to an environment, situation, or idea; familiarize [to *orient* oneself to the ways things are done in college]

☐ **paraphrase** (par´ə-frāz´) *v.* To restate using other words; reword [to *paraphrase* a teacher's statements while taking lecture notes]

☐ **pent-up** (pent´up´) *adj.* Not allowed out; curbed, confined, repressed, held back [a fit or rage resulting from *pent-up* anger]

☐ **perceive** (pər-sēv´) *v.* To acquire knowledge by using the senses of sight, hearing, touch, taste, or smell; to sense, observe, detect [by counting, to *perceive* how much money is in your wallet]

☐ **perception** (pər-sep´shən) *n.* Knowledge gotten by using the senses of sight, hearing, touch, taste, or smell; awareness, comprehension, recognition [the *perception* from the sound of a siren that a fire engine, ambulance, or police car is near]

☐ **perennial** (pə-ren´ē-əl) *adj.* Lasting a long time; permanent, constant, persistent [students' *perennial* complaints about tests]—**perennially,** *adv.*

☐ **phenomenon** (fi-nom´ə-non´) *n.* A happening, occurrence, or event [the *phenomenon* of a snowstorm in winter]—**phenomena,** *n.pl.*

☐ **physiological** (fiz´ē-ə-loj´i-kəl) *adj.* Having to do with the functioning of a living organism or its parts [the *physiological* act of breathing]

☐ **predominant** (pri-dom´ə-nənt) *adj.* Most frequent, noticeable, dominant, important, major [financial necessity as a *predominant* reason to hold a job]—**predominantly,** *adv.*

☐ **prerequisite** (prē-rek´wi-zit) *adj.* Required as a condition of something that follows; necessary, mandatory [a license is a *prerequisite* to marriage]

☐ **prevalent** (prev´ə-lənt) *adj.* Common, frequent, widespread, usual [Tipping is *prevalent* in restaurants.]

☐ **procreation** (prō´krē-ā´shən) *n.* The act of producing children [the *procreation* of the human race]

☐ **profit sharing** (prof´it shar´ing) *n.* A procedure by which employees receive a portion of the profits of a business [to build employee morale with a *profit-sharing* plan]

ə ago/a pat/ā pay/â care/ä arm/e pet/ē be/i pit/ī pie/î pier/o pot/ō toe/ô paw/ōō took/ōō boot/oi boy/ou scout/u cut yōō cute/û firm

☐ **profound** (prə-found´) *adj.* Thoughtful, deep, wise, intense [the *profound* writings of a great philosopher]

☐ **proponent** (prə-pō´nət) *n.* A person who argues in support of something; supporter, advocate, booster [a *proponent* of free health care for all]

☐ **proposition** (prop´ə-zish´ən) *n.* A suggested plan; proposal [the *proposition* that all men are created equal]

☐ **prospect** (pros´pekt) *n.* An expected outcome; possibility, expectation [young people's *prospects* for finding high-paying jobs]

☐ **ratification** (rat´ə-fi-kā´shən) *n.* Approval or confirmation [the *ratification* of an amendment by the legislatures]

☐ **reassess** (re´ə-ses´) *v.* Evaluate, consider, or look over again [to *reassess* one's primary goals]

☐ **reluctant** (ri-luk´tənt) *adj.* Unwilling or resistant [being *reluctant* to comply with his parents' wishes]

☐ **renovation** (ren´ə-vā´shən) *n.* The state of having been remodeled, repaired, or cleaned up; renewal [the *renovation* of a house that was damaged by fire]

☐ **repress** (re´pres´) *v.* To force thoughts into unconsciousness [to *repress* memories of an unhappy childhood]

☐ **sensory** (sen´sə-rē) *adj.* Relating to the senses of hearing, sight, smell, touch, and taste [eating is a *sensory* experience]

☐ **socioeconomic** (sō´sē-ō-ek´ə-nom´ik) *adj.* Involving social and economic factors [the *socioeconomic* consequences of widespread drug use]

☐ **sodium** (sō´dē-əm) *n.* A chemical element found in common table salt [to be on a diet low in *sodium*]

☐ **solidify** (sə-lid´ə-fī´) *v.* To become solid or united [to *solidify* a friendship]

☐ **stamina** (stam´ə-nə) *n.* Strength to withstand illness or hardship; endurance, sturdiness, hardiness [the *stamina* needed to run a marathon]

☐ **strained** (strānd) *adj.* Not relaxed or natural; tense, forced [lack of communication leading to *strained* relations between friends]

☐ **suffrage** (suf´rij) *n.* The right to vote in political elections; franchise [women fought for *suffrage*]

☐ **superego** (soo´pər-e´go) *n.* According to Freud, that part of the personality that represents parental values and societal rules; the conscience [to have a *superego* that prompts one to do her or his best]

☐ **sustain** (sə-stān´) *v.* To maintain, keep up, prolong [to *sustain* a constant speed while driving on a highway]

☐ **taunt** (tônt) *v.* To mock, insult, tease, ridicule [a little boy *taunted* by a big bully]

☐ **technology** (tek-nol´ə-jē) *n.* The application of science to the solution of practical problems [the use of computer *technology* in planning highways]

☐ **theoretical** (thē´ə-ret´i-kəl) *adj.* Based on theory; unproved, hypothetical [a *theoretical* framework for understanding the workings of the human brain]

☐ **transition** (trans-zish´ən) *n.* The passage from one condition to another; changeover, passing, shifting [the *transition* from high school to college]

☐ **trauma** (trou´mə) *n.* A painful emotional experience that has a lasting effect [the *trauma* of seeing one's child killed]

☐ **trite** (trīt) *adj.* Lacking originality because of overuse; worn out, overdone, commonplace ["Quick as a wink" is a *trite*, overworked expression.]

☐ **typify** (tip´ə-fī) *v.* To possess the essential characteristics of something; represent, embody, epitomize [McDonald's *typifies* fast food restaurants.]

☐ **ultimatum** (ul´tə-mā´təm) *n.* A final offer or demand in a negotiation, the rejection of which may lead to a break in relations [an *ultimatum* to pay rent or move out]

☐ **utopian** (yoo-tō´pē-ən) *adj.* Ideal, perfect, but impractical [to conceptualize a *utopian* society]

☐ **valid** (val´id) *adj.* Able to withstand criticism; genuineness, soundness, reasonableness [a *valid* argument]

☐ **volatility** (vol´ə-til´i-tē) *n.* The characteristic of shifting quickly, widely, or unpredictably; variability, instability [the *volatility* of an active volcano]

☐ **vulnerable** (vul´nər-ə-bəl) *adj.* Can be easily hurt or criticized; defenseless, unprotected [a bully attacking a *vulnerable* child]—**vulnerability**, *n.*

Glossary

Words in italics within these definitions are also defined in this *glossary*.

Abstract. A brief statement about the contents of a book, article, or other written material.

Active listeners. Students who, when necessary, verify their understanding by asking appropriate questions and who demonstrate their understanding of what teachers say by making accurate *notes* of lecture content.

Adviser. A teacher assigned to help students select the courses for which they register.

Almanac. An annual publication that contains a variety of information, including facts and statistics about famous people, history, countries, and sports.

Analyze. To separate something into its parts for the purpose of *studying* the parts and understanding how they are related.

Appendix. A part of a book that contains supplementary materials or information; usually located in the back of a book, immediately following the last chapter.

Assistant professor. A teacher who ranks below an *associate professor*.

Associate degree. A *degree* that is usually offered by two-year colleges, often the A.A. (Associate of Arts), A.S. (Associate of Science), or A.A.S. (Associate of Applied Science).

Associate professor. A teacher who ranks below a *professor* but above an *assistant professor*.

Atlas. A book of maps.

Audit. To have official permission to attend a course without receiving a grade or academic *credit*.

Auditory learners. People who prefer to learn by listening and discussing. Compare with *kinesthetic learners* and *visual learners*.

Automatic processing. The effortless *storage* of information in *memory*.

Bachelor's degree. A *degree* offered by four-year colleges and universities, usually the B.A. (Bachelor of Arts) or the B.S. (Bachelor of Science).

Bar graph. A drawing in which parallel bars are used to compare differences in amounts, such as differences in the amounts of fat in various foods.

Bibliography. A list of books, articles, and other sources of information that are referred to by a writer. Same as *references* and *notes*.

Bluebook. A booklet, not necessarily blue, that contains lined paper on which to write.

Bulletin. A booklet published by a college or university that includes information about curriculums, courses, and other important facts; a *catalog*.

Bursar. The title of a person at a college or university who is responsible for money transactions; a treasurer or *cashier*.

Call number. Numbers and letters printed on books to indicate their location in a library.

Card catalog. A file in a library that lists books alphabetically by authors' names, by titles, and by subjects.

Cartoon. A drawing depicting a humorous situation, often accompanied by a caption.

Cashier. Same as *bursar*.

Catalog. Same as *bulletin*.

Chancellor. Sometimes the same as *president* and sometimes the title for special assistant to a president.

Circle graph. A drawing in the shape of a circle that is used to show the sizes of the parts that make up the whole. A circle graph can show what parts of a family's income are used for rent, food, clothing, and other expenses.

Classification chart. A format for recording *notes* about information that explains how two or more people, places, or things are alike or different in two or more ways.

Copyright page. The page of a book that states the year the book was copyrighted or published; follows the *title page*.

Counselors. People who provide students with guidance in achieving their educational and occupational *goals* and in resolving their personal problems.

Credit. A unit given for completion of any study that applies toward a *degree*.

Current goal. A *goal* that helps in accomplishing an *intermediate goal*.

Curriculum. The courses required to earn a particular *degree*.

Database. A collection of data that can be accessed by using a computer.

Dean. A member of the administration of a college or university who is in charge of specified areas of the school's activities, such as a dean of students, a

327

dean of faculty, a dean of instruction, or a dean of a *school* or *division* within a college or a university.

Decay theory. The theory that if we do not use information that is stored in *memory*, we will not be able to *retrieve* it because it fades from disuse.

Degree. A rank given to students who have successfully completed specified courses of study, such as the *bachelor's degree*.

Department. An organizational unit that offers courses in a specific subject or a specific group of subjects. For instance, a foreign language department may offer courses in Spanish, French, German, and other languages.

Diagram. A drawing that explains something by outlining its parts and showing the relationships between them. For example, a diagram may show the relationships between the parts of the human eye.

Direction word. A word in an *essay question* that informs test takers about the type of answer they are to give. The direction word "diagram" usually indicates that students are to draw a picture and label its parts.

Distracter. A choice for a *multiple-choice question* that is not the correct answer.

Division. *Departments* are sometimes organized under larger groups called divisions. For example, the social sciences division may include a psychology department, a sociology department, an anthropology department, and other departments.

Doctor. Title for a person who has earned the highest *degree* awarded by a college or a university.

Doctoral degree. The highest *degree* offered by colleges and universities, such as the Ph.D. (Doctor of Philosophy) or Ed.D. (Doctor of Education).

Double negative. A phrase that contains two negatives, often the word "not" and a negative prefix, such as "un-" ("not unkind").

Elaborative rehearsal. Same as *rehearsal*.

Encoding. The process by which information enters *memory*.

Essay questions. Test items that require students to give written answers that are usually one paragraph or more in length.

Exercise. In a *textbook*, a *problem* or series of problems.

Expressive vocabulary. The words one uses when writing and speaking. Compare with *receptive vocabulary*.

Extreme modifiers. Words such as "always" and "never" that tend to be in false statements. For instance, "**All** children love candy" contains an extreme modifier, and so it is false.

Figure. A photograph, *diagram*, graph, or other illustration in a *textbook*.

Fill-in questions. Statements that have deleted portions that test takers must supply: "There are _____ letters in the English alphabet."

Glossary. A list of words and their definitions; usually located in the back of a book, just in front of the *index*.

Goal. A purpose or objective that is worked toward or strived for.

GPA values. Values given to *letter grades* so that *grade point averages* may be computed. The following values are used at many colleges: A, 4.00; B, 3.00; C, 2.00; D, 1.00; and F, 0.00.

Grade point average (GPA). A number that usually ranges from 0.00 to 4.00 and indicates a student's average course grade.

Grant. A gift that does not need to be repaid, such as a tuition assistance grant funded by state and federal governments to assist students who demonstrate financial need.

Heading. In a *textbook*, a word or words at the beginning of a division within a chapter.

Highlight. To mark important words or sentences in a book using a marker that contains watercolor ink. This is done so that important statements will stand out clearly and not be overlooked while *studying*.

Hour. A unit, usually less or more than sixty minutes, that designates time students spend in classrooms, laboratories, or conferences.

Incomplete grade (INC). A grade given at many colleges and universities when students are doing passing work but have not completed all course requirements. Usually an INC grade is changed to an *F* or to some other grade if incomplete work is not completed within a specified time.

Index. An alphabetically arranged listing of subjects and the page numbers on which they are discussed in a book; usually located at the very end of a book.

Information-processing model. A theory of *memory* that compares the ways that computers and people process and store information.

Insert. Material set off in a *textbook*, which may be enclosed within lines or printed on a shaded background of light blue, yellow, gray, or some other color.

Interference theory. The theory that we sometimes cannot retrieve information in *memory* because other memories stored there interfere.

Intermediate goal. A *goal* that helps in accomplishing a *primary goal*.

Intersession. A short session of study offered between two *terms*, such as a four-week session offered in January between a fall term and a spring term.

Introduction. The part of a book that gives the author's explanation of why the book was written. It often includes a summary of the purposes, philosophy, or contents of a book; usually located right after the *table of contents*. This information may also be located in a *preface*.

Journal. A *periodical* that contains articles about a particular subject, such as a medical journal.

Kinesthesia. The sensory experience that comes from moving muscles, tendons, and joints.

Kinesthetic learners. People who prefer to learn by being physically involved, such as by doing something or by handling and manipulating things. Compare with *auditory learners* and *visual learners*.

Learning goals. A list of statements or questions at the beginning of a *textbook* chapter that summarizes information in a chapter.

Learning strategy. A set of procedures for accomplishing a learning task, such as the procedures that are used to learn information for tests.

Learning style. The set of procedures that a particular person actually uses to accomplish a learning task.

Letter grade. A grade such as A-, B+, or C that designates the quality of work students do. Letter grades have the following meanings at many schools: A, excellent; B, good; C, satisfactory; D, passing; and F, failing.

Line graph. A drawing in which lines are used to show increasing or decreasing amounts. A line graph can show increases or decreases in the numbers of students enrolled at a college over a period of time.

Loan. A lent sum of money that must be repaid with interest.

Long-term memory. The stage of *memory* that holds a vast amount of information for as long as a lifetime.

Map. A *diagram* or other drawing that shows how a topic and details are related.

Marginal note. Material printed in the margins of books or written in the margins of class notes.

Master's degree. A *degree* that ranks higher than a *bachelor's degree* but lower than a *doctoral degree*, usually the M.A. (Master of Arts) or M.S. (Master of Science).

Matching questions. Test items that present two lists and require test takers to associate words or statements in one list with words or statements in the other list.

Matriculate. To be admitted to study in a particular degree program at a college or university.

Memory. The total of what one remembers; same as *long-term memory*.

Midterm. The middle of a *term* or an examination given at this time.

Mnemonic acronym. A *retrieval cue* that is a word made from the initial letters of words to be retrieved.

Mnemonic device. A device used to aid *memory*. "Use i before e except after c" is a mnemonic rhyme for remembering a spelling principle.

Mnemonic sentence. A sentence in which the first letters of words in the sentence are the same as the first letters of words to be recalled.

Modifier. An adjective that qualifies a noun, or an adverb that modifies a verb. In the phrase "young women talking quietly," the adjective "young" is a qualifier of the noun "women," and the adverb "quietly" is a qualifier of the verb "talking."

Multiple-choice questions. Test items written in a format that requires test takers to select a correct answer from among four or five possible answers that are listed.

Name index. An *index* of the authors and other people referred to in a book.

Negative. A word (such as "not") or a prefix (such as "un-") that indicates an opposite.

Notes. Same as *bibliography* and *references*. Also, handwritten summaries of information stated in classes or printed in course *textbooks*.

Number grade. A grade such as 91, 85, or 68 that designates the quality of work students do. Many schools agree on the following correspondences between number grades and *letter grades*: A, 90–100; B, 80–89; C, 70–79; D, 60–69; F, 0–59.

Ombudsperson. A special assistant to a *president*.

Open-book test. A test during which students may refer to books, and sometimes to *notes*, as they answer questions.

Orientation. A period of time or a series of events planned to help students adjust satisfactorily to college or university life.

Outline. A summary of information that lists important points in a well-organized manner. In the traditional outline format, details are labeled with Roman numerals, capital letters, and Arabic numerals.

Paraphrase. To state in one's own words the essential meaning of something heard or read.

Periodicals. Newspapers, magazines, *journals*, and other publications that are published at regular intervals, such as daily, weekly, monthly, and bimonthly.

Preface. Same as *introduction*.

Prerequisite. A requirement that must be completed before a student may take a course. For example, the prerequisite for an intermediate algebra course might be a course in elementary algebra.

President. At a college or university, the chief administrative officer, who has ultimate responsibility for all aspects of the functioning of the school.

Preview of a book. The examination of the major features of a book, such as the *table of contents*, *introduction*, *appendix*, and *glossary*.

Preview of a chapter. The quick examination of introductory paragraphs, headings, illustrations, *tables*, and other features of a chapter to learn what major topics it discusses.

Primary goal. A *goal* that a person hopes to achieve in the future, such as the goal of graduating from college.

Problem. In a *textbook*, a question to answer, a proposition to solve, or other activity to do.

Professor. The highest rank for college and university teachers, also sometimes called full professor to distinguish it from *associate professor* and *assistant professor*. Also a correct form of address for any person who holds any of the three professorial ranks and an honorary or courtesy title at some colleges.

Quarter system. A system that divides a school year into three parts, usually a fall, a winter, and a spring *term* of about ten weeks each.

Reading. The process used to understand information presented in writing. Contrast with *studying*.

Receptive vocabulary. Words one knows when listening or *reading*. Compare with *expressive vocabulary*.

Recitation. The act of repeating information silently or aloud to learn it and to be able to recall it.

References. Same as *bibliography* and *notes*.

Registrar. The title of a person at a college or university who is responsible for registering students in courses and for maintaining their academic records on *transcripts*.

Registration. A period of time during which students register for the courses they will take.

Rehearsal. The act of *analyzing* information and relating it to information that is already stored in *memory*.

Retrieval. The act of recalling or recollecting information stored in *memory*.

Retrieval cues. Words or images that help in recalling information stored in *memory*.

Retrieval failure theory. The theory that information in *memory* sometimes cannot be recalled because proper *retrieval cues* are not available.

Review. The repeated recitation and *rehearsal* of information to ensure that it can be retrieved quickly when it is needed.

Review questions. Questions at the end of a *textbook* chapter that students may answer to determine whether they have understood or learned information in the chapter.

Scholarship. A grant of financial assistance that is awarded to students who meet specific criteria such as outstanding academic, athletic, or artistic achievement.

School. A *division* within a college or university, such as a school of medicine.

Semantic code. A representation of information by its general meaning.

Semester system. A system that divides a school year into two parts, usually a fall and a spring *term* of fifteen to sixteen weeks.

Sensory memory. The stage of *memory* that briefly registers all information received by the senses of sight, hearing, taste, touch, and smell.

Sentence outline. An *outline* in which the statements are all sentences.

Short-term memory. A stage of *memory* that holds up to nine pieces of information for about twenty seconds.

Skill. An ability acquired as a result of training and practice. *Reading* and writing are skills.

Stacks. The places in a library where most books are shelved.

Stem. The part of a *multiple-choice question* that comes before the first answer.

Storage. The act of holding information in *memory*.

Stress. Mental or physical strain that is experienced in response to psychologically or physically demanding events.

Stressors. Events or situations that induce *stress*.

Studying. The strategies used to remember and recall information. Contrast with *reading*.

Subject index. An *index* of the subjects discussed in a book.

Summary. A section at the end of a *textbook* chapter that provides an overview of the contents of the chapter.

Summer session. A period in the summer during which students may take courses for academic *credit* but that is usually not considered a *semester*, *quarter*, or *trimester* for the purposes of a school's business.

Syllabus. A summary or outline distributed by an instructor that states the main topics to be discussed in a course.

Table of contents. A list that shows the page numbers on which chapter headings and subheadings of a book appear; usually located in the front of a book, right after the *copyright page*.

Table. A systematic listing of statistical information that is presented in orderly columns and rows to facilitate comparisons among data.

Take-home test. A test for which students are given questions to answer at home or to study at home before answering them in class.

Tenure. A status in which faculty members, having fulfilled certain requirements, hold their positions permanently.

Term. A period of study that usually ends with the administration of final examinations.

Terminology. Words or phrases that are used with specific meanings when a subject is discussed. The important terminology used in a *textbook* is usually defined in a *glossary*.

Test anxiety. Uneasiness or apprehension students experience because they must take a test.

Textbook. A book that summarizes information about course subject matter. This book is a *textbook*.

Thesaurus. A book of synonyms.

Title page. The page of a book that gives information about the title, author, and publisher; usually the second or third printed page of a book.

Topic outline. An *outline* in which the statements are all phrases.

Transcript. The official record of courses taken, grades received, and *grade point averages*. Transcripts are maintained by a *registrar*.

Trimester system. Same as *quarter system*.

True-false questions. Test items that are statements that test takers must decide are either true or false.

Tutor. A person who gives individual instruction to students.

Underline. To draw lines under important words or sentences in a book so they stand out clearly and will not be overlooked while *studying*.

Vice chancellor. Sometimes the same as *dean*.

Vice president. Sometimes the same as *dean*.

Visual code. A mental image of information or an event.

Visualization. An image that can be pictured in the mind and used to recall information. If you picture in your mind the room in which you sleep, you can use the image to recall the information about the room.

Visual learners. People who prefer to learn by *reading* and watching demonstrations. Compare with *auditory learners* and *kinesthetic learners*.

Withdrawal grade (W). A grade given at many colleges and universities so that students may drop courses when they have good reasons for doing so. Usually W grades do not lower *grade point averages* when they are requested within specified time limits or when students are doing passing work at the time of withdrawal.

Index

Assignment Form*

Course Name	Monday *Date:*	Tuesday *Date:*	Wednesday *Date:*	Thursday *Date:*	Friday *Date:*

*You may photocopy this form.

Study Schedule*

	MON	TUE	WED	THU	FRI	SAT	SUN
7–8							
8–9							
9–10							
10–11							
11–12							
12–1							
1–2							
2–3							
3–4							
4–5							
5–6							
6–7							
7–8							
8–9							
9–10							
10–11							
11–12							

*You may photocopy this form.